W9-AWM-009

PRAISE FOR
WORDS ON FIRE

"Many of us were taught a lie as youngsters that sticks and stones can break our bones, but words will never hurt us. Garcia courageously, graphically, and powerfully illustrates that it is words on fire that cause deep internal permanent damage while often triggering accompanying physical damage. *Words On Fire* should be mandatory reading and a guide book for every journalist, business school, religious leader, and elected official. Important institutions in our society and culture have the affirmative responsibility to stand up and speak out against the users and use of dangerous language."

—James E. Lukaszewski,
America's Crisis Guru®

"Drawing on history and his deep expertise in communications, Helio Fred Garcia documents how Trump's barrage of hate, divisiveness, and falsehoods are even uglier and more dangerous than we thought, right out of the autocrat's playbook. This is a highly readable guide to how we can call out and combat Trump's toxic language and malignant agenda, and push back against the corrosive forces that enable Trumpism and put our country in peril."

—Evan Wolfson,
Founder, Freedom to Marry

"Garcia, a proven scholar on communication, enables his readers to understand both the benefits and threats of words that inevitably alter the direction and the values of a nation. He identifies rhetoric that breeds violence, affirms autocracy, and prompts terrorism as well as critical responses to those developments that serve as antidotes to trouble and strategies for building a more equitable, united world."

—Rev. Dr. C. Welton Gaddy,
President Emeritus, Interfaith Alliance

"Language is powerful. It can uplift or harm. Helio Fred Garcia is an astute student of language and communication. This book offers historic examples, keen insights, and valuable advice on recognizing patterns of language that can lead to violence."

—David Lapan, Colonel, USMC (ret),
Former Pentagon and DHS spokesman

"In this dark moment of hateful and divisive rhetoric in our blessed country, at a time when such original analyses and solutions are scarce, *Words on Fire* serves as a guiding light. Garcia details the incendiary language used by our leaders and offers practical tools for leaders and citizens to combat it. Every American should read this timely, imperative book if we are to save our democracy."

—Khizr Khan, Gold Star Parent,
Immigrant American

WORDS
ON FIRE

To VICTORIA,

WORDS ON FIRE

The Power of Incendiary Language and How to Confront It

HELIO FRED GARCIA

RADIUS BOOK GROUP
NEW YORK

Radius Book Group
A Division of Diversion Publishing Corp.
New York, NY
www.RadiusBookGroup.com

Copyright © 2020 by Helio Fred Garcia

All rights reserved, including the right to reproduce this book or portions thereof in any form whatsoever. No part of this publication may be reproduced or transmitted in any form or by any means, electronic or mechanical, including photocopying, recording, or any other information storage and retrieval, without the written permission of the author.

For more information, email info@radiusbookgroup.com.

First edition: June 2020
Trade Paperback ISBN: 978-1-63576-902-9
eBook ISBN: 978-1-63576-903-6

Library of Congress Control Number: 2020901883

Manufactured in the United States of America

10 9 8 7 6 5 4 3 2 1

Cover design Tom Lau
Interior design by Neuwirth & Associates, Inc.

Radius Book Group and the Radius Book Group colophon are registered trademarks of Radius Book Group, a Division of Diversion Publishing Corp.

This book is dedicated to all who
were ever labeled any form of the Other,
and to those who stood up to bullies,
either for themselves or to protect those at risk.

CONTENTS

Preface   xi

PART I COMMUNICATION AND CONSEQUENCES
Introduction to Part I   1

1   The Power of Communication   5
2   Less Than Human   19
3   Stochastic Terrorism and Lone Wolves   43

PART II TRUMP
Introduction to Part II   63

4   Divide to Conquer   73
5   American Carnage   93
6   What Is Trump Up To?   139

PART III BELIEVING ABSURDITIES
Introduction to Part III   165

7   Trump Not a Cause but a Consequence   169
8   Why People Believe What They Believe   191

PART IV A CALL TO ACTION:
PRACTICAL TOOLS FOR LEADERS AND CITIZENS

Introduction to Part IV   207

9   Leadership and Accountability   209

10 Be on the Lookout   229

Acknowledgments   247

Notes   249

PREFACE

I am an immigrant to the United States, an American by choice.

I choose to be an American because, of all the places in the world—and I've been fortunate to have visited or worked in dozens of countries on six continents—this is one of the few places where your birth circumstances do not determine the rest of your life. And where the national aspiration, still a work in progress, encourages us to be our better selves.

I have been able to build a good life here. I married a wonderful person, and together we've raised two remarkable young women. I graduated from two of the finest universities in the land and am a professor at both. I've worked with or for some of the best companies in the world.

I pass as an American, and I carry with me all the manifestations of white privilege. But it wasn't always so.

When I arrived from South America as a young child, I was different from the other kids. I was an easy mark. Scrawny. With an unpronounceable name, a heavy foreign accent, and a very weak command of the English language.

I was the Other. And I was a target. I was tormented for years by a pack of boys who saw in me an opportunity to feel superior. I was constantly told to go back to where I came from. But what began with taunting and insult and name-calling metastasized into physical violence and sexual humiliation. I was beaten. I was held down by the boys, who took turns peeing on me and then ran off, laughing.

More than fifty years later, I carry scars around my eyes where I was kicked with a heavy boot. Now that I no longer have hair, many other scars are noticeable, especially on the top and back of my head, where I was hit with sticks, with rocks, and in at least one instance, with a brick. I also have scars on my soul.

But I was also very lucky. I had several caring and gifted teachers who made me their project, investing time and love not only in school but also beyond the classroom. Because of them I came of age working on the floor of the US House of Representatives as a page, watching the House consider articles of impeachment against President Richard Nixon. Since then I've met presidents and prime ministers, one king, several princes, one pope, and hundreds of religious leaders of most of the world's faith traditions. I've advised hundreds of CEOs and public officials. I've visited the White House on business three times, under three presidents.

But in my seventh decade, I still have a visceral fear of being alone with men with whom I don't have a relationship of authority. I avoid sporting events; I don't hang out with groups of men. I have only a handful of male friends. My therapist advises me that more than fifty years after the assaults I still suffer from a form of post-traumatic stress disorder. I'm still the cowering little boy terrified of the bullies.

My father worked for nearly thirty years for the United States Army, teaching soldiers and soldiers-in-training. He and my mother, who never became citizens, are buried in the cemetery of the United States Military Academy at West Point. My dad always told me that there is no greater honor than to teach people who wear the uniform of the armed forces of the United States.

When I was twenty-one, I became an American citizen. I took an oath affirming that I would protect and defend the Constitution and serve the nation. I have done so.

Although I have never worn the uniform myself, for almost thirty years I have taught and advised senior officers of the United

States military—mostly Marines. I have taught dozens of generals and thousands of senior officers and NCOs, as well as senior members of each of the other armed services. Almost all this teaching has been on a pro bono publico basis. It's my form of national service.

Most of my career has been a form of overcompensation for being inarticulate and powerless as a child. For twenty years I worked for some of the top communication consulting firms, advising and representing companies and leaders in the public square. Since 2002, I've owned and run a crisis management and leadership communication consulting and coaching firm. Our work helps leaders become more effective by harnessing their own power with humility and empathy, building trust by connecting meaningfully with others. I've written four books about how to use the power of communication for good.

I have also deployed my gifts to help members of marginalized communities protect themselves. I served as a faculty member, board member, and board chair of a progressive seminary preparing religious leaders to counter oppression. I spent fourteen years on the board of Freedom to Marry, which successfully created the conditions that led to both majority public support and Supreme Court affirmation of gay couples' legal right to marry. I have spent thirteen years on the board, and three as board chair, of Interfaith Alliance, which, among other things, helps promote and protect America's religious pluralism and protect at-risk religious communities. And I've spent nineteen years advising, and seven years on the Board of International Trustees of Religions for Peace, the largest multi-religious organization in the world. Religions for Peace helps leaders of religious communities around the world harness the moral authority of their faith traditions to prevent violence, transform conflict, and provide sustainable development.

Since 1988, I have been an adjunct associate professor of management and communication in the school of professional studies at New York University. Since 2003, I have also been an adjunct professor of management at NYU's Stern School of Business, executive MBA program. Since 2017, I've been an adjunct associate professor of professional development and leadership at Columbia University's Fu Foundation School of Engineering and Applied Sciences. For twenty years I've been a contract lecturer in leadership communication at the Wharton School of the University of Pennsylvania, and for eight years I've been a contract lecturer at the United States Defense Information School, teaching senior military officers about the drivers of trust.

In my teaching and research, I study patterns: patterns that help leaders enhance competitive advantage, build trust and loyalty, and change the world for the better. I study the patterns of audience engagement and audience reaction. I study persuasion and influence, and the power of language to change people, mostly for the better.

But I've also been acutely aware of the use of communication to hurt, to harm, and to humiliate, and of how dehumanizing and demonizing language can lead some people to commit acts of violence. I typically don't teach those things in a classroom, but I often send up a flare, warning students, former students, and others of the predictable, if unintended, consequences of speech that, under the right conditions, can influence people to accept, condone, and commit violence against members of a group.

I have found myself sending up many flares in the past few years. But my concern grew into alarm as the 2018 midterm elections approached and as President Trump's language crossed a line. I worried that someone would be killed by Trump followers who embraced his increasingly incendiary rhetoric about immigrants, Mexicans, Muslims, and critics. And in a single week, about ten days before the midterms, two separate terror attacks took place. One killed eleven people at worship in a synagogue. One failed but had targeted a dozen Trump critics with mail bombs. In both cases the perpetrators justified their actions by quoting Trump language. One of them, the mail bomber, described his conversion from being apolitical to being "a soldier in the war between right and left" that resulted from his several years in Trump's orbit.[1]

The following day, I posted a blog describing the relationship between language and violence. This book is the continuation of that original blog post. In reflecting on the president's language, I noticed another pattern: The forms of his language were familiar. I quickly noticed that he was using the very same rhetorical techniques that had preceded previous mass murders, including genocides. I worried that, left unchecked, he would continue, with increasingly dire consequences.

This book documents those forms of language, and the consequences of that language, both before Trump and by Trump. But it does more. It assesses how American political life came to this dangerous and demoralizing place. And it offers hope, a path forward: a framework, a mindset, and a set of techniques to help civic leaders and informed citizens recognize the patterns of dangerous speech early, intervene early, hold those who use such language accountable for the consequences, and ideally prevent such violence in the first place.

Being an immigrant, or any other manifestation of the Other, is hard enough. It's made even more difficult when political leaders encourage their followers to take the initiative to harm the Other. However bad my childhood experience may have been—and it was bad—back then there was no president of the United States inspiring insult, humiliation, and violence against me and others like me.

WORDS
ON FIRE

PART I
COMMUNICATION
AND CONSEQUENCES

Communication is an act of will directed toward a living entity
that reacts. —HELIO FRED GARCIA, *The Power of Communication*

This book is about the power of communication to do great
harm, and how civic leaders and engaged citizens can hold
leaders accountable to prevent such harm.

Part I sets the context for the rest of the book. It establishes the
principles of leadership communication, good and bad, and identifies patterns that help citizens make sense of the bigger issues
when a leader begins using language in dangerous ways.

Chapter 1 is about how all effective leadership communication
helps to secure an outcome: a change in people. Inspired leaders
use communication to rally people to be their better selves

despite adversity. Malign leaders use communication to divide, to frighten, and to acquire power. The chapter begins with profiles of three national leaders who took the reins when things looked bleak. I look at effective leaders who used communication, as well as other leadership skills, to guide citizens to positive outcomes that seemed practically impossible when the leaders took over. I use these three positive examples to be able to draw a sharp contrast with what follows.

The chapter also describes framing, the establishment of context, that drives meaning. Framing triggers worldviews that determine the meaning of all that follows and establishes what makes sense. If surrender means annihilation, then refusal to surrender makes sense. If a group of people is evil, determined to wipe us out, an immediate threat to our safety and security, then committing violence against them makes sense. Leaders use framing to move audiences to action but can do so in either honorable or dishonorable ways.

Chapter 2 opens with a summary of one of the largest atrocities in recorded human history, the Holocaust. It then defines dangerous speech as communication that creates a social context that conditions an audience to accept, condone, and commit violence against a targeted group. The chapter then provides a summary of a more recent atrocity, the genocide of Rwandan Tutsi by the Hutu in 1994.

Most of the chapter is a demonstration of twelve forms of communication that provide the social conditions that lead people to accept, condone, or commit violence. Examples of each of the forms of communication are drawn from *Mein Kampf,* from Holocaust scholarship, and from scholarship on Hutu propaganda. The chapter closes with an observation that the twelve forms of communication serve as a kind of playbook that engaged citizens and civic leaders can use to recognize dangerous speech early, to call attention not only to the speech but to how it constitutes a danger, and to hold leaders accountable for the consequences of their speech.

Chapter 3 opens with vignettes of violence caused by such language in the United States in the last ten years. It introduces the concept of *stochastic terrorism*, the use of communication in ways that trigger lone wolves to commit acts of violence, up to and including terrorism, that are collectively predictable but not individually predictable. The phrase *stochastic terrorism* is difficult to grasp, and even to say, and tends to limit discussion. I propose a different way to describe the phenomenon, based on who is motivated to act on the communication—lone wolves—and what triggers them to so act—a kind of dog whistle that I call a lone-wolf whistle. The rest of the chapter looks at patterns of lone-wolf terrorism, and the characteristics of the lone wolves who commit these acts of violence. This includes models that show how a terrorist's mindset is created, as well as the activation process that turns a latent lone wolf into someone who commits mass murder.

Not all lone-wolf terrorism is triggered by dangerous language. But all lone-wolf-whistle terrorism, "stochastic terrorism," is triggered by such language. Knowing this, we can begin to apply both the concept of "dangerous speech" from Chapter 1, the playbook—the twelve forms of language that provoke violence—from Chapter 2, and both the terrorist mindset model and the lone-wolf terrorism escalation model to the campaign and presidency of Donald Trump, which is the longest part of the book and the entirety of Part II.

1

The Power of Communication

COMMUNICATION AND OUTCOMES

Communication has power.

Communication has the power to influence outcomes.

Communication creates competitive advantage: for a leader, for a group, for an enterprise, or for society at large.

Communication has the power to change people, to change societies, and to change the world. Communication has the power to comfort, to inspire, to liberate. Communication also has the power to terrify, to demoralize, and to oppress.

Some leaders use communication to help their followers overcome fear. Some use communication to provoke fear.

Some leaders use communication to unite; some to divide.

Some leaders use communication to appeal to the better angels of our nature; some to appeal to the worst demons within us.

This is a book about the predictable consequences of incendiary rhetoric.

I will begin by profiling three leaders who used communication in times of adversity to inspire, to align people to a difficult challenge, to protect the world from great harm, and to change the world in positive ways. Each did so at the very beginning of his tenure in senior executive office.

These examples of leaders who used communication for noble and honorable purposes provide a starting point to explore the opposite.

Fear Itself

Franklin Delano Roosevelt became the thirty-second president of the United States during the worst economic depression in the nation's history. The country was reeling. People were out of work; they couldn't support their families; homelessness was rampant. Roosevelt knew that things would get worse before they got better, and that major changes in both government and society were needed to turn the tide.

He knew that people were afraid: afraid of whether they could feed themselves and their families; afraid of whether they'd be able to get a job; afraid for both the short term and the long term. They could see no light at the end of the tunnel. However, those changes that FDR knew were necessary would be very difficult to achieve.

The moment FDR took office, in his inaugural address in March 1933, he took these challenges head-on. His inaugural began with a note of reassurance: "I am certain that my fellow Americans expect that on my induction into the presidency I will address them with a candor and a decision which the present situation of our Nation impels. This is preeminently the time to speak the truth, the whole truth, frankly and boldly. Nor need we shrink from honestly facing conditions in our country today.

This great Nation will endure as it has endured, will revive and will prosper."[1]

He then spoke the words that defined his presidency, and that became the animating spirit he brought to all adversity, starting with leading the nation out of the Great Depression and continuing through his leading the nation to war in Asia and Europe after Japan attacked and Hitler declared war in December 1941: "So, first of all, let me assert my firm belief that the only thing we have to fear is fear itself—nameless, unreasoning, unjustified terror which paralyzes needed efforts to convert retreat into advance."[2]

He then drew a connection with the citizenry, naming the people's problems as his own: "In such a spirit on my part and on yours we face our common difficulties. They concern, thank God, only material things. . . . More important, a host of unemployed citizens face the grim problem of existence, and an equally great number toil with little return. Only a foolish optimist can deny the dark realities of the moment."[3]

He then pivoted to what would be needed: "This Nation asks for action, and action now. Our greatest primary task is to put people to work. This is no unsolvable problem if we face it wisely and courageously."[4]

FDR then laid out his blueprint for how to get the country back to work, including government projects to directly employ millions in creating an infrastructure that would outlive Roosevelt and those he led.

It was the beginning of a turnaround that, by the time Roosevelt died in 1945, had converted the United States into the most powerful nation on Earth.

We Shall Fight

Consider also Roosevelt's contemporary, British prime minister Winston Churchill. He became prime minister suddenly on May 10, 1940. That same day, Germany, under Adolf Hitler, invaded

Belgium, Holland, and France. Germany had already gobbled up much of central and eastern Europe. It was clear that Hitler had his sights on Britain. Germany was an existential threat.

At the time, there was still significant disagreement in Parliament about whether it made sense to resist a German invasion. Many hoped that a negotiated agreement could prevent the slaughter that an invasion would certainly bring. Churchill's nascent government was a multi-party coalition. His own party was not in control of Parliament. As Churchill took office, he needed to rally both the British Parliament and the British people to resist a likely invasion and to be ready for a long war.

In his first five weeks, he gave three speeches that turned British public opinion around. Three days after Churchill's taking office, May 13, 1940, Hitler's forces were advancing through Holland, Belgium, and France, and Churchill did not believe they would stop at the water's edge. Churchill needed to build support for resisting the Germans. He asked Parliament for a vote of confidence in his new government. That day he addressed the House of Commons with a speech that was also broadcast that evening to the nation. He then outlined the steps he had taken since King George VI had asked him to form a government three days earlier. These included the appointment of a War Cabinet that consisted of leaders from all the major political parties.

He then laid out his intention as prime minster. It was not some negotiated settlement that would result in some benign form of German occupation, nor some negotiated treaty that would keep Germany across the English Channel but still menacing Britain. Rather, it was nothing short of defeating the Germans. He told the House,

> We have before us an ordeal of the most grievous kind. We have before us many, many long months of struggle and of suffering. You ask, what is our policy? I can say: It is to wage war, by sea, land, and air, with all our might and with all the strength that God can give us; to wage war against a

monstrous tyranny, never surpassed in the dark, lamentable catalogue of human crime. That is our policy.

You ask, what is our aim? I can answer in one word: It is victory, victory at all costs, victory in spite of all terror, victory, however long and hard the road may be; for without victory, there is no survival.[5]

Three weeks later, the situation in Europe had gotten worse. France was on the brink of falling, and the German army would soon be at the English Channel and poised to invade. During this time, a significant portion of the British army was trapped on a beach in Dunkirk, northern France, along with thousands of French and Belgian troops. They faced imminent slaughter. The loss of that many troops would dramatically lower the odds of Britain's successful defense against a German invasion.

On June 4, 1940, Churchill again addressed Parliament. He needed to report on the success in saving most of the British army from slaughter. But he also needed to gird the nation for a likely German invasion. A British public opinion research company had reported that, despite the rescue of the British Expeditionary Force, morale in Britain was low, at zero in some parts of the country. Less than half the British public believed the nation should continue fighting.

Churchill exhorted the British people to persevere, in what has become his most quoted passage:

Even though large tracts of Europe and many old and famous States have fallen or may fall into the grip of the Gestapo and all the odious apparatus of Nazi rule, we shall not flag or fail. We shall go on to the end, we shall fight in France, we shall fight on the seas and oceans, we shall fight with growing confidence and growing strength in the air, we shall defend our Island, whatever the cost may be, we shall fight on the beaches, we shall fight on the landing grounds, we shall fight in the fields and in the streets, we shall fight in the hills; we shall never surrender, and even if, which I do not for a moment believe, this Island or a large part of it were subjugated and starving, then our Empire beyond the seas, armed and guarded by the British Fleet, would carry on the struggle, until, in God's good time, the New World, with all its power and might, steps forth to the rescue and the liberation of the old.[6]

According to news accounts of the day, several members of the House of Commons were in tears by the time Churchill finished. One wrote him a letter that said, "My dear Winston. That was worth 1,000 guns and the speeches of 1,000 years."[7]

The speech had its desired effect. Although it was not broadcast live, the speech was read aloud by news hosts on the evening radio broadcasts. One listener wrote, "Even repeated by the announcer, it sent shivers (not of fear) down my spine. I think that one of the reasons why one is stirred by his Elizabethan phrases is that one feels the whole massive backing of power and resolve behind them, like a great fortress: they are never words for words' sake."[8]

An American journalist later noted that the full refrain that began "We shall fight . . ." was printed with Churchill's picture and could be found in many homes and offices throughout Britain.[9]

Two weeks later, Churchill again took to the floor of the House of Commons to continue to rally the nation despite further bad news in the war. France was about to fall—it surrendered to Germany two days later.

So began the turnaround in British fortunes. Germany eventually attacked Britain by air, but there was no invasion of German troops onto British soil. About eighteen months later, the United States entered the war, and three and a half years after that, Germany was defeated.

Because They Are Hard

John F. Kennedy became the thirty-fifth president of the United States on January 20, 1961. Eight weeks later, the Soviets sent a human being—cosmonaut Yuri Gagarin—into space and safely back to Earth. The Space Race between the United States and the Soviet Union was fully underway. And putting humans in space and bringing them back served as a proxy for scientific capacity. The symbolic meaning went way beyond adventure or exploration; it was about the ability to deliver weapons of mass destruction from space.

In 1958, President Eisenhower had founded the National Aeronautics and Space Administration (NASA) to coordinate the nation's space initiatives.

Three weeks after the Russians put a human in space, the United States matched that achievement. On May 5, 1961, Alan B. Shepard rode the *Freedom 7* capsule into suborbital space flight, and back down to Earth. Three weeks later, President Kennedy addressed a joint session of Congress. On May 25, 1961, he laid out an audacious idea:

> I believe that this nation should commit itself to achieving the goal, before this decade is out, of landing a man on the moon and returning him safely to the Earth. . . . No single space project in this period will be more impressive to mankind, or more important for the long-range exploration of space; and none will be so difficult or expensive to accomplish. . . . In a very real sense, it will not be one man going to the moon. If we make this judgment affirmatively, it will be an entire nation. For all of us must work to put him there.[10]

This was a lofty ambition, and it would take a lot of work, both in engineering and in persuasive terms. And he set out to sell the idea to the American people.

Four months later, in September, President Kennedy made his case during a speech at the football stadium at Houston's Rice University. Among other things, he addressed the geopolitical reasons to win the Space Race—to prevent the Soviets from weaponizing space. He closed his speech with an exhortation. He noted that the nation had a history of overcoming obstacles. "But why, some say, the moon? . . . We choose to go to the moon in this decade and do the other things, not because they are easy, but because they are hard, because that goal will serve to organize and measure the best of our energies and skills, because that challenge is one that we are willing to accept, one we are unwilling to postpone, and one which we intend to win, and the others, too."[11]

President Kennedy did not live to see his dream become a reality; he was assassinated in November 1963. But just seven years after the speech at Rice University, on Christmas Day, 1968, Apollo 8, piloted by US Air Force colonel Frank Borman, orbited the moon. Seven months later, two American astronauts stepped onto the surface of the moon. US Navy commander Neil Armstrong became the first human on the moon, followed twenty minutes later by US Air Force fighter pilot Buzz Aldrin. They returned safely to Earth on July 24, 1969, well before the end of the decade.

Each of these national leaders—Roosevelt, Churchill, and Kennedy—came into office with their citizens afraid. Each had a vision, each had confidence, and each could comfort people even as he exhorted them to move beyond their fears. Each could inspire people to a higher aspiration. At the time, each goal seemed out of reach.

It wasn't just talk. Each leader managed complex governmental processes that organized his nation's resources toward fulfillment of that difficult goal. Each successfully aligned communication with action to reach the goal sooner.

Each harnessed the power of communication.

The words of these three leaders demonstrate that communication has the power to rally people to overcome adversity, even in the worst of times. Communication has the power to align people around a vision, to move people toward a common goal.

Words Matter

Words are carriers of meaning well beyond the literal.

The most effective leaders—both benevolent and malevolent—use a rhetorical technique known as framing to move people. Framing creates context.

Frames trigger worldviews that determine what other meanings are possible. One of the fathers of framing is George Lakoff, a professor emeritus at the University of California, Berkeley. He observes that frames trigger the "cognitive unconscious" in people's brains.[12] He notes that most thinking—about 98 percent—is unconscious.[13] Only about 2 percent of human thought is conscious.

Lakoff describes frames as mental structures that trigger worldviews.[14] Once a frame is triggered, an entire worldview is triggered, and that determines the meaning of everything that follows. It determines what makes sense: Whatever is consistent with the frame makes sense; what is inconsistent with the frame does not make sense.[15]

FDR used framing in the very beginning of his inaugural address. At a time when people were afraid, discouraged, and in great distress, his first words were to point to a future state and to remind citizens that such a future state is consistent with the past that is only just remembered: "This great Nation will endure as it has endured, will revive and will prosper." This frame creates a context: We have a reason to hope; it is within us to rebuild.

Similarly, Churchill faced a scared and fractious population that was witnessing Germany occupy entire parts of Europe. Despite a divided country and government, he asked for a vote of Parliament giving him unequivocal authority to go to war against Germany. Notice the language of his resolution was not merely to declare war; rather, it focused on an outcome: "the united and inflexible resolve of the nation to prosecute the war with Germany to a victorious conclusion."[16] Notice the power of the frames. He asks Parliament first to affirm that they are united. Second, that their resolve is inflexible: They will do whatever it takes. And, finally, going to war is not merely a defensive act, to protect the nation from invasion. Rather, it is to prosecute the war to a "victorious conclusion," to eliminate the German threat altogether.

Framing determines what makes sense. Once survival depends on victory, then surrender puts survival at risk. In that context, "we shall never surrender" becomes a perfectly reasonable conclusion.

And JFK also used framing. The nation was scared. First the Soviets had beaten the US into space. Then, on JFK's own watch, they had beaten the nation in putting a human in space. JFK needed both to raise the stakes and to get a commitment for the massive investment of capital, attention, and political will that would be necessary to overtake the Soviets in space. So, he framed the quest as something every citizen should be part of: "In a very real sense, it will not be one man going to the moon. If we make this judgment affirmatively, it will be an entire nation. For all of us must work to put him there."[17]

Four months later, he differentiated how the American quest for space dominance would differ from the Soviets':

We have vowed that we shall not see space filled with weapons of mass destruction, but with instruments of knowledge and understanding. Yet the vows of this Nation can only be fulfilled if we in this Nation are first, and, therefore, we intend to be first. In short, our leadership in science and in industry, our hopes for peace and security, our obligations to ourselves as well as others, all require us to make this effort, to solve these mysteries, to solve them for the good of all men, and to become the world's leading spacefaring nation.[18]

That reminded the nation that this was a national security issue, and not a boondoggle or a project to enhance his own political fortunes. So, when he proposed massive spending and accelerated timelines to get American astronauts in space, it made sense.

Framing has power because it changes what people feel, before changing what people think or know. And, unlike facts, which typically are processed in the brain's neocortex—the thinking part of the brain—frames are processed in the limbic part of the brain, the emotion-provoking part of the brain. And when the emotion-provoking part of the brain is stimulated, it tends to shut down critical thinking.[19] As Lakoff describes it, when facts are inconsistent with the frame, the facts bounce off and the frame remains.[20] And once they are in one frame, people cannot make sense of a contrary frame.[21]

Metaphor is one framing technique. Metaphor—in which a word stands in for something much broader than its literal meaning—is a particularly powerful carrier of content, triggering emotional resonance.[22]

Power Corrupts

Communication has power.

FDR, Churchill, and JFK used that power to help lead their nations through adversity. They were honorable people who behaved honorably.

But power can corrupt, and corrupt leaders can harness power as effectively as honorable leaders, but to dishonorable ends, or through dishonorable means, or both.

Leaders can change what people feel, think, know, and believe through deception, through dishonesty, through pursuing hidden agendas.

Leaders can also change what people feel, think, know, and believe by pitting groups against each other: divide and conquer.

This is often a way for leaders to acquire power at the expense of their own people. They create contention, suspicion, fear. They keep people so focused on the danger of the Other that they have no time or ability to hold the leader accountable. Such leaders can also use communication to target their political adversaries.

Yale University philosopher Jason Stanley describes this technique as "fascist politics." Stanley is a scholar whose area of focus is the use of fascist politics as a mechanism to achieve or maintain power.

He observes that the techniques of fascist politics apply even when a fascist state does not arise. Rather, fascist politics is a method of getting or keeping power. He says, "The most telling symptom of fascist politics is division. It aims to separate a population into an 'us' and a 'them.' Many kinds of political movements involve such divisions; for example, Communist politics weaponizes class divisions. . . . [F]ascist politics . . . distinguishes 'us' from 'them,' appealing to ethnic, religious, or racial discrimination, and using this division to shape ideology and, ultimately, policy. Every mechanism of fascist politics works to create or solidify this distinction."[23]

Stanley helps us understand why otherwise good people might tolerate inhumanity directed toward other human beings: "The dangers of fascist politics come from the particular way in which it dehumanizes segments of the population. By excluding groups, it limits the capacity for empathy among other citizens, leading to the justification of inhumane treatment, from repression of freedom, mass imprisonment, and expulsion to, in extreme cases, mass extermination."[24]

Both benevolent and malevolent leaders use framing to change what people feel. This book focuses on the use of communication to divide, to sow suspicion and fear of the Other. Leaders who do so use framing and other communication techniques to shut down thinking and to provoke fear and hate.

Framing triggers a worldview in which certain things make sense. If a suspect group is understood to be less than human—

referred to as animals, as vermin, as carrying disease and infesting the nation—then it makes sense to try to exclude them, or worse. In that context, exterminating vermin makes sense.

If a political rival is said to hate the country, and to be putting the nation in danger, it makes sense not to support that leader or to try to remove that leader. If the providers of information are understood to be reporting fake news or to be enemies of the people, and if their criticism of the leader constitutes treason, then it makes sense for citizens to stop relying on those sources of information, and for the leader to use instruments of government to suppress that information.

Such forms of communication follow persistent patterns, with predictable consequences.

Tone at the Top

In all organizations—families, companies, nations—the leader sets the tone at the top: what we care about; the values that drive our decision-making and behaviors; what we reward; what we avoid; and what we punish. Leaders create a culture that sends such signals throughout the organization.

Researchers at the communication advisory firm MG Strategy analyze the drivers of culture. In their book *Five Frequencies: Leadership Signals That Turn Culture into Competitive Advantage*, they observe that the leader is constantly transmitting culture-defining signals, intentionally or otherwise, through decisions and actions.[25] They argue that the best leaders self-monitor their signals and are deliberate in what they broadcast, to create a culture by design rather than by default.[26]

In their book, they point to an analysis by Axios of Donald Trump's presidency and the culture he has created. Authors Jim VandeHei and Mike Allen write: "All habits, good and bad—in all organizations, big and small—flow down fast from the top."[27]

They note that this phenomenon applies to Donald Trump: "This dynamic is particularly true in the White House, and *unmistakably* true in this Trump White House. . . . Trump's lifelong habits—to improvise, to attack, to deny the undeniable, to leak—spread fast through the White House, metastasized in the agencies, and infected Republicans in Congress."[28]

The authors describe how staff members go through a cycle of being enamored of Trump and his persona. But many become frustrated by the environment around them, and often become angry at him. This leads many to leave and others to leak information outside the White House. The authors quote a senior administration official who describes the culture: "It's the Donald Trump culture. It's every man for himself—do what's best for me, not for the organization."[29]

For the purposes of the book you are reading, regarding Donald Trump and others, I will show how when a leader creates a culture that makes clear that some people are not only undeserving of dignified treatment but are an outright danger to the nation, some of the leader's followers may then feel empowered to take matters into their own hands, in the service of their leader. They get the signal from the top.

2

Less Than Human

GERMANY AFTER THE GREAT WAR

The mood was dour. Germany had been bitterly defeated in World War I. Allied sanctions had crippled German commerce and industry. The postwar government had led the country into a severe economic depression. Millions were out of work. Citizens had lost confidence in the Weimar Republic. In that vacuum a man emerged with a plan to make Germany great again and to provide the country with someone to blame for its woes.

Adolf Hitler had started to position himself in politics shortly after the war. As a returning veteran, he joined the National Socialist German Workers Party, what would become the Nazi Party, in 1919. He quickly demonstrated his leadership ability by devising the party's political program within that first year. He officially became the Führer, or leader, of the Nazi Party in 1921, and quickly increased its support.

In November 1923, the party sought to overthrow the German government through a coup d'état, which ultimately failed. Hitler and his co-conspirators were convicted of treason. During his prison sentence, Hitler used his confinement to put pen to paper and write a book that served as both his autobiography and his political vision for the future of his party and of Germany. The book laid out a set of ideas not simply political, but also revolutionary.

A key theme of the book was that Jews were to blame for the destruction of the former German political system and were the cause of both the economic and social woes faced by the masses. Playing on existing anti-Semitism within the country, Hitler suggested that to restore Germany to glory would require fighting back against the oppressive and destructive forces posed by those he described as being inferior to true Germans.

Mein Kampf was published in 1925 and, according to the US Holocaust Museum, sold more than twelve million copies and was translated into more than a dozen languages between 1925 and the summer of 1945.[1] The book today is a staple for neo-Nazis, anti-Semites, and racists around the world.

After Hitler was released from prison, he reorganized and rejuvenated the Nazi party and began the work to win over the German electorate. In 1933, after the Great Depression intensified the economic hardships within Germany and as the Nazi party steadily increased its electoral support, Hitler was made chancellor. In the years that followed, Hitler laid the foundations of the Nazi state, which led to a war that spread across the globe as well as one of the most brutal genocides in history. Six million Jews and millions of people from other persecuted groups were killed.[2]

How did Hitler and the Nazi party convince millions of Germans to actively participate in the systematic extermination of their fellow citizens?

They systematically dehumanized, demonized, and delegitimized Jews and other groups. It is part of a predictable pattern.

Patterns of Dehumanization

The US Holocaust Museum Simon-Skjodt Center for the Prevention of Genocide defines "dangerous speech" as "speech that increases the risk for violence targeting certain people because of their membership in a group, such as an ethnic, religious, or racial group. It includes both speech that qualifies as incitement and speech that makes incitement possible by conditioning its audience to accept, condone, and commit violence against people who belong to a targeted group."[3]

One of the key elements of creating such conditions is to dehumanize others. Rachel Brown, author of the center's handbook, *Defusing Hate*, notes that: "Dangerous speech often dehumanizes the group it targets (e.g., by calling its members rats, dogs, or lice), accuses the target group of planning to harm the audience, and presents the target group's existence as a dire threat to the audience."[4]

But Brown notes that speech by itself is not enough to lead people to commit violence. Four other elements are needed.

- A speaker who is influential or popular with the audience
- A medium (the means used to communicate a message) that makes the audience more likely to access, believe, or spread the speech
- A context that increases the risk that the speech will provoke violence toward a group
- An audience that is receptive to speech that promotes violence, fear, or hatred toward a group[5]

Hitler and the Nazi leadership had all of these.

Rwanda and the Genocide of the Tutsi

Around 8:30 p.m. on April 6, 1994, a plane carrying Rwandan president Juvénal Habyarimana and Burundi president Cyprien

Ntaryamira was hit by a ground-to-air missile and exploded while returning to the Rwandan capital of Kigali. Everyone on board was killed.

To understand the significance of this, and what came after, it is necessary to understand the tensions that had long existed in the central African nation of Rwanda. In 1994, Rwanda was a country in which ethnic Hutu represented 85 percent of the population, ethnic Tutsi represented 14 percent, and Twa just 1 percent.[6] There had long been tensions between the Hutu and Tutsi, solidified and amplified during colonization, first by Germany in 1884, and then by Belgium after World War I.

In the late nineteenth century, Rwanda had been organized under the ruler Kigeri Rwabugiri into tightly organized administrative divisions, mainly headed by Tutsi. When Rwanda came under European domination, the colonial powers formalized Tutsi rule and made the once-fluid social and ethnic distinctions between the Hutu and Tutsi far more rigid, with far-reaching consequences.

The Hutu took power from the Tutsi during the so-called Social Revolution of 1959. Many Tutsis were forced to flee into neighboring countries.

The plane that was shot down in 1994 was returning from a meeting of regional heads of state, at which the Rwandan president agreed to implement the Arusha Accords of August 1993. The Accords established a tentative peace between Rwanda and the Rwandan Patriotic Front, a pro-Tutsi group that had invaded Rwanda in 1990 with an aim of securing a right of return for refugee Rwandan Tutsis who had fled the country during the Social Revolution. The Accords also outlined a shift in the political structure from a presidential system to a parliamentary system, with a Council of Ministers taking on many of the responsibilities previously held by the president. This Accord represented a major threat against the ruling Hutu elite.

Within an hour after the plane crashed on April 6, before the government officially announced the crash, the news spread through radio broadcasts, roadblocks began being set up, and the genocide began. During the next hundred days, approximately eight hundred thousand people were systematically killed, primarily Tutsi men, women, and children, as well as Hutu opposition party members.[7]

This genocide is well known both for the carnage that ensued over a short period of time and for the lackluster and delayed international response to this violence. It is also notable because the genocide was committed not only by Rwandan armed forces, but also by civilians who at times brutally killed their own friends, family members, and neighbors.

What compelled thousands of people to take up arms to slay their fellow citizens?

As early as 1990, a propaganda campaign, led by those who supported the Hutu Power movement and the Hutu political establishment, began to sow suspicion against all Tutsis within the country and to encourage violence against them.

Rachel Brown of the Simon-Skjodt Center for the Prevention of Genocide notes, "Hutu extremists were able to incite genocide in Rwanda in part because years of propaganda had influenced Hutus to view Tutsis as less than human and so dangerous that they must be eliminated from the country. The propagandists' goal may not have been genocide, but their work prepared Hutus to understand and answer the call to act when extremist leaders launched the genocide."[8]

In fact, the Hutu used the same techniques the Nazis had sixty years earlier. For example, Yale's Jason Stanley notes that, "In Hutu power ideology, Hutu women exist only as wives and mothers, entrusted with the sacred responsibility of ensuring Hutu ethnic purity. This pursuit of ethnic purity was a key justification for killing Tutsis in the 1994 genocide."[9]

In 1990, the anti-Tutsi propaganda campaign took off with the publication in the Hutu newspaper *Kangura* of "Ten Commandments of the Hutu." This was quite similar to Hitler's 1935 Nuremberg Laws that systematized oppression of people who were

Jewish, including restricting marriage between Jews and non-Jews. The First Hutu Commandment was to label as a traitor any Hutu man who married or had sexual relations with a Tutsi woman.[10]

Similarly, Holocaust scholar Sarah Ann Fisk, in a thesis about Hitler's language, notes: "For Hitler, the Jew's supposed life-draining nature is comprehensive in its corruptibility. Tainted heavily by miscegenation with black people, Jews had developed a strong, insatiable sensuality and sexuality that had traditionally been associated with black people. . . . Hitler continues this tradition of portraying Jewish sexuality as extremely base and perverted; sounding more like a novelist, he illustrates the merciless predation of the Jew. . . . Hitler depicts even the young Jew as a threat, preying upon and ruining Germany's innocent maidens."[11]

Forms of Dangerous Speech: Dehumanization and Other Techniques

Dangerous speech begins with dehumanization but doesn't end there.

As I have studied the language that preceded the Holocaust, the Rwanda genocide, and similar mass killings, I have identified twelve distinct communication techniques that collectively create conditions where systematic violence against others, up to and including genocide, becomes possible. These twelve communication techniques individually and collectively create a social context that conditions an audience to accept, condone, and commit violence against people who belong to a targeted group. Each technique is a bit different from the others, although the individual techniques have elements in common. The twelve techniques are as follows:

1. **Dehumanize.** Calling groups of people animals or vermin who are infesting the nation.

2. **Demonize/Delegitimize.** Attributing to a group or rival a menacing, evil identity or calling into question the legitimacy or qualifications of a group or rival.

3. **Scapegoat.** Blaming a group for all or many of the nation's problems.

4. **Public Health Threat.** Claiming that members of a group are carrying or transmitting dangerous diseases.

5. **Safety Threat.** Claiming that a group, rival, or critic is a threat to public safety—likely to cause death or injury to the nation or to the dominant group—or is a threat to civic order.

6. **Violent Motive.** Claiming that a group has violent or hostile intentions toward a dominant group.

7. **Severely Exaggerating Risk.** Labeling a minor issue or routine event a major threat.

8. **Sinister Identities.** Attributing vague or sinister identities to a group or its members.

9. **Conspiracy.** Saying that something is part of a sinister conspiracy.

10. **Discredit Information.** Discrediting the source of objective information or of information critical of the leader.

11. **Conflation.** Conflating the leader and the state, so that any criticism of the leader is seen as an attack on the nation.

12. **Menacing Image.** Juxtaposing a menacing image (noose, swastika, flaming cross) with a person or person's image, a location, or a facility associated with the target.

Let's take a look at examples of each technique from the different incidents of genocide. The Nazi examples come from *Mein Kampf,* and the Rwanda examples come from scholarship on Hutu propaganda.

Technique #1: Dehumanize

Calling groups of people animals or specific animals (rat, monkey, ape, snake), parasites, vermin, or referring to their presence as an infestation.

From *Mein Kampf*:

[The Jew] is and remains a parasite, a sponger who, like a pernicious bacillus spreads over wider and wider areas according as some favorable area attracts him.[12]

This pestilential adulteration of the blood, of which hundreds of thousands of our people take no account, is being systematically practiced by the Jew to-day. Systematically these negroid parasites in our national body corrupt our innocent fair-haired girls and thus destroy something which can no longer be replaced in this world.[13]

From Scholarship on Hutu Propaganda:

In Rwanda, political figures, editors, and broadcasters famously described Tutsi people as inyenzi, or cockroaches. A 1993 *Kangura* newspaper article, "A Cockroach Cannot Give Birth to a Butterfly," describes Tutsi as biologically distinct from the Hutu inherently marked by malice and wickedness.[14]

As one announcer said, using the term inyenzi or cockroach to refer to [Tutsi], "the cruelty of the inyenzi can be cured only by their total extermination."[15]

Technique #2: Demonize/Delegitimize

Attributing a menacing or evil identity to a rival or group or calling into question the legitimacy or qualification of a rival or group.

From *Mein Kampf*:

The Jew essentially lacks those qualities which are characteristics of those creative races that are the founders of civilization. . . . No; the Jews have not the creative abilities which are necessary to the founding of a civilization; for in them there is not, and never has been, that spirit of idealism which is an absolutely necessary element in the higher development of mankind. Therefore the Jewish intellect will never be constructive but always destructive.[16]

For, under the cloak of purely social concepts there are hidden aims which are of a Satanic character. These aims are even expounded in the open with the clarity of unlimited impudence. This Marxist doctrine is an individual mixture of human reason and human absurdity; but the combination is arranged in such a way that only the absurd part of it could ever be put into practice, but never the reasonable part of it.[17]

From Scholarship on Hutu Propaganda:

The core of the Hutu Power ideology was the conviction that the Tutsi were a race alien to Rwanda, and not an indigenous ethnic group. In defining the Tutsi as a foreign race, the Hutu extremists were reaffirming the colonial legacy and constructing their identity the same way that Belgian colonizers had constructed them prior to independence. . . . In the Hutu Power ideology, the Tutsi were demonized by the Hutu as a foreign invading power with no entitlements in Rwanda. They had no right to power in a country where they were aliens.[18]

From the "Ten Commandments of the Hutu": 4. All Hutus must know that all Tutsis are dishonest in business. Their only goal is ethnic superiority. We have learned this by experience from experience. In consequence, any Hutu is a traitor who: Forms a business alliance with a Tutsi; Invests his own funds or public funds in a Tutsi enterprise; Borrows money from or loans money to a Tutsi; Grants favors to Tutsis (import licenses, bank loans, land for construction, public markets . . .).[19]

Technique #3: Scapegoat

Blaming a group for all or many of the nation's problems.

From *Mein Kampf*:

The division created between employer and employees seems not to have extended to all branches. How far this Judaizing process has been allowed to take effect among our people is illustrated by the fact that manual labor not only receives practically no recognition but is even considered degrading. That is not a natural German attitude. It is due to the introduction of a foreign element into our lives, and that foreign element is the Jewish spirit, one of the effects of which has been to transform the high esteem in which our handicrafts once were held into a definite feeling that all physical labor is something based and unworthy.[20]

Look at the ravages from which our people are suffering daily as a result of being contaminated with Jewish blood. Bear in mind the fact that this poisonous contamination can be eliminated from the national body only after centuries, or perhaps never.[21]

From Scholarship on Hutu Propaganda:

The Tutsi became those "who took everything," "who are everywhere," who control the business sector, who govern despite appearances, who constitute the majority in the school system, both in terms of teachers and students, in the church and within all spheres that symbolize progress. . . . *Kangura* [newspaper] was active in a context wrought with undeniable difficulties, where increasing poverty hindered access to education, health care, and employment and within a society that lived by agriculture, while land became less and less available and fertile. Within this setting, accusing Tutsi of grabbing all privileges and identifying them as scapegoats was a sure-fire mobilization tactic.[22]

Technique #4: Public Health Threat

Saying that a group of people are carrying and transmitting dangerous diseases.

From *Mein Kampf*:

Here was a pestilence, a moral pestilence, with which the public was being infected. It was worse than the Black Plague of long ago. And in what mighty doses this poison was manufactured and distributed. . . . Sometimes it went so far that one of these fellows, acting like a sewage pump, would shoot his filth directly in the face of other members of the human race. . . . One ought to realize that for one Goethe, Nature may bring into existence ten thousand despoilers who act as the work kind of germ-carriers in poisoning human souls. It was a terrible thought, and yet it could not be avoided, that the greater number of the Jews seemed specially destined by Nature to play this shameful part.[23]

There is no equivalent example from Hutu propaganda.

Technique #5: Safety Threat

Claiming that a group, rival, or critic is a threat to public safety—likely to cause death or injury to the nation or to the dominant group—or is a threat to civic order.

From *Mein Kampf*:

Whenever we read of attacks against Germany taking place in any part of the world the Jew is always the instigator.[24]

The Jewish way of reasoning thus becomes quite clear. The Bolshevization of Germany, that is to say, the extermination of the patriotic and national German intellectuals, thus making it possible to force German Labor to bear the yoke of international Jewish finance—that is only the overture to

the movement for expanding Jewish power on a wider scale
and finally subjugating the world to its rule.[25]

From Scholarship on Hutu Propaganda:

[Hutu radio] warned [in February 1994] that the [Tutsi]
were going to attack the capital, a report that was false. It
demanded that listeners protect themselves against [Tutsi]
in certain parts of the city. Hutu in those neighborhoods, led
by militia, killed about seventy people, thus foreshadowing
the bloody events to come two months later.[26]

Tutsi [said a Rwanda politician] were going to "exterminate you until they are the only ones left in the country so
that they can keep for a thousand years the power that their
fathers had kept for four hundred."[27]

Technique #6: Violent Motive

Claiming that a group or rival has violent motives, including want-
ing to supplant, wipe out, replace, eliminate, harm, or kill members of the dominant group.

From *Mein Kampf*:

In accordance with the general brutality and rapacity of his
nature, he turns the trades union movement into an organization for the exercise of physical violence. The resistance of
those whose common sense has hitherto saved them from
surrendering to the Jewish dictatorship is now broken down
by terrorization.[28]

Out of the democratic Jew, the Jew of the People, arises
the "Jew of the Blood," the tyrant of the peoples. In the
course of a few years he endeavors to exterminate all those
who represent the national intelligence. And by thus depriv-
ing the peoples of their natural intellectual leaders he fits

them for their fate as slaves under a lasting despotism. Russia furnishes the most terrible example of such a slavery.[29]

From Scholarship on Hutu Propaganda:

[Hutu radio] emphasized the message that all Hutu were at risk of being attacked, overwhelmed, recolonized, and exploited by all Tutsi and that appropriate measures should be taken to prevent this.[30]

The "10 [Hutu] Commandments" were presented as a response to an earlier article published in *Kangura*, entitled the "Plan de colonisation des Tutsi" ("Tutsi colonization plan"), a clearly fictitious account about how, supposedly, the Tutsi were planning to colonize the entire region of Central Africa and enslave the Hutu. . . . *Kangura*'s message echoed official government propaganda about the RPF: "Since the Social Revolution of 1959, the Tutsi have never relinquished their plan to take over the country, to exterminate the intellectuals, and to dominate the Hutu farmers."[31]

Technique #7: Severely Exaggerating Risk

Labeling a minor issue or a routine event a major threat.
From *Mein Kampf*:

[W]henever Aryans have mingled their blood with that of an inferior race the result has been the downfall of the people who were the standard-bearers of a higher culture. . . . The act which brings about such a development is a sin against the will of the Eternal Creator. And as a sin this act will be avenged.[32]

From Scholarship on Hutu Propaganda:

While the Rwandan authorities exaggerated the size of attack and the threat of the Rwanda Patriotic Front itself,
Kangura tried to persuade its readers that the rebel invasion
was only one part of a larger plan by the Tutsi to "dominate"
the Hutu.[33]

Technique #8: Sinister Identities

Attributing vague but sinister identities to a group or its members.
From *Mein Kampf*:

The effect produced by [the Jew's] presence is also like that
of the vampire; for wherever he establishes himself the people who grant him hospitality are bound to be bled to death
sooner or later.[34]

For only in the brain of a monster, and not that of a man,
could the plan of this organization take shape whose work-
ings must finally bring about the collapse of human civilization and turn this world into a desert waste.[35]

From Scholarship on Hutu Propaganda:

Tutsi leaders were portrayed as cunning, bloodthirsty, un-
trustworthy, and natural power mongers. These negative
representations tap into Rwandan history and old stereo-
types exemplified in such sayings as "You give shelter to a
Tutsi in your living room, he chases you out of your bed-
room" and "You cure a Tutsi of inflammation of the genitals,
he makes love to your wife."[36]

The general picture painted of the Tutsi community by
[Hutu radio] was that of a treacherous people, people who
had hoodwinked the Hutu, living with them in apparent
peace while all the while planning an attack.[37]

Technique #9: Conspiracy

Claiming that something is part of a larger sinister conspiracy to do harm to the nation, or that some sinister puppet-master is controlling members of the group.

From *Mein Kampf*:

Aided by international influences, [the Jew] forms a ring of enemies around those nations which have proved themselves too sturdy for him in withstanding attacks from within. He would like to force them into war and then, if it should be necessary to his plans, he will unfurl the banners of revolt even while the troops are actually fighting at the front.[38]

In peace-time, as well as during the War, the Jewish-Marxist stock-exchange Press systematically stirred up hatred against Germany, until one State after another abandoned its neutrality and placed itself at the service of the world coalition, even against the real interests of its own people.[39]

From Scholarship on Hutu Propaganda:

Kangura [newspaper] criticized the country's authorities for a lack of vigilance and for providing Tutsi with identity cards attesting that they were Hutu, which made control and discrimination impossible. "Due to the practice of identity falsification, the policy aiming for ethnic balance has failed. This explains why the Tutsi—those who kept their identity and those who modified it—now make up 80 per cent of staff in our schools. But who would be surprised by this? Those who should implement this policy are themselves Tutsi, pretending they are Hutu."[40]

Allegations that RPA [armed wing of Tutsi Rwanda Patriotic Front] members were not Rwandans and formed part of a regional conspiracy to dominate Hutu and set up a Tutsi-Hima empire in central Africa took up 7.05 per cent of the broadcasts; allegations that the RPA wanted to take over the country and reinstate the monarchy, subjugating all Hutus accounted for 5.89 per cent [of Hutu radio] broadcasts.[41]

Technique #10: Discredit Information

Discrediting or refusing to accept the accuracy of objective information or information that is critical of the leader.

From *Mein Kampf:*

The deeper my soundings went the lesser grew my respect for the Press which I formerly admired. Its style became still more repellent and I was forced to reject its ideas as entirely shallow and superficial. To claim that in the presentation of facts and views its attitudes was impartial seemed to me to contain more falsehood than truth. The writers were—Jews.[42]

The function of the so-called liberal Press was to dig the grave for the German people and Reich. No mention need be made of the lying Marxist Press. To them the spreading of falsehood is as much a vital necessity as the mouse is to a cat. Their sole task is to break the national backbone of the people, thus preparing the nation to become the slaves of international finance and its masters, the Jews.[43]

From Scholarship on Hutu Propaganda:

In mid-1991, the creation of Radio Muhabura [a Tutsi-leaning station] was reported by Radio Rwanda, Reuters, and the Ugandan government daily newspaper, *The New Vision*. Radio Rwanda immediately instructed listeners not to believe anything which they heard on the rebel radio broadcasts and warned: "whenever you will hear anything from that radio station, try to understand their aim which is . . . to divide our country and try to put back our country in to the thirties."[44]

[T]he Hutu radio broadcast from April 11, 1994, read a declaration from the Ministry of Defense which stated no less than four times that the [Tutsi-sponsored] radio station was lying: "The population and the army are requested not to believe the lies of Radio Muhabura and other radios which monitor news from [Tutsis] because their aim is nothing else than to divert, divide, and threaten Rwandans."[45]

Technique #11: Conflation

Conflating the leader with the state, so that any criticism of the leader is seen to be an attack on the state itself.

From the US Holocaust Museum:

After the Nazi rise to power in Germany in the 1930s, it became common for Germans to greet each other with a stiff-armed salute and the words "Heil Hitler." The "German Greeting," as it became known, was a ritual of the cult of Adolf Hitler. Under the Nazi regime, Germans were expected to pay public allegiance to the "Führer" (leader) in quasi-religious forms. For example, they even saluted statues of Hitler.[46]

From Holocaust Scholarship:

To begin with, people often rendered the gesture under duress. Particularly in the first months of Nazi power, when dissidents and opponents of the regime were liable to be beaten up by storm troopers or hauled off to a concentration camp, many people conformed simply out of fear. The posters put up along Germany's streets proclaiming "Germans use the German Greeting!" implied that anyone who did not use it could not be counted as part of the "national community" of Germans, and was an outsider, an outcast, even an enemy.[47]

Technique #12: Menacing Image

Juxtaposing a menacing image (noose, crosshairs, animal, vermin) with the image of a person or location, facility, or institution associated with the target.

From Holocaust Scholarship:

A Nazi propaganda poster shows a microscope and a slide with germs on it. On close inspection, each of the germs is in the shape of the Star of David.

Another Nazi propaganda poster juxtaposes the image of Christ on the cross and a burning city. Looking over it is a Jew portrayed as a sinister-looking vampire figure, and, in Polish, the words "Enemy of Christianity."[48]

From Scholarship on Hutu Propaganda:

In November 1991, Hassan Ngeze asks one question: "What tools will we use to defeat the Inyenzi once and for all?" The answer is in the adjacent illustration where Kayibanda and a "beautiful" machete appear alongside each other [1991 issue of *Kangura*]. This allegory intends to demonstrate the rationale for the elimination of Tutsi by means of murder, implying that this is inscribed in the republic's history and that it is based on the need to protect the Hutu from the permanent threat of feudal bondage.[49]

In 1991, *Echo de Milles Collins*, a newspaper that supported [the] Habyarimana regime, published a cartoon showing a Tutsi massacring Hutu with [the] caption, "Flee! A Tutsi will exterminate the Hutus."[50]

Understanding the Power of These Twelve Techniques

These twelve techniques, collectively and over time, create the very conditions that the US Holocaust Museum Simon-Skjodt Center for the Prevention of Genocide refer to as "dangerous speech": "speech that increases the risk for violence targeting certain people because of their membership in a group, such as an ethnic, religious, or racial group. It includes both speech that qualifies as incitement and speech that makes incitement possible by conditioning its audience to accept, condone, and commit violence against people who belong to a targeted group."[51]

And the consequences were real. More than ten million killed in the Holocaust; nearly a million killed in the hundred days of the Rwanda Genocide.

We often hear calls of "Never Again" when commemorating the Holocaust and other genocides. But they keep happening. One way to be vigilant is to recognize the power of dangerous speech to create conditions that make such outcomes possible, and then to point to the patterns. Left unchecked, this language can have escalating consequences.

We can see these twelve techniques as constituting a playbook that malicious leaders can use to divide communities and to accumulate power. We can see that the Nazis used all twelve techniques—plays—over more than fifteen years. The Hutu used ten of the twelve over a four-year period.

The playbook has explanatory power: It can help us make sense of the causes of violence in the past and even in the present. But it also has predictive power: We can anticipate the future consequences of the use of such language on society at large, and on the targets of that language.

We can use both this explanatory and predictive power to call attention to the patterns when they arise, and to hold those who use the playbook accountable.

THE PLAYBOOK

TWELVE RHETORICAL FORMS THAT MAY PROVOKE VIOLENCE

1. DEHUMANIZE: Calling groups of people animals or vermin who are infesting the nation.

- **Nazis:** Jews are animals, vermin, rats, lice, leeches, parasites.
- **Hutu:** Tutsi are cockroaches.

2. DEMONIZE/DELEGITIMIZE: Attributing to a rival or group a menacing or evil identity or calling into question the legitimacy or qualification of a rival or group.

- **Nazis:** Jews are great masters of lies; Jewish intellect is always destructive; Jews are responsible for Marxism, Bolshevism; Jews as Satan; Jews as sexual predators.
- **Hutu:** Tutsis are foreign, not real Rwandans; Tutsis as alien race reaffirming colonial legacy.

3. SCAPEGOAT: Blaming a group for all or many of the nation's problems.

- **Nazis:** Jews cause estrangement between workers and employers; Jews are responsible for the downfall of the German people; Jews are profiting from the decline of the German economy.
- **Hutu:** Tutsi took everything; Tutsi are responsible for Hutu poverty, lack of access to education, healthcare, and employment.

4. PUBLIC HEALTH THREAT: Saying people are carrying or transmitting dangerous diseases.

- **Nazis:** Jews are a pestilence, spreading infection, depicted as germs, as parasitic disease-carrying organisms, a gangrenous appendix.

5. SAFETY THREAT: Claiming that a group or people or a political rival is a threat to public safety or civic order.

- **Nazis:** Jews will force Germany into war; Jews sabotage social enterprises; Jews try to exterminate all who represent national intelligence; Jews are always the instigator in any attack on Germany; Jews are exterminating German intellectuals.
- **Hutu:** Tutsi will kill Hutu, so Hutu need to act first; Tutsi will exterminate Hutu; Tutsi will take up arms against Hutu.

6. VIOLENT MOTIVE: Claiming that a group has violent or hostile intentions toward a dominant group.

- **Nazis:** Rapacious by nature, Jews turn trade union movement into organization for physical violence; Jews will stop at nothing; Jews consider as enemies not only those who attack but anyone capable of resisting; Jews want to bastardize German people; Jews systematically endeavor to lower the racial quality of the German people.
- **Hutu:** Tutsi want to enslave Hutu; Tutsi children, women, and old men will take up arms; All Tutsi will attack all Hutu; Tutsi want to colonize Rwanda as part of Central African region.

7. SEVERELY EXAGGERATING RISK: Labeling a minor issue or routine event a major threat.

- **Nazis:** Jews invariably lead to the downfall of higher culture; intermarriage would lead to the collapse of beauty, nobility, and humanity.
- **Hutu:** Tutsi castrated Burundi president, will castrate Rwandan Hutu; RPF invasion part of larger plan to dominate Hutu.

(continues)

TWELVE RHETORICAL FORMS
THAT MAY PROVOKE VIOLENCE (CONT.)

8. SINISTER IDENTITIES: Attributing vague or sinister identities to a group or its members.

- **Nazis:** Jews are vampires, are Satan; Jews' very existence is a denial of God's image; Jews are Communists, Bolsheviks, Marxists.
- **Hutu:** Tutsi leaders are cunning, bloodthirsty, power mongers; Tutsi are treacherous.

9. CONSPIRACY: Saying that something is part of a sinister conspiracy.

- **Nazis:** Jews bring about destruction of the state; undermine foundations of national resistance; Jewish-Marxist stock-exchange; Press systematically stirred up hatred against Germany so neutral states joined coalition against Germany.
- **Hutu:** Belgian peacekeepers with Tutsi shot down president's plane; Rwandan government with Tutsis provided identity cards identifying Tutsi as Hutu.

10. DISCREDIT INFORMATION: Discrediting the source of objective information or information critical of the leader.

- **Nazis:** All journalists are controlled by Jews; the function of a liberal press is to dig a grave for the German people; the sole task of the press is to break the backbone of the people, to have Germans become slaves of international finance and its masters, Jews; through the press, the Jew is always spreading falsehoods.
- **Hutu:** Do not believe negative comments by foreigners on Tutsi radio; do not believe anything on Tutsi radio.

11. CONFLATION: Conflating the leader and the state, so that any criticism of the leader is seen as an attack on the nation (i.e., negative media coverage of the leader is cast as media being an enemy of the people or unpatriotic).

- **Nazis:** "Heil Hitler," so-called "German Greeting," mandatory; Rudolf Hess: The Party is Hitler, Hitler is Germany, Germany is Hitler.

12. MENACING IMAGE: Juxtaposing a menacing image (noose, crosshairs, flaming cross, swastika, etc.) with a person or person's image, a location, or a facility associated with the target.

- **Nazis:** Jews depicted as a variety of animals; as vampires, rodents; Jews depicted as germs; Jews depicted as enemies of Christianity.
- **Hutu:** Illustrations of machete; cartoon depicting Tutsi using machete to exterminate Hutus.

3

Stochastic Terrorism and Lone Wolves

FROM DOG WHISTLES TO LONE-WOLF WHISTLES

I t was an ordinary Sunday at the Reformation Lutheran Church in Wichita, Kansas. It was the last Sunday in May 2009. The 10:00 a.m. service had just begun. Just inside the church foyer a sixty-seven-year-old usher was handing out leaflets to latecomers about the day's events at the church. A visitor approached, held a .22 caliber pistol to the side of the usher's head, and shot him at point-blank range. The usher died instantly.

The shooter pointed his weapon at two others who tried to come to the usher's aid, and then ran from the church and escaped in his car. He was later arrested.

The usher was Dr. George Tiller, the only provider of abortions in the Wichita area, and one of only three physicians in the country to perform late-term termination of pregnancy, a procedure that is legal.

Dr. Tiller was aware that he was in danger. He was wearing body armor, as he had been since the FBI first advised him to do so eleven years earlier. Dr. Tiller had been attacked before. In 1993, while in his car, he had been shot five times by an anti-abortion activist and had survived. The activist, Shelley Shannon, was later convicted of attempted murder. At her trial, Shannon said that there was nothing wrong with trying to kill Dr. Tiller, because of the work he did. She was sentenced to eleven years in prison. Dr. Tiller then started driving an armored SUV.

In 1986, Dr. Tiller's clinic had been firebombed. As it was being rebuilt, he put up a sign reading, "Hell no, we won't go!"[1]

But that Sunday in 2009, Dr. Tiller was assassinated. The killer was Scott Roeder, fifty-one years old, who lived in a Kansas City suburb more than 150 miles from the church. During his trial Roeder told the judge that he was protecting children so he was justified in killing Dr. Tiller. The judge disagreed, noting that abortion, including late-term abortion, is legal in Kansas. He also said, "There is no immediate danger in the back of a church."[2] Roeder said that he had been contemplating killing Dr. Tiller for at least sixteen years.

Roeder was convicted of first-degree murder and other charges and sentenced to life in prison without chance of parole for fifty years.

The assassination of Dr. Tiller was not a surprise. He had been the subject of a vigorous campaign to demonize him. Anti-abortion groups such as Operation Rescue had targeted his clinic for years, including blocking access to the clinic and acts of sabotage against it. After the killing, Operation Rescue founder Randall Terry, who had led many of the protests, issued a statement via *ChristianNewsWire*:

George Tiller was a mass-murderer. We grieve for him that he did not have time to properly prepare his soul to face God. I am more concerned that the Obama Administration will use Tiller's killing to intimidate pro-lifers into surrendering our most effective rhetoric and actions. Abortion is still murder. And we still must call abortion by its proper name; murder.

Those men and women who slaughter the unborn are murderers according to the Law of God. We must continue to expose them in our communities and peacefully protest them at their offices and homes, and yes, even their churches.[3]

That kind of language, that abortion is murder and that Dr. Tiller was a mass murderer, was part of a campaign by several anti-abortion groups to close abortion clinics in the United States. It was part of what Terry called his movement's "most effective rhetoric and actions."

One group had distributed posters with a picture of Dr. Tiller and the words *WANTED: Auschwichita Abortionist*, combining the place names for the Nazi death camp and the city where Dr. Tiller lived. Similar "wanted" posters had preceded the murders of other abortion doctors: Dr. George Gunn and Dr. George Patterson in 1993, and Dr. John Britton in 1994. The posters claimed that the doctors killed babies, and listed their work and home addresses, pictures of their faces, and their phone numbers. After Dr. Tiller's murder, one doctor in North Carolina, who had been similarly portrayed, told CBS News, "I am always looking over my shoulder. I know they know my car. They know my face. They've been to my house. They've put these posters in my neighborhood. So yeah, I look over my shoulder. . . . These posters are a call for my murder."[4]

In Dr. Tiller's case it wasn't just anti-abortion activists who used this kind of language. Fox News late-night host Bill O'Reilly had made Dr. Tiller the subject of his commentary for years. O'Reilly called the doctor "Tiller the baby killer." An analysis by PolitiFact found that O'Reilly had mentioned Dr. Tiller by name forty-two times. On twenty-four of those occasions, he used the phrase "baby killer." On one show O'Reilly said, "In the state of Kansas, there is a doctor, George Tiller, who will execute babies for $5,000 if the mother is depressed."[5]

No one, including O'Reilly, explicitly called for Dr. Tiller's murder, but O'Reilly's and the anti-abortion groups' language and images had the effect of mobilizing people to commit such acts of violence against him and other abortion providers.

The idea that abortion doctors kill babies became a flashpoint in the early days of the campaign for the 2016 presidential nomination. And it also put at risk the lives of reproductive health workers.

Selling Baby Parts?

On July 14, 2015, an anti-abortion group called The Center for Medical Progress (CMP) released the first of a series of videos purporting to show that Planned Parenthood was illegally selling fetal tissue from aborted fetuses.[6] The video, titled "Planned Parenthood Uses Partial-Birth Abortion to Sell Baby Parts," showed footage taken secretly of a senior Planned Parenthood executive allegedly discussing the sale of fetal tissue.[7] It ended with the message, "Share this video. Hold Planned Parenthood accountable for their illegal sale of baby parts."[8] The video also launched the hashtag #PPSellsBabyParts.[9]

Eventually, the video would be exposed as a hoax, and the claims of those who promoted the video would all be discredited. At the time, the video created a sensation that became irresistible for some of the early candidates for the Republican presidential nomination.

Former Florida governor Jeb Bush tweeted that the video was a "shocking and horrific reminder that we must do so much more to foster a culture of life in America."[10] Wisconsin governor Scott Walker called the video "absolutely horrifying and disgusting," adding that, "Planned Parenthood and the Democrats who vote to fund this organization owe the American people an explanation for these heinous, and possibly illegal, actions."[11] Senator Ted Cruz called for Congress to investigate and defund Planned Parenthood, saying, "There is no place for taxpayer funding of organizations that profit from taking away innocent life, much less profiting off the bodies of the lives they have stolen."[12] Kentucky senator Rand Paul circulated a petition to defund Planned Parenthood.[13] And Louisiana governor Bobby Jindal directed his state health department to investigate local Planned Parenthood chapters.[14]

Several weeks after the video's release, several dozen attorneys called on California's attorney general, Kamala Harris, to investigate CMP and noted that the video and commentary about it put the safety of reproductive health workers at risk. They argued, "Given the unique risks that abortion providers face of being targeted by anti-abortion extremists, abortion providers whose images and names are blasted across the internet in this fashion face grave threats to their and their family's safety."[15]

In late August, a federal judge issued an emergency restraining order against CMP, forbidding it from releasing any more videos.[16] Despite the court order, CMP posted more videos—but rather than publish them openly they posted them on their attorney's website. The head of CMP and his attorney were later found to be in contempt of court.

A month after the first video was released, CMP released a new video that suggested that some fetuses are aborted with their hearts still beating. The video included an interview with a woman identified as an ex-procurement technician for a biospecimen company. She described an alleged instance where she was tasked with harvesting the brain from a well-formed male fetus whose heart was still beating after being aborted. The video also included a clip of a fully formed fetus in a metal bowl.[17] There was also a photo of adult hands holding a well-formed fetus.

A woman in Pennsylvania recognized that image as a video taken by her family as she went into premature labor in her nineteenth week of pregnancy, resulting in a miscarriage. CMP had

used her family photo without permission and had mischaracterized it as an abortion.[18]

At the Republican presidential debate in September, Carly Fio-
rina falsely claimed that the video showed "a fully formed fetus on
the table, its heart beating, its legs kicking while someone says we
have to keep it alive to harvest its brain."[19]

Between July and September 19, 2015, after the initial release
of the CMP videos, there were nine reported criminal or suspicious incidents against Planned Parenthood, including cyberat-
tacks, threats, and arson.[20] Three days after the debate, the FBI
released an Intelligence Assessment, warning: "[I]t is likely criminal or suspicious incidents will continue to be directed against
reproductive health care providers, their staff and facilities."[21]

The FBI also noted that the attacks they had seen already
against Planned Parenthood facilities were "consistent with the
actions of lone offenders using tactics of arsons and threats all of
which are typical of the pro-life extremist movement."[22]

The FBI was right to be concerned. Several weeks later, on
Friday, November 27, a lone gunman began firing inside a
Planned Parenthood clinic in Colorado Springs, leading to a
five-hour standoff with police.[23] He was carrying six rifles, five
handguns, a shotgun, and more than five hundred rounds of
ammunition. The shooter, Robert Lewis Dear Jr., left three dead,
including one police officer, plus nine injured.[24] Investigators reported that during his questioning Dear rambled about "no
more baby parts."[25] The *Washington Post* reported that Dear told
police he was a "warrior for babies" and was upset with Planned
Parenthood for "performing abortions and selling baby parts."[26]
Dear had an affinity for the extremist anti-abortion group Army
of God, whom he described as "heroes," and thought that those
who attacked abortion providers were doing "God's work."[27] The
Army of God had taken credit for a number of abortion clinic
bombings and killings.

More than a dozen state attorneys general investigated the
charges made against Planned Parenthood by CMP. None found

any evidence of improper or illegal activity by Planned Parenthood.[28] One Texas grand jury that had been asked to indict Planned Parenthood chose instead to indict the head of CMP and one of his employees for making and using fake driver's licenses to get access to a Planned Parenthood facility.[29]

The US House of Representatives Oversight and Reform Committee investigated the allegations against Planned Parenthood and concluded, in part:

* The CMP videos include no credible evidence that Planned Parenthood profits from its fetal tissue donation program.
* Planned Parenthood receives reasonable reimbursement for its tissue donation services, as expressly permitted by law.
* There is no credible evidence that Planned Parenthood doctors change the method, timing, or procedure of abortions solely for the purpose of obtaining fetal tissue in violation of federal law.
* There is no credible evidence that Planned Parenthood collects fetal tissue without obtaining proper consent.
* Planned Parenthood does not conduct partial birth abortions.
* The videos have been heavily edited and deceptively manipulated.
* [CMP founder David] Daleiden created the Center for Medical Progress in 2013 with the sole purpose of entrapping Planned Parenthood.
* Daleiden's tactics are potentially criminal.
* Planned Parenthood does not use federal funds in this manner.
* Abortion services make up a minuscule percentage of Planned Parenthood's services.
* No federal funds are used to support Planned Parenthood's fetal tissue donation programs.

- Only a small fraction of Planned Parenthood affiliates currently participates in fetal tissue research.[30]

In 2017, David Daleiden, the founder of CMP, and one of his employees were indicted on fifteen felony charges including conspiracy to invade privacy. On December 5, 2019, a California judge dismissed five of those charges. As of this writing they are awaiting trial for the remaining charges.[31] In November 2019, a federal jury in San Francisco awarded Planned Parenthood more than two million dollars in a suit against Daleiden and others. The jury found that Daleiden and his colleague had violated state and federal laws against trespassing, fraud, clandestine recording, and racketeering. The same week a federal appellate court upheld the injunction against posting any videos of abortion providers.[32]

Robert Dear, the Colorado Planned Parenthood shooter, was diagnosed with a delusional disorder and found incompetent to stand trial. He spent four years at the Colorado Mental Health Institute in Pueblo.[33] In December 2019, he was indicted on sixty-eight federal charges. During his hearing, he insisted that he is competent to stand trial, saying, "I'm not crazy, I'm just a religious zealot."[34]

Stochastic Terrorism

The killing of abortion doctors and the Colorado Springs Planned Parenthood attacks follow a pattern: Individuals, without direction from a central authority, responded to the language of baby killing and the selling of baby parts and took matters into their own hands.

The framing is very powerful. The phrases "baby killer," "mass murderer," and descriptions such as "a fully formed fetus on the table, its heart beating, its legs kicking while someone says we have to keep it alive to harvest its brain" provoke deep emotional reactions. So does Fox News's Bill O'Reilly's claim that a doctor will "execute babies for $5,000 if the mother is depressed."[35]

These are the acts of monsters. They put at risk all children, not just fetuses. Frames trigger worldviews that determine what makes sense. If someone is an imminent threat, it makes sense to try to neutralize the threat. The woman who first tried to assassinate Dr. Tiller said she had no remorse, because he was a baby killer. The man who succeeded in killing Dr. Tiller justified his act as protecting babies from slaughter. In their frame, such actions make sense. Once in those frames, people are unlikely to consider evidence that is contrary to those frames.

"Dangerous speech," under the right conditions, can influence people to accept, condone, and commit violence against members of a group.[36] In the aftermath of the Tiller shooting, the use of language that provokes some people to commit acts of violence was named *stochastic terrorism* by an anonymous blogger.

The phrase *stochastic terrorism* had initially been coined in 2002 by a mathematical physicist and expert in catastrophes, Dr. Gordon Woo. Dr. Woo is an expert in risk management with a specialty in quantifying catastrophic risks. He wrote in the *Journal of Risk Finance* about heightened security in the aftermath of the 9/11 attacks. Dr. Woo noted that after such a major terror attack, as Western societies increased security, it was likely that groups like Al-Qaeda would shift their focus from highly directed attacks to more decentralized targets of opportunity.[37]

The name *stochastic terrorism* is drawn from a principle in statistics about seemingly random things still being predictable. Despite the unfamiliarity many people have with the word *stochastic*, the name caught on in the aftermath of the killing of Dr. Tiller. Social scientists, commentators, and journalists began to use it to describe violence provoked by language.

In their book, *The Age of Lone Wolf Terrorism*, Indiana State University criminologist Mark S. Hamm and Australia's Victoria University sociologist Ramon Spaaij define stochastic terrorism as, "[T]he use of mass media to provoke random acts of ideologically motivated violence that are statistically predictable but individually unpredictable."[38]

Hamm and Spaaij observe that ISIS has used stochastic terrorism through the broadcasting of beheading videos and extensive use of social media in multiple languages. They argue that the stochastic terrorist indirectly enables the expression of violence through persuasive communication, without knowing who will pick up on the messages and commit violence, when, or against whom. They refer to people who pick up on messages as "emergent lone wolves."[39] "What often matters most in stochastic terrorism is the emotional intensity of the messaging and the way it is socially constructed and interpreted by the consumer, not the intentions of the messenger. In other words, the messenger does not have to actively promote violence for violence to occur."[40]

Stochastic terrorism doesn't make a direct call to violence. Rather, it infuriates, frightens, and mobilizes people to take matters into their own hands. So, stochastic terrorist violence is statistically predictable, even if it will not predict that a certain individual will commit a certain act against a certain person or group or place.

The stochastic terrorist uses incendiary rhetoric in the full expectation or with a recognition that it may trigger someone somewhere to act out in some way. Such rhetoric increases the likelihood that someone, for ideological, political, religious, or personal reasons, will react. For politicians, that explicit desired reaction may simply be to gain votes. For single-issue organizations, such as anti-abortion activists, the desired reaction may be to mobilize people to picket at clinics or to lobby for tougher legislation. In all these instances, a foreseeable consequence of demonizing, dehumanizing, or delegitimizing language is that some people may go a step further and commit acts of violence that they otherwise would not have committed.

Stochastic terrorism has plausible deniability built in. Stochastic terrorists can deny having anything to do with the violence that occurs from their language and may even condemn such acts. But they are unlikely to change their rhetoric, even when the link between the language and the violence is called to their attention.

The First Amendment protects free speech but not calls to violence that create a clear and present danger to people. We are not permitted to yell "fire" in a crowded theater that is not on fire, for example. A foreseeable consequence of such use of language is panic, leading to a stampede that may endanger the lives of people in that theater. But stochastic terrorism is insidious because it is a clear but indirect, yet still predictable, danger.

Notice that the phrase itself, *stochastic terrorism*, tends to confuse and makes discussion of the phenomenon difficult. The name puts the emphasis on the statistical predictability of an act of violence. That may not be the most productive way to call attention to this phenomenon. I propose addressing the issue from a different direction, from the people who are motivated by language to commit such violence, and what causes that motivation.

There is a well-known phenomenon in American politics where politicians use coded language that conveys one meaning, usually benign, to most people, but a different meaning to members of a certain group or followers of a certain ideology. This is known as "dog whistle politics," from the metaphor of a whistle that is audible to dogs but not to people.

Language that provokes violence is of this type, but such language does more than convey a private meaning. It encourages, provokes, or invites individuals to act in response to that language. It triggers lone individuals, people who are not directed by a central authority, to commit acts of violence. This is what happened in both the people who shot Dr. Tiller, years apart, as well as what happened in the shooter in the Colorado Springs Planned Parenthood attack. They thought they were doing something noble, in preventing the killing of babies and the selling of baby parts. That they were committing—or attempting to commit—murder as simply a means to an end.

Those who respond to such signals are lone wolves, predators who operate independently of an authority. Hamm and Spaaij describe this phenomenon as follows: "Lone-wolf terrorism is political violence perpetrated by individuals who act alone; who do not belong to an organized terrorist group or network; who act without the direct influence of a leader or hierarchy; and whose tactics and methods are conceived and directed by the individual without any direct outside command or direction."[41]

Other experts on lone-wolf terrorism, often called "lone-actor terrorism," expand on this definition a bit, to include a pair of individuals or very small groups. But the key is that they operate without direction from a central authority, choose the targets themselves, and equip themselves independently of some larger resource.

Not all lone wolves are triggered by language. Some are simply triggered by ongoing commitment to a terrorist cause, and act when they see an opportunity to do so. Others are triggered by events in the world. So, not all lone-wolf terrorism is stochastic terrorism, but all stochastic terrorism is lone-wolf terrorism. Stochastic terrorism is a subset of the larger category of lone-wolf terrorism.

Those who commit violence triggered by language are not directed to do so. Rather, they take it upon themselves to do so. But the people who send such signals either intend the violence, or act in reckless disregard of the likelihood that such language may foreseeably lead to such violence.

I propose a new name for such violence-provoking language: *lone-wolf-whistles*. Acts of violence triggered by such language I call *lone-wolf-whistle violence*. When the target of the violence is political—in the service of a political, ideological, or similar motive—I call it *lone-wolf-whistle terrorism*.

In law enforcement and counterterrorism vernacular, lone wolves are individuals who take it upon themselves to commit violence for political or ideological reasons. They also typically have some form of grievance against a group or government. Some are emotionally unstable. Hamm and Spaaij conclude that there is a 50 percent chance that those who respond to what I call lone-wolf whistles by committing acts of political violence either have a criminal record or a mental illness or both.[42]

Lone-Wolf Terrorism After 9/11

The attacks on the World Trade Center and Pentagon on September 11, 2001, were planned with military precision and carried out by terrorists at the direction of Osama bin Laden, head of Al-Qaeda. But in the years following the attack, Al-Qaeda adapted its methods, relying less on a traditional command-and-control method of attack and rather using the internet and social media to radicalize potential followers and providing online instruction on the building of bombs and other forms of mass murder. This is precisely what Dr. Gordon Woo had predicted in his *Journal of Risk Finance* article in early 2002.

Ten years after the 9/11 attacks, President Barack Obama noted, "The biggest concern we have right now is not the launching of a major terrorist operation, although that risk is always there, the risk that we're especially concerned over right now is the lone-wolf terrorist, somebody with a single weapon being able to carry out wide-scale massacres. . . . You know, when you've got one person who is deranged or driven by a hateful ideology, they can do a lot of damage, and it's a lot harder to trace those lone-wolf operators."[43]

A year earlier, CIA director Leon Panetta had told Congress that the main threat to the United States was lone-wolf terrorism.[44] In the years since 9/11, lone-wolf terrorism has been the subject of significant study by scholars and national security experts.

One such expert is Jeffrey D. Simon, president of Political Risk Assessment Company, Inc., and a terrorism expert. Simon notes that traditional terrorist group members pledge their loyalty to the group or its leaders, and then are expected to carry out orders with strict obedience. This was the case in Al-Qaeda's attacks on 9/11. Simon notes, "The lone wolf, however, doesn't have to make any pledges to a leader or make his or her desires align with that of a group. While lone wolves often perpetrate their violence for political, religious, ethnic-nationalist, and other 'traditional' terrorist-group objectives, some of them have a personal, psychological, criminal, or idiosyncratic motive for their violence."[45]

One of the findings that surprised Simon in his study of lone wolves is that they like to talk a lot: "Even loners have a basic human need for contact with others. It was harder in the days before the internet, since they could not just sit at home and send emails around the world, post YouTube videos, create Facebook pages, or engage in other online activity to satisfy their need to express their views on various issues. But they still found ways to communicate their messages or sentiments to whoever would listen. . . . The internet, however, has made it easier and faster for lone wolves to communicate whatever messages and statements they want."[46]

Simon believes that understanding the patterns of lone-wolf behavior can help prevent lone-wolf attacks: "Many people assume that the lone-wolf terrorist is a wildcard, unpredictable, and usually mentally ill, and because of that, there is little that anybody can do to prevent an attack. I believe . . . that perception is wrong"[47]

The Making of a Terrorist

Professor Randy Borum is the Coordinator of Strategy and Intelligence Studies at South Florida University in Tampa. After the 9/11 attacks he published an analysis of the process by which people develop the mindset that makes becoming a terrorist possible. In the *FBI Law Enforcement Bulletin* he noted that it is tempting to assume that ideology drives terrorists. But he admonished that ideology is not enough. He described a four-stage process by which people develop a terrorist mindset, whether members of terrorist organizations such as Al-Qaeda or ISIS, or lone wolves who are not formally affiliated with any group. The process "begins by framing some unsatisfying event or condition as being unjust, blaming the injustice on a target policy, person, or nation, then vilifying, often demonizing, the responsible party to facilitate justification of aggression."[48]

Borum's four stages are:

1. **Social and Economic Deprivation.** The process begins with an individual or group experiencing some social or economic phenomenon that he or they consider undesirable. It could be a social restriction, or economic hardship, or government policy. They conclude, "It's not right."[49]

2. **Inequality and Resentment.** The second phase begins with identifying the undesirable condition as fundamentally unfair, as an injustice. Those involved perceive the experience as more than not right. They conclude, "It's not fair."[50]

3. **Blame.** Once the experience has been defined as unfair, the disaffected person or group tries to identify who is responsible for the injustice. Once they find a person or group they consider responsible, they attribute blame: "It's your fault."[51]

4. **Dehumanization.** The final stage is the attribution of evil and the dehumanization, demonization, or delegitimization of that person or group. The disaffected person or group attributes malicious motive: "You're evil."[52] The demonization or dehumanization of the target is a process of framing. It is a form of language that creates social conditions in which killing or harming the person or group is seen to be an honorable thing: the remedying of an injustice by neutralizing the evil person or people who perpetuate the injustice.

Whether organized acts of terror planned by traditional terrorist groups, or lone-wolf terror carried out by individuals without central direction, such terrorists believe they are acting as warriors in a struggle against evil. They may be mistaken, delusional, or evil themselves, but they think their acts are good. The ends justify the means.

We can apply this framework to understand how the killers of abortion doctors and the Planned Parenthood shooter came to become terrorists.

1. They believed that abortion should not be legal.
2. They further believed that a fetus is a person, equivalent to a born child, and that terminating a pregnancy is the equivalent of killing a fully formed and live baby.
3. They blamed the doctors and health providers who perform such acts.
4. They demonized the reproductive health workers as "baby killers." The Colorado shooter believed the rhetoric that Planned Parenthood was illegally selling baby parts, and he was committed to stopping it. Hence, his justifying his attack by saying "no more baby parts" and that he was a "warrior for babies."[53]

Although most terrorists go through those four stages, simply doing so does not make one a terrorist. Going through the stages does not necessarily lead someone to commit political violence. That takes something more. In the case of members of traditional terrorist groups, they become formal members, and obey authority. When they are directed to commit terrorist acts, they do. If sent on a suicide mission, they often justify such acts as martyrdom.

But lone wolves do not act on direction from others. The anti-abortion terrorists noted above were not following orders. Rather, lone wolves are inspired by others. They, too, however, go through a process that leads them to commit acts of violence.

In 2015, Hamm and Spaaij first published the results of their extensive study of American lone-wolf terrorism. Their research was funded by the US Department of Justice and included interviews with several lone wolves who had been convicted of their crimes. They concluded that most lone wolves in the United States are unemployed, single white males with a criminal record. They tend to be older, less-educated, and more prone to mental illness than members of terrorist groups.[54] The authors report that nationalist movements tend to produce terrorists from the lower socioeconomic classes, while religious terrorists come from all classes.

They note that half of pre-9/11 lone wolves suffered from a documented mental illness; 42 percent of post-9/11 lone wolves did. But mental illness alone is not the cause of such violence. Hamm and Spaaij conclude: "In order to commit terrorism, an extremist must first dehumanize his victim and then raise himself to the position of moral superiority. Internalizing these psychological pre-conditions, extremists begin to think of themselves as soldiers."[55]

Hamm and Spaaij harvested the patterns that their research reveals and developed a radicalization model that describes, in five stages, the predictable phases that lead to someone becoming a lone wolf and committing an act of terrorism:

1. **Personal and political grievance.** The authors argue that lone-wolf terrorism is caused by relative deprivation. Lone wolves tend to combine personal and political grievances, and then conclude that violence is the only just alternative. About 80 percent of both pre- and post-9/11 lone wolves mixed personal and political grievances.[56]

2. **Affinity with extremist groups.** The authors write: "Affinity implies that lone wolf terrorists are in sympathy with extremist groups; that their beliefs are in accordance with a clearly defined organizational entity. . . . [T]he overall finding implies that lone wolves may be seeking direction through venues other than organizations: namely, via networks of like-minded activists found online or on cable television. This finding is consistent with radicalization patterns among recent organized terrorists."[57] About two-thirds of pre-9/11 lone-wolf terrorists had an explicit affinity with extremist groups; about half of post-9/11 lone-wolf terrorists did.[58]

3. **Identification with an enabler.** Hamm and Spaaij claim: "Lone wolves are enabled through either *direct* means in the form of people who unwittingly assist in planning attacks, or *indirectly* by people who provide inspiration for terrorism. Whereas affinity for extremist groups is a vicarious experience best understood as ideological validation of beliefs, an enabler is best understood at a personal level as someone who either unknowingly performs tasks that make an attack possible, or someone who indirectly encourages terrorism by example. Enablers are also common among group actors."[59]

They note that indirect enablers may no longer be alive. For example, Adolf Hitler, dead for seventy-plus years, continues to inspire acts of lone-wolf terrorism around the world.[60] Fifty-seven percent of pre-9/11 lone-wolf terrorists had an identification with an enabler; 70 percent of post-9/11 lone-wolf terrorists did.[61]

4. **Broadcasting terrorist intent.** Hamm and Spaaij explain: "While lone wolves physically isolate from society, at the same time they communicate with outsiders through spoken statements, threats, letters, manifestos, and videotaped proclamations, similar to the jihadist martyrdom videos uploaded to the internet by members of al-Qaeda and ISIS. Broadcasting intent may occur in the weeks, days, and even hours before an attack. Broadcasting intent may be the most important commonality from the standpoint of prevention: If lone wolves announce their violent intentions beforehand, then presumably steps can be taken to stop them."[62]

Not all lone wolves broadcast their intent, but many do. Eighty-four percent of pre-9/11 lone-wolf terrorists broadcast their intent; 70 percent of post-9/11 lone-wolf terrorists did.[63]

5. **Triggering event.** Finally, "The triggering event is a catalyst for lone-wolf terrorism and such events are common among terrorist group members. For lone wolves, triggering events may be personal or political or some combination of the two. Triggering events are sometimes 'sharp' or immediate. Other times events slowly accumulate over time (through a series of 'escalation thresholds') until the lone wolf snaps under the pressure, triggering the act of terrorism."[64]

In lone-wolf-whistle terrorism, the triggering event is intensified rhetoric that asserts that a person or group is an immediate threat. Eighty-four percent of pre-9/11 lone-wolf terrorists had an identifiable triggering event; 73 percent of post-9/11 lone-wolf terrorists did.

We can apply the Hamm and Spaaij activation model to the Colorado shooter.

1. **Personal and political grievance.** Robert Lewis Dear Jr. was a longtime foe of abortion. He had been diagnosed with a delusional disorder.
2. **Affinity with an extremist group.** Dear was a fan of the anti-abortion extremist group Army of God, whom he described as "heroes" doing "God's work."
3. **Identification with an enabler.** He was inspired by Paul Hill, an anti-abortion activist who attacked an abortion clinic in 1994, killing two people.
4. **Broadcasting terrorist intent.** In this instance, Dear did not broadcast his intent publicly. He is among the 30 percent of post-9/11 lone-wolf terrorists who do not broadcast intent.
5. **Triggering event.** It is clear from Dear's comments after being arrested that the triggering event was the persistent references in the 2015 presidential election

primary campaign to Planned Parenthood allegedly selling baby parts for profit and harvesting such parts from live babies. At about the same time, there was also increased personal stress on Dear. His girlfriend had become ill and was hospitalized at the time he committed the attacks.

This escalation model applies to all lone-wolf terrorists, including those for whom the triggering event is not a lone-wolf whistle. All lone-wolf-whistle terrorism, what is currently called stochastic terrorism, is triggered by such language. We can begin to apply the concepts of "dangerous speech," the twelve forms of language that provoke violence (the playbook), and the Borum terrorism mindset model along with the Hamm and Spaaij lone-wolf terrorism escalation model to the campaign and presidency of Donald Trump.

PART II
TRUMP

I'm very highly educated. I know words, I have
the best words. But there's no better word than stupid.
—DONALD J. TRUMP, *campaign rally, December 16, 2015*

Donald Trump's language is often incendiary. Sometimes it goes further. Sometimes his words are on fire.

His language divides. His language frightens. Trump plays to the worst angels of our nature. He uses language in ways that dehumanize, demonize, and delegitimize political opponents, critics, and minority groups. He unleashes words that cannot be unsaid and that are not easily erased from memory, words that make citizens less empathetic toward one another. These words empower some people to exclude and oppress others. Sometimes these words can lead a lone wolf to commit acts of violence.

His language riles up the disaffected. His language resonates with those who carry a grievance; it stirs something in loners. It may delude or inspire individuals who seek a purpose into thinking they need to take matters into their own hands in service of what they perceive to be Trump's goals.

In fact, Trump uses language that aligns completely with the Borum sequence of how people develop a mindset that leads to violence: It's not right ➡ It's not fair ➡ It's their fault ➡ They're evil/less than human.[1]

And, yet, Trump's language is familiar. We have heard it before, from other leaders. It is the language of dictators, of tyrants, of authoritarians who conflate themselves with the state. We heard similar language in the 1930s and 1940s before and during the Holocaust. We heard it in the 1990s before and during the Rwanda genocide. We heard it before Dr. George Tiller was killed and before the Colorado Planned Parenthood clinic was attacked.

Trump uses language that the media reports and thereby amplifies. And when the mainstream media repeats these words, they bounce around conservative and white nationalist spheres until they become a chorus of hate. In these echo chambers, language that was previously unacceptable becomes the new normal.

Trump uses all twelve forms of language in the lone-wolf-whistle playbook. He speaks in ways that are consistent with each play:

1. **Dehumanize.** Trump dehumanizes groups: Mexicans, Muslims, migrants. He says they are not people. He calls them animals and calls their presence among us an infestation.

2. **Demonize/Delegitimize.** He demonizes and delegitimizes rivals and critics. He tells four congresswomen of color to go back to where they came from; all are American citizens, and three were born in this country. He says those congresswomen are not capable of loving America. He refutes the legitimacy of a sitting president, says the Speaker of the House wants terrorists,

drug kingpins, and human traffickers to enter the country to wreak havoc. He calls for his opponent in the 2016 presidential election to be imprisoned.

3. **Scapegoat.** He claims that groups such as immigrants and Muslims are responsible for many of the nation's problems, from unemployment to the opioid epidemic to terrorist attacks.

4. **Public Health Threat.** Members of certain groups—Mexicans, Muslims, migrants—are spreading disease, he says.

5. **Safety Threat.** He says that a group, rival, or critic is a threat to public safety—likely to cause death or injury to the nation or to the dominant group—or is a threat to civic order.

6. **Violent Motive.** He attributes violent motives to entire groups of people: Mexicans, migrants, Muslims. He says they want to kill Americans, to attack America from within, to change Americans' religion.

7. **Severely Exaggerating Risk.** He inflates a relatively harmless event—a scraggly group of impoverished migrants walking thousands of miles to seek legal asylum—and calls it a caravan, an invasion, funded by mysterious sources, infiltrated by dangerous people, worthy of mobilizing the military.

8. **Sinister Identities.** He makes vague references to sinister identities, saying that the sitting president is secretly a Muslim or secretly Kenyan; that a prominent Jewish investor and philanthropist is secretly providing funding for an invasion of the nation; that people of "Middle Eastern origin" have infiltrated the group of Central American migrants seeking asylum.

9. **Conspiracy.** He says that the Jewish investor is funding the invaders. He calls a counterintelligence investigation and a special counsel investigation a witch hunt, an attempted coup. He claims that his opponent in his

presidential campaign was secretly conspiring with both the FBI and the Russian government. He says that immigration across the southern border is the result of the Mexican and Central American nations intentionally sending the worst elements of their societies to hobble America.

10. **Discredit Information.** He labels any story he doesn't like fake news, and reporters who investigate him personal enemies. He challenges the legitimacy of those who investigate him and of information that is critical of him.

11. **Conflation.** He conflates his own identity with the state. A proper search with a judicial warrant of his lawyer's office he calls an "attack on the nation." He calls tepid applause at his State of the Union address "treason." He calls negative coverage of him unpatriotic. He says the media who are critical of him are "enemies of the people."

12. **Menacing Image.** He juxtaposes a rival or critic's image against a stereotype. Hillary Clinton's face appears against a backdrop of cash with the Star of David. A Muslim congresswoman in a hijab is juxtaposed against the World Trade Center under attack on 9/11.

Any one of these statements from the playbook does not necessarily put lives at risk. Even moderate instances of all these plays may not necessarily create a crisis of fear and division.

Yet, "dangerous speech," under the right conditions, can influence people to accept, condone, and commit violence against members of a group.[2]

In the three chapters that constitute Part II, we will see how Trump's persistent use of the techniques outlined in the playbook, and the escalation of both frequency and intensity over his time in office, has had the effect of creating just these kinds of conditions: a social context in which violence against members of a suspect group is normalized. I argue that Trump's language may have led to deaths that would not have happened but for his language. It has demonstrably led to death threats against the rivals and critics he has denounced, and because he could get away with it early, he has intensified the language he uses, right up to the present day.

In an analysis in Chapter 6, I conclude that Trump does not necessarily intend the violence. Rather, I believe that he is indifferent to the violence that often arises in the aftermath of his communication. He uses such language because it helps him accumulate power, animate his base, and distract the media and critics, without regard to the consequences of that language. Even when put on notice of the likely consequences, he continues using such language. Sometimes he even intensifies the dehumanization or demonization. The way Trump uses language, the consequences of his language, and his indifference to those consequences are all unprecedented for a president of the United States.

Trump persistently uses techniques outlined in the playbook. The more heated his language and the more often he uses it from his pulpit in the White House, the more likely his language is to create a social context in which violence against members of a suspect group is normalized.

The civic institutions that are supposed to hold a leader in check—from the media to political rivals to career government officials to engaged citizens—did not recognize the pattern for too long. Once the pattern became clear, these institutions and individuals have been unable to hold the president accountable. So far.

The first two chapters in Part II lay out in chronological form key examples from Trump's run for president through the middle of his third year in office. This is not a comprehensive review but a representative one consisting of ten vignettes that show both Trump's use of language and the reaction to that language. Some of the vignettes are about Trump, others discuss reactions to Trump. Taken together, the vignettes reveal the progression of a pattern. Over time, the frequency and intensity of Trump's language changed. Without anyone or anything to stop it, Trump's language moved beyond incendiary.

He became more aggressive and his language more directly incendiary when discrediting his political rivals. For example, for more than five years Trump questioned President Barack Obama's legitimacy, usually in indirect ways. He challenged the legitimacy of a state-issued birth certificate and made conditional statements, such as, *if* Obama wasn't born in the United States *then* he cannot be president. After two years in the White House, Trump was using direct, incendiary, and often false statements about rivals. Rather than the innuendo he used to cast doubts about Obama, he went on a different kind of attack. He told CBS News that House Speaker Nancy Pelosi wants open borders, doesn't mind human trafficking, and is responsible for people dying all over the country. These are allegations presented as facts and an attribution of dangerous motives to a rival.

The aftermath of Trump's dehumanizing communication saw a corresponding increase in violence. Insult or exclusion of certain groups metastasized into a spike of hate crimes against those groups. What began as mostly individual, isolated, and opportunistic acts of violence began to intensify into attempted and planned assassinations of large numbers of people. The perpetrators who attempted or committed violent acts, however unstable or filled with hatred, had never committed violence before. They seem to have been motivated, triggered, or emboldened by Trump's rhetoric. Their attacks have been labeled domestic terrorism by the FBI. As outlined in Chapter 3, I call this kind of violence lone-wolf-whistle terrorism.

At least one of those people explicitly said he was moved to violence by Trump. Others justified their acts by invoking Trump or his language. Although justifying violence by referring to the president is not proof of motive, a pattern emerges that is repeated over time, across many people. This pattern includes people who invoke Trump while they plan acts of violence; people who use Trump's name while committing the act, as if the name itself is part of the assault; and some who, when caught, justify the violence by invoking Trump or his language. Some people do all three. All of those who committed or attempted acts of domestic terrorism followed the Hamm and Spaaij activation model that describes how an emergent lone wolf goes from latent hate to active violence.

Justifying violence by invoking a president is unprecedented: We do not have prior instances of violent individuals justifying their actions by invoking Presidents Obama, or Bush, or Clinton, or by invoking candidate Hillary Clinton. Invoking the president in this way is a phenomenon unique to the Trump era.

As Trump ratcheted up his language, the negative reaction to his speech grew stronger in response. Shock that a candidate would say such things soon changed into expressions of concern. Journalists, public officials, and experts wondered whether Trump's demonization of certain people was encouraging death threats or acts of violence. Fox News journalist Chris Wallace first publicly expressed his concerns soon after Trump became president. And more and more journalists asked whether Trump was culpable for the acts of violence and attempted violence in the wake of the 2018 midterms. By early 2019, journalists, civic leaders, and targets of the president began explicitly linking his words to potential violence. Citizens began to see a link as well. In July 2019, after the president persistently demonized three congresswomen of color, political leaders, journalists, and foreign leaders criticized him for putting lives at risk. More than three-quarters of Americans surveyed in the middle of 2019 said that "heated or aggressive" language directed by elected officials against certain people or groups makes violence against them more likely.

The vignettes in Chapter 4 start in the late winter of 2011, when Trump told a conservative group that he was running for president against incumbent Barack Obama, and continue through his 2016 campaign.

Trump's use of language that provokes fear and incites violence began well before his 2015 campaign for the presidency.

The vignettes in this chapter:

1. **Winter 2011**—Questioning President Obama's legitimacy
2. **June 16, 2015**—"Mexico sends rapists"
3. **2015**—Total and complete shutdown of Muslims entering the US
4. **November 2016**—Trump's election unleashes a wave of hate crimes

In Chapter 4, I show how Trump's language led to lone-wolf-whistle violence, primarily in the form of hate crimes, individualized acts of oppression or violence that were directed at individuals or symbolic targets such as synagogues or mosques. Occasionally they moved to lone-wolf-whistle terrorism: carefully planned and coordinated acts of mass violence against groups or people whom Trump had called out in his lone-wolf whistles.

The vignettes in Chapter 5 cover the first years of Trump's presidency, ending in August 2019.

1. **August 2017**—"Blood and soil" in Charlottesville
2. **Spring to Fall 2018**—Caravan, invasion, and the congressional midterm elections
3. **October 27, 2018**—Terrorist attack at the Tree of Life Synagogue
4. **October 2018**—Soros, Obama, Clinton, and others receive bombs in the mail
5. **March–July 2019**—Trump attacks a freshman congresswoman who wears a hijab
6. **August 3, 2019**—White nationalist terrorist attack kills twenty-two in El Paso

Chapter 5 shows a dramatic escalation in lone-wolf-whistle terrorism and attempted terrorism. It also shows that those so provoked to commit violence followed the Hamm and Spaaij radicalization model, including, in the fifth step, a triggering event that was Trump's use of lone-wolf whistles.

Chapter 6 shows how Trump's language follows each of the plays in the lone-wolf-whistle terrorist playbook, analyzes Trump's language more generally, and reaches conclusions.

4

Divide to Conquer

Winter 2011—
Questioning President Obama's Legitimacy

Michelle Obama was concerned. It was the late winter of 2011, about eighteen months before the 2012 presidential election in which President Barack Obama would likely seek reelection. Real estate mogul and *The Apprentice* TV host Donald Trump announced he was running for president to take on the incumbent.

He made the announcement on February 11, 2012, at the Conservative Political Action Conference (CPAC). He began by raising questions about whether President Obama was born in Hawaii. He argued, without evidence, that no one in Hawaii knew who Obama was. He said, "Our current president came out of nowhere. Came out of nowhere. In fact, I'll go a step further: The people that went to school with him, they never saw him, they don't know who he is. It's crazy."[1]

This was an oblique reference to what had become known as the "birther" movement, claiming that Obama was not born in the United States and was secretly a Muslim. The CPAC audience would recognize the signal for what it was.

This theme had first emerged in 2004 when Obama was serving in the Illinois Senate and running for the US Senate. A candidate for the Republican primary for the US Senate, Anthony Martin-Trigona, suggested that Obama was secretly a Muslim. Martin-Trigona was a deeply controversial figure from the political fringes, who persistently ran for office in several states. He was a white supremacist who had been renounced by the Republican Party of Florida in his 1996 campaign for Florida State Senate after the party learned that Martin-Trigona's campaign committee was named "The Anthony R. Martin-Trigona Congressional Campaign to Exterminate Jew Power in America and to Impeach the Judges of the US Court of Appeals in New York City."[2]

The birther movement took off significantly when Obama ran for president in 2008, morphing beyond Obama's religious identity to claim that he had not been born in Hawaii but rather in Kenya. If true, this would make him ineligible to serve as US president. The birther rumors reached such a peak of visibility that, eleven months before the 2008 election, the *Los Angeles Times* published an editorial denouncing the rise of birther commentary:

[I]t's worth considering the persistence of the internet rumors that Obama, well known to Chicagoans as a Christian, is actually a stealth Muslim, a "Manchurian candidate" who would take the presidential oath with his hand on the Koran. The rumors first surfaced during Obama's run for Senate but took off in a viral email campaign in 2006. One email called Obama "The Enemy Within." GOP strategist Ed Rogers also pointedly mentioned Obama's middle name, Hussein. In January, the Obama campaign was forced to denounce Fox News for repeating a false *Insight* magazine report that he had spent four years in an Indonesian

madrasa, an Islamic school. Though CNN sent out a reporter who found that the school Obama had attended had
nothing in common with the Pakistani incubators for jihad-
ists, and though his campaign has set the record straight
repeatedly, last week the *Washington Post* ran a front-page
story about Obama's "Muslim ties."[3]

In fact, Obama was born in Hawaii and was a member of the
Trinity United Church of Christ in Chicago, where he and Michelle Obama were married. Obama's membership in that church
had become a controversial issue in his 2008 campaign when his
rivals tried to discredit Obama because of divisive statements by
the church's pastor, Rev. Jeremiah Wright.

But the birther theme was kept alive throughout the 2008 campaign. To quell the rumors that Obama was from Kenya, the
Obama campaign released his official birth certificate, called a
"Certificate of Live Birth," in 2008. The state of Hawaii confirmed
its authenticity. The Obama campaign made clear that the rumors
"aren't actually about that piece of paper—they're about manip-
ulating people into thinking Barack is not an American citizen."[4]

Even after the election, conservative media and politicians continued to fan the birther flames. This often took the form of de-
manding to see his birth certificate, even though he had already
released it. Some challenged the validity of the short-form certificate that Hawaii had issued.

By the time Donald Trump revived the birther theme in early
2011, Republican luminaries ranging from former House Speaker
Newt Gingrich to 2008 vice presidential candidate Sarah Palin to
former Arkansas governor Mike Huckabee had raised questions
about Obama's birthplace and whether he was really American.

About a month after telling CPAC that he was running for president, Trump questioned the validity of Obama's certificate of live
birth, which he said was not the same as an official birth certificate. He told *Fox & Friends*, "They give you a certificate of live
birth, which anybody can get, just walk into the hospital, and you

get a certificate of live birth. It's not even signed by people. Now, this guy either has a birth certificate or he doesn't. And I didn't think this was such a big deal, but I will tell you, it's turning out to be a very big deal because people now are calling me from all over saying, please don't give up on this issue. If you weren't born in this country, you cannot be president."[5]

Later in April, Trump claimed that he had sent investigators to Hawaii to look into the birth certificate claims, and that "they can't believe what they're finding." He repeated this line many times over many interviews, but never provided evidence that he had sent investigators, or what those investigators found.

As Trump continued making statements questioning President Obama's legitimacy as president, the First Lady became increasingly concerned. Not about the politics. But about the safety of her family. She wrote in her memoir, "The so-called birthers had tried during the previous campaign to feed a conspiracy theory claiming that Barack's Hawaiian birth certificate was somehow a hoax and that he'd in fact been born in Kenya. Trump was now actively working to revive the argument, making increasingly outlandish claims on television, insisting that the 1961 Honolulu newspaper announcements of Barack's birth were fraudulent and that none of his kindergarten classmates remembered him. All the while, in their quest for clicks and ratings, news outlets—particularly the more conservative ones—were gleefully pumping oxygen into his groundless claims."[6]

Mrs. Obama then revealed the root of her concern:

The whole thing was crazy and mean-spirited, of course, its underlying bigotry and xenophobia hardly concealed. But it was also dangerous, deliberately meant to stir up the wingnuts and kooks. I feared the reaction. I was briefed from time to time by the Secret Service on the more serious threats that came in and understood that there were people capable of being stirred. What if someone with an unstable mind loaded a gun and drove to Washington? What if that person went looking for our girls? Donald Trump, with his loud and reckless innuendos, was putting my family's safety at risk. And for this, I'd never forgive him.[7]

She recognized the lone-wolf whistle signal and feared that it would encourage violence against her family: It was deliberately meant to stir up people who are unstable or who carry a grievance, and according to the Secret Service there were people capable of being stirred.

When her book was launched, Mrs. Obama told Oprah Winfrey, "[T]o think that some crazed person might be ginned up to think my husband was a threat to the country's security; and to know that my children, every day, had to go to a school that was guarded but not secure, that they had to go to soccer games and parties, and travel, and go to college; to think that this person would not take into account that this was not a game—that's something that I want the country to understand. I want the country to take this in, in a way I didn't say out loud, but I am saying now. It was reckless, and it put my family in danger, and it wasn't true. And he knew it wasn't true."[8]

It's important to pause and to reflect on what Mrs. Obama said. She was calling out Donald Trump for putting her family in danger by persistently claiming something that he knew not to be true.

She also shared this story with Oprah: While the Obamas lived in the White House, a gunman had shot a bullet into the window of the Truman Balcony, where her family often sat. No one was hurt and the shooter was arrested. But because the window was custom-made of bombproof glass, it took several months to replace. She recounted, "I had to look at that bullet hole, as a reminder of what we were living with, every day."[9]

In April 2011, in response to the controversy created by Trump, President Obama asked the state of Hawaii to release the long form of his birth certificate, which it did. Contrary to Trump's claim that a long-form birth certificate is different from a "Certificate of Live Birth," this longer document also was called a

"Certificate of Live Birth." But despite that evidence, birthers—including Trump—persisted. The following month a Gallup poll showed that 13 percent of all Americans, and 23 percent of Republicans, believed that President Obama was not born in the United States.[10]

Trump continued insisting that Obama was not born in America for five full years. It was not until the very last weeks of the 2016 campaign that he grudgingly admitted that Obama was born in the US. Naturally, he blamed Hillary Clinton for having started the birther rumors.[11]

June 16, 2015—"Mexico Sends Rapists"

Candidate Donald J. Trump opened his 2016 campaign for president with a live televised event in the lobby of Trump Tower in New York. On June 16, 2015, he and his wife, Melania Trump, descended an escalator to a cheering crowd of actors paid to pretend to be his supporters.[12]

About a minute into the speech, Trump cast Mexico as an existential threat to the United States. He asked the crowd, "When do we beat Mexico at the border? They're laughing at us, at our stupidity. And now they are beating us economically. They are not our friend, believe me. But they're killing us economically. The US has become a dumping ground for everybody else's problems."[13]

He then spoke the lines that defined his campaign: "When Mexico sends its people, they're not sending their best. They're not sending you. They're not sending you. They're sending people that have lots of problems, and they're bringing those problems with us [*sic*]. They're bringing drugs. They're bringing crime. They're rapists. And some, I assume, are good people."[14]

He continued this theme: "They're sending us not the right people. It's coming from more than Mexico. It's coming from all over South and Latin America, and it's coming probably from the

Middle East. But we don't know. Because we have no protection and we have no competence, we don't know what's happening. And it's got to stop and it's got to stop fast."[15]

This formulation itself is peculiar. Much has been written about Trump's calling Mexicans rapists and criminals, but Trump's claim is bigger than this. It's about more than immigration, which involves people choosing, on their own, to move to another country. Trump claimed that Mexico, and other Latin American countries, was intentionally sending violent people to the United States who could commit crimes against Americans. And he even included a vague reference to the Middle East. By and large, the news media did not focus on this part of his statement. Why would they? It made no sense. Immigration is not about nations sending their people to another country, about one nation beating another at their shared border. Could Trump simply have been confused?

Several weeks after his initial announcement, Trump released a written statement doubling down on his claim, expanding the reference from the nation of Mexico in general to the government itself: "I don't see how there is any room for misunderstanding or misinterpretation of the statement I made on June 16th during my Presidential Announcement speech. What can be simpler or more accurately stated? The Mexican Government is forcing their most unwanted people into the United States. They are, in many cases, criminals, drug dealers, rapists, etc."[16]

This statement, absurd on its face, has rhetorical force. It establishes a context in which violence is seen to be an appropriate response to a threat. The statement creates a frame that immigrants are part of some larger sinister plot to harm the nation, that they are agents of a foreign power that is intent on destabilizing American society. This provokes both fear and a desire to fight back: to punish Mexico for its act of aggression. And to suspect all Mexican immigrants—and those thought to be Mexican immigrants—of being part of this invasion.

His statement continues, "In other words, the worst elements in Mexico are being pushed into the United States by the Mexican government. The largest suppliers of heroin, cocaine, and other illicit drugs are Mexican cartels that arrange to have Mexican immigrants trying to cross the borders and smuggle in the drugs."[17]

This rhetoric serves as a kind of dog whistle that white supremacists in his base, who are highly attuned to the idea of invasions, are likely to recognize. But it's also a signal to lone wolves. And some chose to act on that signal. In the months following the announcement, Trump continued to make similar attacks against Mexicans, other Latin American immigrants, and the government of Mexico. And he rolled out a theme that continued throughout the campaign and his presidency: the imperative to protect the nation by building a wall along the entire two-thousand-mile stretch of southern border.

One of the effects of Trump's language was that people who otherwise would resist the temptation to insult, confront, or commit acts of violence became less inhibited. With this disinhibition, the incidence of hate crimes against people perceived to be Mexican or Hispanic rose significantly, starting in 2015. According to a report by the Center for Public Integrity, the targeting of Latino communities was on the rise: "Hate incidents targeting Latinos and immigrants often go beyond name-calling and intimidation. Victims and advocates also say they are too often the targets of assault, robberies and even murder. . . . 'In immigrant communities, the fear is palpable,' said Monica Bauer, director of Hispanic affairs at the Anti-Defamation League (ADL). 'It's so much fear that I think the word doesn't really convey. It's almost terrified, like it's beyond fear. It's paralyzing fear.'"[18]

One example. About six weeks after Trump began the campaign by saying Mexicans are rapists, two brothers in Boston, ages thirty and thirty-eight, came upon a homeless man sleeping in a subway station. They urinated on him. As he woke up, they kicked and punched him, and one of the brothers repeatedly hit him with a metal pole. They then walked away laughing. They were soon arrested and told the police that they had targeted the man because they thought he was an illegal immigrant. One of them told the police, "Donald Trump was right. All of these illegals need to be deported."[19]

In fact, the victim was a legal permanent resident. The older brother was sentenced to three years in prison, the younger to a year and a half.

2015—Total and Complete Shutdown of Muslims Entering the US

Trump soon expanded his focus from Mexicans to Muslims. He told a false narrative about Syrian Christians being blocked from entering the United States, but Syrian Muslims being fast-tracked. He told the crowd at his July 11, 2015, rally: "If you're from Syria and you're a Christian, you cannot come into this country, and they're the ones that are being decimated. If you are Islamic . . . it's hard to believe, you can come in so easily."[20]

In fact, both Muslim and Christian refugees from Syria had recently entered the United States. Trump intensified his rhetoric about Syria during a New Hampshire rally in September, warning that refugees could be part of a secret army invading the country: "I'm putting people on notice that are coming here from Syria as part of this mass migration, that if I win, they're going back! They could be ISIS. . . . This could be one of the great tactical ploys of all time. A 200,000-man army maybe, or if you said 50,000 or 80,000 or 100,000, we got problems and that could be possible. I don't know that it is, but it could be possible so they're going back—they're going back."[21]

This is a common pattern in Trump's language: He identifies a genuinely dangerous group or individual, and then generalizes them to an entire population. Here, he invoked ISIS, a terrorist organization responsible for killing thousands and creating havoc that led to the Syrian refugee crisis. But he conflates those fleeing ISIS with ISIS itself, noting that perhaps upward of two hundred thousand ISIS soldiers may be infiltrating the country.

It's a lone-wolf whistle. And those who hear the signal generalize it to a wider universe of people. And some commit lone-wolf-whistle violence.

For example, in early December 2015, a nineteen-year-old Penn State student named Nicholas Tavella followed a fellow student across campus. The student tried to keep his distance, but Tavella kept taunting him, asking him whether he was going to rape a girl, and whether he was from the Middle East. A Penn State police officer then witnessed Tavella grabbing the student by the neck, with two hands, and choking him. As the police officer approached, Tavella threatened the student: "If you get away I'll put a bullet in you."[22]

The officer intervened and took Tavella into custody. He later noted that Tavella seemed intoxicated. Tavella confessed that he had pursued the student because he "looked suspicious" and "appeared to be of Asian or Middle Eastern descent."

In the initial hearing, Tavella's lawyer attributed the assault to the defendant's "love of country" and "Donald Trump rhetoric covered in the media that may have incited fear of suspicious individuals."[23]

Tavella pleaded guilty to charges of felony ethnic intimidation, misdemeanor terroristic threats, and summary harassment, among other crimes.[24] He was sentenced to just under two years in prison.[25]

Donald Trump intensified his anti-Muslim rhetoric even more on December 6, 2015, the day after the Penn State assault and four days after two terrorists killed fourteen people and injured twenty-two in San Bernardino. At a rally in South Carolina, while holding a piece of paper in his hand, Trump read an announcement: "Donald J. Trump is calling for a total and complete shutdown of Muslims entering the United States until our country's representatives can figure out what the hell is going on."[26]

Of the 7.4 billion people in the world, about 1.8 billion, or 24 percent, are Muslim. Trump's ban would prohibit a quarter of the world's population from attempting to enter the country. "Total and complete shutdown" would prevent even Americans who are Muslim from reentering their own country. There are about 3.45 million Muslims living in the United States, or about 1 percent of the population. At the time Trump called for a total and complete ban, there were five thousand Muslims serving in the United States armed forces. A literal reading of Trump's proposed ban would suggest that none of these five thousand would be able to return to the country after being deployed overseas in the service of the nation.

Trump spoke with ABC's George Stephanopoulos on *Good Morning America*. Stephanopoulos pointed out that many people, including Republicans, said that Trump's proposal was both un-constitutional and un-American. He asked, "Do you have any second thoughts at all that you may have gone too far?"[27]

Trump responded by describing Muslims already living in this country, and by citing a discredited poll he had quoted in his announcement: "We have people in this country who want to blow up our country. . . . The polls have come out, and various polls I quoted, where 25 percent of those polled agreed that violence against Americans here in the United States is justified, and they're looking at the jihad, and they want global jihad. . . . George, we can take it sitting back, you'll have many more World Trade Centers. It'll get worse."[28]

This statement, in response to a question about a ban on non-American Muslims entering the country, seemed to be about Muslims who were already here. Stephanopoulos seemed confused, and asked Trump whether an American Muslim traveling outside the United States would be able to come back. Trump tried to have it both ways, saying that citizens were good people, but that Muslims living here wanted to cause harm. He said, "No they can come back. We're talking about all good people. This is not only—if a person is a Muslim and goes overseas and comes back, they can come back. They're a citizen. That's different. But we have to figure things out. We didn't know. . . . We have people that want to blow up our buildings, our cities."[29]

Stephanopoulos shifted his questions to criticism of Trump's proposed ban. He said, "You're increasingly being compared to Hitler. Does that give you any pause at all?"[30]

Trump responded by invoking former president Franklin Delano Roosevelt. "No, because what I am doing is no different than what FDR—FDR's solution for Germans, Italians, Japanese, you know, many years ago."[31]

Stephanopoulos asked whether Trump was in favor of internment camps. Trump responded with a somewhat incoherent description of measures during World War II that prohibited people of German, Japanese, and Italian descent from having radios or flashlights. He compared the need for his ban with those wartime restrictions: "We are now at war. We have a president who doesn't want to say that, but we are now at war."[32]

At the time he said this, the United States was still in a war in Afghanistan and conducting a somewhat secret war against ISIS, using American and allied troops based in Iraq and elsewhere. We were fighting alongside our Muslim allies, in Afghanistan, Iraq, and elsewhere. But Trump's answer seemed not to be about those wars. He suggested, rather, that the ban was necessary because we were at war against Islam, and that President Obama didn't want to admit it. But we were in no way at war against Islam. If anything, we relied upon Muslim allies in the wars we were fighting.

Trump then invoked the terrorist attack in San Bernardino: "We just had a case where people were killed. We're going to have many more cases like that. We had somebody in this country that shouldn't be. And she came in, he came in, they were radicalized, they were looking at doing something. . . . There are many, many other people like him in this country, right now."[33]

The San Bernardino shooter's wife was indeed an immigrant from Pakistan. But the shooter himself was an American citizen, born in Chicago. Based on Trump's earlier response to Stephanopoulos's question, the ban would not have applied to him.

Stephanopoulos noted that a quarter of the world's population is Muslim. He asked about the likely reaction to the ban outside the United States: "Aren't you concerned at all that you're going to make the United States a pariah nation and play right into ISIS's hands?"[34]

Trump responded with a rambling false narrative that Muslim infiltration of Britain and France was so severe that police refused to enter some Muslim neighborhoods in those countries. (Both countries quickly denied such claims.)

Stephanopoulos asked one final question: "So one more time, no second thoughts? Any Muslim coming into the United States is banned for now?"[35]

Trump replied, "We have to look at people, we have to use vigilance in our country, or we're going to have many more World Trade Centers and our country will never be the same. We will have many, many more World Trade Centers as sure as you're sitting there. Our country will never be the same."[36]

A week after his announcement, Trump spoke with Jake Tapper on CNN. He told Tapper that he has many Muslim friends who are happy that he called for a Muslim ban. An incredulous Tapper questioned how that could be true. Trump changed the subject to radicalism, and then said something that could lead people to suspect the legitimacy of Americans who are Muslims and who have a valid American passport. He said, without offering evidence, "I just read where ISIS has gotten a hold of a passport-printing machine for the migrants to get them into the United States. Now maybe that's true, maybe it's not. It's an early report. But how crazy are we allowing ourselves to be subject to this kind of terror."[37]

Tapper didn't respond to the statement about a passport-printing machine. He did acknowledge the legitimacy of concerns about extremism. But he asked whether a blanket ban on all Muslims was the right solution. Trump replied, "We have a real problem. We have people coming into the country, getting into airplanes, and flying them into the World Trade Center."[38]

That statement is stunning. Fourteen years had passed since the 9/11 attacks. The nation had gone to war in 2001 against Al-

Qaeda and the Taliban in Afghanistan. The US and NATO had partnered with the political leadership in Afghanistan and had created, trained, and equipped a domestic Afghanistan army, all Muslim, that continues to fight alongside American and NATO troops. The United States has been able to differentiate between terrorists and the community in which the terrorists operate. Trump was conflating the two.

The US also went to war in Iraq in 2003, nominally to prevent the use of weapons of mass destruction but in any event to oust Saddam Hussein from power. An insurgency arose and what we now know as ISIS was formed in Iraq in 2004. The United States has been able to differentiate between the insurgents, ISIS, and the communities in which the terrorists operated. And again, Trump was conflating them.

Indeed, the 9/11 terrorists were Muslim. However, they did not commit their acts of terror because of their religion but because they were terrorists. In fact, more Muslims than Christians have been killed by Al-Qaeda and ISIS. Saying all Muslims are or could be terrorists because the 9/11 terrorists were Muslim is the equivalent of saying that all Christians are or could be terrorists because Timothy McVeigh was Christian. McVeigh blew up the Murrah Federal building in Oklahoma City in 1995, killing 168 people in what was until 9/11 the worst terrorist attack in American history.

But Trump told Jake Tapper that a defining trait among Muslims, which justified preventing any of the world's 1.8 billion Muslims from entering the country for any purpose, is that they get into planes and fly into the World Trade Center. As a lone-wolf whistle, it is strong. And its effect has lasted long after the presidential campaign. Indeed, for years afterward, much criticism of Muslims, including from Trump, included visual imagery of or explicit reference to the World Trade Center attack. And the reference to ISIS running a passport-printing machine, even with some hedging, could easily cause frightened people to wonder about whether any American Muslim was an ISIS operative. It could have the effect of making all Muslims suspect.

November 9, 2016—Trump's Election Unleashes a Wave of Hate Crimes

Many people went to sleep on Tuesday, November 8, 2016, thinking they knew who would win the election. But on the morning of Wednesday, November 9, they woke up to a jolt. To almost everyone's surprise—including Trump's—Donald J. Trump was elected president of the United States.

The day after the election, thirty mosques received an identical letter warning that "President Trump will do to you what Hitler did to the Jews." The letter, published in its entirety in the Council on American-Islamic Relations report *The Empowerment of Hate*, read,

> To the Children of Satan,
> You Muslims are a vile and filthy people. Your mothers and your fathers are dogs. You are evil. You worship the devil. But your day of reckoning has arrived.
> There's a new sheriff in town—President Donald Trump. He's going to cleanse America and make it shine again. And he's going to start with you Muslims. He's going to do to you Muslims what Hitler did to the Jews. You Muslims would be wise to pack your bags and get out of Dodge.
> This is a great time for patriotic Americans. Long Live President Trump and God Bless the USA.
> Americans for a Better Way.[39]

According to the *Washington Post*, reported hate crimes with a racial or ethnic bias increased the day after the election to the highest level of the year. And for ten days the level of such crimes remained higher than on Election Day itself.[40] It was as if the election liberated people who had been holding back, giving them implicit permission to target people Trump had identified as enemies, dangerous, or less than human.

The Los Angeles County Commission on Human Relations published its *2016 Hate Crimes Report*, in which it noted not only that hate crimes rose to their highest levels in the days after the election but revealed a pattern of hate crimes in which Trump's name was specifically invoked. These included:

- An Asian woman walking her dog was assaulted by two white men who also shouted, "Go back to Chink town, you slant eye bitch. Take your Chink dogs with you! Trump town!"
- The home of three Asian victims was ransacked, and graffiti that included swastikas, "KKK," "White Power," and "Trump" was written throughout the house.
- A Latino family's home was spray-painted with the word "Trump," and a warning reading, "Mixed race breeding. Keep your spic children off our property or there will be consequences." The letter x in the word "mixed" was written as a swastika.

The report noted that, "These reported hate crimes had a direct reference by the perpetrator(s) to Trump or the presidential election. As we have noted in our annual report with regard to hate crimes with anti-immigrant slurs, other hate crimes could have been motivated by the election, but the perpetrators did not communicate or express it to the victims."[41]

The day after the election, three men were arrested for plotting to bomb a mosque and refugee residence in Kansas. One defendant was quoted in court documents discussing killing Muslims with weapons dipped in pigs' blood. For months in his rallies Trump had praised the apocryphal claim that US general John J. Pershing had killed Muslims in the Philippines with bullets dipped in pigs' blood.[42] Trump told the story: "Take this bullet back to all the people who are causing the problem. And for forty-two years they didn't have a problem."[43]

One of the defendants was recorded by the FBI calling Muslims "cockroaches" and saying, "The only good Muslim is a dead Muslim. . . . If you're a Muslim, I'm going to enjoy shooting you in the head. . . . The only fucking way this country's ever going to get turned around is it will be a bloodbath and it will be a nasty, messy motherfucker. Unless a lot more people in this country wake up and smell the fucking coffee and decide they want this country back . . . we might be too late, if they do wake up. . . . I think we can get it done. But it ain't going to be nothing nice about it."[44]

In their March 2018 trial, their defense lawyer's opening statement argued that the defendants were early and avid supporters of Trump who were "influenced by the charged discourse of the [2016 presidential] campaign."[45]

The lawyer said the defendants "were hoodwinked by fake news on Facebook and unfairly exploited by a federal government targeting them for their conservative beliefs."[46]

The *Huffington Post* reported,

The country was sharply divided during the 2016 election, [defense attorney James] Pratt argued, and the media fed into the division by reporting on it non-stop. If you read conservative news, the lawyer said, you thought Hillary Clinton was a criminal, Obama was letting in hordes of Muslim immigrants, and the federal government was coming to get your guns. If you read liberal news, he said, you thought Trump was a racist unqualified to be president who planned to kick out Mexican immigrants and impose a Muslim ban. "Hate ruled the day and the ratings. Left hating right, right hating left. And it was into this mix that we land," Pratt said.[47]

The men were convicted. In a sentencing memo to the judge, their defense attorneys argued, "2016 was 'lit.' The court cannot ignore the circumstances of one of the most rhetorically mold-breaking, violent, awful, hateful and contentious presidential elections in modern history, driven in large measure by the rhetorical China shop bull who is now our president."[48]

In the court filing defense attorneys James Pratt and Michael Shultz wrote, "A person normally at a 3 on a scale of political talk might have found themselves at a 7 during the election. A person, like [defendant] Patrick [Stein], who would often be at 7 during a normal day, might go to 11."

The three were each sentenced to at least twenty-five years in prison. By the end of 2016, according to the Southern Poverty Law Center, the number of anti-Muslim hate groups in the United States had tripled, from 34 at the end of 2015 to 101. The Center published its annual *Intelligence Report* in early spring 2017, with a picture of Donald Trump on the cover with the caption "The Year in Hatred and Extremism."

"'2016 was an unprecedented year for hate,' said Mark Potok, senior fellow and editor of the *Intelligence Report*. 'The country saw a resurgence of white nationalism that imperils the racial progress we've made, along with the rise of a president whose policies reflect the values of white nationalists. In [Trump campaign chairman and White House senior strategist] Steve Bannon, these extremists think they finally have an ally who has the president's ear.'"

The report directly links the increase in hate and hate crimes to Trump's language: "The increase in anti-Muslim hate was fueled by Trump's incendiary rhetoric, including his campaign pledge to bar Muslims from entering the United States, as well as anger over terrorist attacks such as the June massacre of forty-nine people at a gay nightclub in Orlando."[49]

Just one example: Five days after Trump was inaugurated, a Muslim contract employee of Delta Air Lines, who wears a headscarf known as a hijab, was assaulted by a passenger while sitting in her office in the airline lounge at JFK Airport. The Queens

County District Attorney announced that the passenger, Robin Rhodes, shouted at her through the office door:

> "Are you [expletive deleted] sleeping? Are you praying? What are you doing?" Rhodes then allegedly punched the door, which hit the back of the victim's chair. [W]hen the victim asked Rhodes what she did to him, he stated, "You did nothing but I am going to kick your [expletive deleted] ass." Rhodes then allegedly kicked the victim in the right leg. In an effort to get away, the victim moved to a corner of the office. However, Rhodes allegedly kicked the door, stepped into the office and blocked her from leaving the office. . . . When an individual came over to the office and tried to calm Rhodes down, Rhodes moved away from the door and the victim ran out of the office to the lounge's front desk. . . . Rhodes followed her and got down on his knees and began to bow down in imitation of a Muslim praying and shouted, "[Expletive deleted] Islam, [expletive deleted] ISIS, Trump is here now. He will get rid of all of you."[50]

5

American Carnage

Donald J. Trump was inaugurated president of the United States on January 20, 2017.

His inaugural speech was unlike any prior. He described a dystopian present, a failed America. He painted a dichotomy between Washington and its politicians and American citizens. He said that Washington had prospered while citizens had suffered. He described the current state of affairs as "American carnage."[1]

He said that the government had enriched foreign industry at the expense of American industry, defended other nations' borders but refused to defend our own. He said the government had spent trillions on overseas investment while American infrastructure was in decay and disrepair. He said American middle-class wealth had been ripped from Americans and sent across the world.

He put the world's leaders on notice that from now on it would be America First. He said he would protect America's borders from the ravages of other countries. He said that he would eradicate radical Islamic terrorism from the face of the earth.[2]

The first months of Trump's presidency were consumed with forming his government, scandal involving his National Security Advisor suddenly being fired for lying about contact with the Russian government during the transition, the firing of FBI Director James Comey, and the appointment of Special Counsel Robert Mueller. It also included various attempts to impose travel bans preventing people from several Muslim-majority countries from entering the country. Most of these attempts were blocked by courts.

But in midsummer a defining event in Trump's use of language and relationship with white nationalists occurred, in Charlottesville.

August 2017—
"Blood and Soil" in Charlottesville

Charlottesville, Virginia, is home of the University of Virginia, an architectural masterpiece and major academic institution. Founded by Thomas Jefferson after the conclusion of his two terms as the third president of the United States, it is referred to by locals as Mr. Jefferson's University. Nearby, at Monticello, the gravestone Jefferson designed himself lists three things for which he wished to be remembered: "Author of the Declaration of Independence [and] of the Statute of Virginia for religious freedom & Father of the University of Virginia." President didn't make the list.

Virginia became a Confederate state in the Civil War; its capital, Richmond, was the capital of the Confederacy for most of the war. Feelings about the war and nostalgia for the South that lost it run deep in parts of Charlottesville. In the winter of 2017, the Charlottesville City Council voted to take down a statue of Confederate general and native Virginian Robert E. Lee and move it to another part of the city, while stripping Lee Park of its name. Backlash, in the form of a lawsuit, was immediate. Two months later, the council voted to sell the statue but was swiftly barred from doing so by court order.

The possible removal of the statue sparked protests. Richard Spencer, who had coined the term "alt-right" to replace "white nationalist," led a torchlit rally through Lee Park on May 13, 2017. Chants of "You will not replace us" and "Blood and Soil" filled the night air.

"You will not replace us" is new in the lexicon of white supremacy, coined a few months before the rally by another white nationalist. The slogan spread like wildfire on social media and became a feature of alt-right and white supremacist protests and communications.[3]

"Blood and Soil" is the translation of the German phrase *Blut und Boden*, words intended to invoke identification with a race— in this case, white—and a place, the countryside. Founded on virulent anti-Semitism and racism, this official Nazi slogan became a key component of Adolf Hitler's "*Lebensraum*," justification for German territorial expansion and a major factor in the Holocaust.[4]

After the chants and speeches fell silent, Spencer and his supporters put out their torches and left Lee park. The following night, Lee Park lit up again, this time with candles. A hundred or so city residents, including the mayor, held a silent vigil in protest of Spencer's actions. Organizations in favor of keeping Robert E. Lee's statue in the park distanced themselves from Spencer, too.

The possible sale of the Robert E. Lee Monument remained an attractive rallying cry for white hate groups. On July 8, about fifty Loyal White Knights of the Ku Klux Klan protested the removal of the bronze statue.[5] Some wore hoods, others waved the

Confederate flag. More than a thousand counterprotesters surrounded the Klansmen, jeering at them. Police dispersed the crowd with tear gas.

Then the hate groups joined forces. Richard Spencer and Jason Kessler, founder of Unity & Security of America, a white nationalist group, filed a permit for a "free speech rally in support of the Lee monument" on August 12.[6] But the rally morphed into something larger, something called Unite the Right, which described itself thus: "[A]n event which seeks to unify the right-wing against a totalitarian Communist crackdown, to speak out against displacement level immigration policies in the United States and Europe and to affirm the right of Southerners and white people to organize for their interests just like any other group is able to do, free from persecution."[7]

Displacement is a common theme among white nationalists, referring to the trend of immigrants replacing whites as the dominant community. A key part of the displacement theme is that such immigration is sponsored, funded, or otherwise caused by Jewish billionaires.

Four days before the rally, The Daily Stormer posted, "Although the rally was initially planned in support of the Lee Monument, which the Jew Mayor and his Negroid Deputy have marked for destruction, it has become something much bigger than that. It is now an historic rally, which will serve as a rallying point and battle cry for the rising alt-right movement."[8]

The Daily Stormer posted on its Facebook page, "Next stop: Charlottesville, VA. Final stop: Auschwitz."[9] One of the organizers, Michael Hill, president of the white nationalist group League of the South, tweeted to his followers, "If you want to defend the South and Western civilization from the Jew and his dark-skinned allies, be at Charlottesville on 12 August."[10]

The permit obtained and prominent white supremacist speakers confirmed, the organizers decided to hold a secret rally by torchlight the night before their official event. Participants were asked to keep the details secret so as not to attract law enforcement or counterprotesters. They were advised that they could buy torches from Walmart, Lowe's, or Home Depot. On August 11, several hundred torchbearers marched through the night, chanting, "Blood and Soil" and "Jews will not replace us." This last chant was not about Jews replacing whites themselves; rather, about Jews replacing whites with immigrants of other races. The chants got louder and louder.

Marching in their midst was a twenty-year-old who had driven from Ohio to attend the rally. James Alex Fields Jr. described himself as a neo-Nazi. In photos from the event, Fields holds a shield bearing a neo-Nazi logo. In video footage, Fields is chanting, "Jews will not replace us!"

By the time the marchers reached the Jefferson Monument, counterprotesters, most of whom were university students, were waiting. The two groups traded taunts, shoved one another, and sprayed mace. Skirmishes broke out. The demonstrators shouted at counterprotesters, "White lives matter," and made "monkey noises" at black counterprotesters.[11]

The following morning, protesters and counterprotesters began gathering across Charlottesville. Each side had its own security. Security for Unite the Right was armed with rifles. Prominent white nationalist and alt-right leaders were present, including Richard Spencer, Mike Enoch, David Duke, and Jason Kessler. Many protesters carried Nazi and neo-Nazi flags and imagery. The neo-Nazi website The Daily Stormer live-blogged the rally and sent instructions on where to assemble and how to respond to police and counterprotesters.

At the same time, counterprotesters, including interfaith clergy, Black Lives Matter, Antifa, and others were gathering. Unite the Right protesters chanted "You will not replace us," "Build the wall," and "Commie scum off our streets."[12] A few shouted "Hail, Trump!"[13] Counterprotesters responded, "Love has already won!"[14] and "Fuck you, Nazis."[15]

Things escalated fast. At 10:45 a.m., hundreds of Unite the Right protesters brawled with counterprotesters, using flagpoles and pepper spray as weapons. Similar violent clashes erupted around town.

The Daily Stormer posted: "THIS IS THE BEGINNING OF A WAR! WE HAVE AN ARMY!"[16] By 11:31 a.m., the Charlottesville police chief announced that the gathering had become an unlawful assembly and was to disperse. At that moment someone threw a smoke grenade.[17] Between the announcement and the grenade, protesters and counterprotesters began to scatter out of Emancipation Park. At 12:06 p.m., the governor of Virginia declared a state of emergency.[18]

At 12:13 p.m., the streets of Charlottesville were filled with violence.[19] In a crowd, a counterprotester sprayed flames at demonstrators with a homemade flamethrower. Telling him to stop, a Klansman drew his handgun, fired a shot next to the man, and then left. As the protesters were regrouping, Richard Spencer and David Duke spoke to them. Then a rally organizer told everyone to return to their cars and leave.

About an hour later, several hundred counterprotesters still milled about downtown Charlottesville, figuring out where to go next. A few cars tried to move through the crowds. At 1:41 p.m., a gray Dodge stopped in front of a group of counterprotesters. The car backed up a bit. Then it sped up and slammed into the crowd, flinging bodies into the air. Then it backed up again. This was an intentional attack. The car was a weapon, ramming into people and other cars. The driver was the twenty-year-old neo-Nazi from Ohio who had marched the night before.

Nineteen people were injured.[20] Heather Heyer, who had come out to show solidarity with the counterprotesters, was killed. She was thirty-two years old. Police apprehended the driver in four minutes. The rally made headlines in national and international media for days.

The day of the rally, President Trump, while visiting the Trump National Golf Club in Bedminster, New Jersey, said: "We are closely following the terrible events unfolding in Charlottesville, Virginia. We condemn in the strongest possible terms this egregious display of hatred, bigotry, and violence on many sides. On many sides. . . . What is vital now is a swift restoration of law and order and the protection of innocent lives."[21]

Trump said nothing about the death of a young woman; neither did he condemn white nationalism. His omissions and his stated equivalence between the sides provoked widespread criticism.

The next day, Vice President Mike Pence claimed Trump had called for unity. He also stated, "We have no tolerance for hate and violence from white supremacists, neo-Nazis, or the KKK."[22] But the president had not mentioned white supremacists, neo-Nazis, or the KKK. The neo-Nazi website Daily Stormer decoded Trump's dog whistle:

> Trump comments were good. He didn't attack us. He just said the nation should come together. Nothing specific against us.
>
> He said that we need to study why people are so angry, and implied that there was hate . . . on both sides! So he implied the antifa are haters.
>
> There was virtually no counter-signaling of us at all. He said he loves us all. Also refused to answer a question about White Nationalists supporting him. No condemnation at all. When asked to condemn, he just walked out of the room.[23]

Two days after the rally and the death of Heather Heyer, President Trump issued a written statement. "Racism is evil. And those who cause violence in its name are criminals and thugs, including the KKK, neo-Nazis, white supremacists, and other hate groups that are repugnant to everything we hold dear as Americans."[24]

The remarks may have been "too little, too late," NPR commented. Trump responded on Twitter: "Made additional remarks on Charlottesville and realize once again that the #Fake News Media will never be satisfied . . . truly bad people!"[25]

The next day, President Trump once again tried to equate the two groups of protesters. "What about the alt-left that came charging at—as you say, the alt-right. Do they have any semblance of guilt? What about the fact they came charging with clubs in their hands, swinging clubs? Do they have any problem? I think they do."

Not all of the protesters were neo-Nazis or white supremacists, Trump said. Some of them, he claimed, were there simply to protest the removal of the statue of Robert E. Lee. "And you had some very bad people in that [Unite the Right] group, but you also have people that were very fine people, on both sides."[26]

This equivalence has become a defining moment of the Trump presidency. The phrase "very fine people, on both sides" allowed white nationalists and others to believe the president, either explicitly or tacitly, endorsed their actions. Former Klan leader David Duke tweeted a thank-you to the president. The rally's two key organizers interpreted Trump's "both sides" remark as support for the white supremacist cause. Richard Spencer, as a 2019 *Atlantic* article noted, said, "The alt-right found something in Trump. He changed the paradigm and made this kind of public presence of the alt-right possible."[27]

But there is more to Trump's reluctance to condemn white nationalism and neo-Nazis right after Charlottesville: his political base. Trump did not want to alienate this block of voters. In fact, the white supremacists themselves describe their relationship with Trump as a series of coded messages. Andrew Anglin of The Daily Stormer described Trump's signals as "wink-wink-wink." He said this many times during Trump's campaign and presidency. *Mother Jones* magazine described the pattern this way: "Signal to the extremists; deny it when forced to, but with a transparently meaningless excuse; wait for the media to move on; leave the extremists reassured that you didn't really mean it."[28]

Daryl Johnson is a former domestic terrorism expert at the US Department of Homeland Security who left the government after a report he wrote warning of right-wing domestic terrorism provoked a backlash among Republican political leaders and conservative media. Just after Charlottesville, he wrote a *Washington Post* column in which he noted the alignment of the white nationalist agenda and Trump's policies and priorities: "Neo-Nazis, Ku Klux Klan members, militia extremists, and other radical right-wing zealots march side-by-side at pro-Trump rallies across the country. Trump's endorsement of the border wall, the travel ban, mass deportations of illegal immigrants—these ideas were touted on white supremacist message boards merely ten years ago. Now they're being put forth as official US policy. Such controversial plans have placated white supremacists and anti-government extremists and will draw still more sympathetic individuals toward these extremist causes along with the sort of violent acts that too often follow, like Charlottesville."[29]

He added, "Rhetoric from the president has further emboldened the alt-right."[30]

Two years after Charlottesville, former FBI counterintelligence chief Frank Figliuzzi wrote in the *New York Times* about Trump's flirtation with white supremacists: "It doesn't really matter whether Mr. Trump is truly a racist or merely playing one on television to appeal to his base. Either way, his path can lead to bloodshed. When that happens, we will hear White House officials and the Republican leadership claim their hands are clean because malicious people can't be stopped from acting out."[31]

The ashes of Heather Heyer, the young woman killed at the rally, were buried in a secret place to protect them from neo-Nazis. Fields, the man who killed Heather Heyer and injured many others, was sentenced to life in prison on federal hate crime charges in July 2019. At his sentencing, prosecutors told the judge that, according to a classmate, Fields announced on a high school trip to a German concentration camp: "This is where the magic happened."[32]

Spring to Fall 2018—Caravan, Invasion, and the Congressional Midterm Election

In the spring of his second year in office, Donald Trump returned to the theme that had launched his campaign nearly three years earlier, one that he had never really let go: the threat to the nation at the southern border. He seized on a group of people who had joined together as they walked through Central America toward the United States, hoping for security in numbers. The walkers in this ragtag column came from Honduras, El Salvador, and Guatemala. They were fleeing violence and starvation, economic collapse, political instability, and violent crime. At the time that Trump began to talk about them as a threat to the nation, they were on foot, thousands of miles from the border.

Many of them planned to apply for asylum in the United States. Asylum is a protected status granted by a government to an individual who has been persecuted, or fears persecution, by their government or another entity because of "their race, religion, nationality, membership in a particular social group, or political opinion."[33] Under American and international law, people who meet this criterion are considered refugees. The United States has legal obligations to protect them.

A person must apply for asylum in person, in the country where he or she is requesting protection. If the person is already in that country, the request for asylum is made at an airport or a border crossing. That is the law.

In April 2018, President Trump said the group of asylum seekers walking north through Central America was trying to enter the United States illegally. He began describing the group as a *caravan*. He claimed that the migrants' home countries were sending them to the United States and he said Democrats allowed "open borders, drugs, and crime."[34]

This is all false. Those walking had not been sent by their governments; they were coming of their own volition, seeking legal asylum. Not a single prominent Democrat has proposed open borders. Open borders are what we find in the European Union, where someone passes from France to Italy without going through an immigration process. Democrats do not favor anyone entering the country without a passport or a visa.

As part of his theme about the dangers of immigration, President Trump renewed his attacks on so-called sanctuary cities. Sanctuary cities or states or counties limit how much they cooperate with federal immigration authorities to prevent low-priority immigrants from being deported. But they typically turn over immigrants accused of serious crime.[35]

Trump mischaracterized California's sanctuary laws at the White House in May 2018: "California's law provides safe harbor to some of the most vicious and violent offenders on Earth, like MS-13 gang members putting innocent men, women, and children at the mercy of these sadistic criminals."[36]

MS-13 is a frequent focus of Trump's fearmongering about immigration. The gang was formed in Los Angeles in the 1980s, mostly by immigrants from El Salvador, and it spread to cities across the US. Ironically, as gang members began to be deported to El Salvador, Honduras, and Guatemala, the gang grew into an international criminal force known for its brutality, especially toward children. MS-13 is the reason some Central Americans flee to the United States.

As Trump did with the call to ban all Muslims from entering the United States, with MS-13 Trump conflated genuinely dangerous people with the broader population. Starting in May 2018 Trump made frequent references to MS-13 but in ways that seemed to describe Latin American immigrants more generally. The typical formulation is: The caravan is dangerous and is invading the southern border. It includes dangerous gangs like MS-13; these aren't even people, they are animals. Audiences are left with a sense that MS-13 defines the group as a whole.

In May 2018, he said: "We have people coming into the country, or trying to come in—and we're stopping a lot of them—but we're taking people out of the country. You wouldn't believe how bad these people are. These aren't people. These are animals."[37]

In a June 2018 speech, he once again conflated immigrants in general with MS-13: "People who come in violate the law. They endanger children in the process. And frankly, they endanger all of our children. You see what happens with MS-13, where your sons and daughters are attacked violently. Kids that never even heard of such a thing are being attacked violently, not with guns, but with knives because it's much more painful."[38]

Trump also said of MS-13, "They've literally taken over towns and cities of the United States."[39] There is no evidence that MS-13 has taken over towns and cities in the US. When pressed to identify those cities, President Trump changed the subject.

In addition to calling would-be immigrants from Central America criminals, gang members, and animals, Trump also said they are infesting our country. That kind of language, using that word to dehumanize people, is a common play in the lone-wolf-whistle terrorist playbook.

Trump stated: "Democrats are the problem. They don't care about crime and want illegal immigrants, no matter how bad they may be, to pour into and infest our Country, like MS-13."[40]

Note in this example that Trump generalizes about immigrants, who he says are allowed to pour in and infest the country, and then uses the phrase "like MS-13." It isn't MS-13 who are infesting, it's immigrants in general. MS-13 is used as an example to describe those immigrants.

As the midterm congressional elections approached in the fall, Trump announced that his campaign to help Republicans increase their control of both houses of Congress would have two themes: newly appointed Supreme Court Justice Brett Kavanaugh and the caravan.

Pretty quickly the focus on Kavanaugh faded, and much of the president's energy went to reviving public fear of a caravan. For Trump it became all caravan, all the time. Republican candidates for both the House of Representatives and the Senate picked up the theme. As the election got closer, the frenzy of Trump's language, both in intensity and in quantity, increased dramatically. And that increase was reflected in the media and social media echo chamber.

In an October 6 rally in Kansas City, Trump said the nation was under foreign invasion:

> Democrats also support deadly sanctuary cities that release violent predators and blood-thirsty killers like MS-13 into our communities. . . . And they go into these communities, and these are rough, rough people, MS-13. How they even come in—and we stop them at the border, but there's so many here from before us. . . . But they come in. We send ICE and they get in there and they get them out and it's like we're liberating a town. In this day and age. It's like in a war, where a foreign invader, a foreign invader finally is being taken out. They're liberating a country or liberating a city or a town. These people are liberating these towns. And you know the story, and you've heard it. It's all over.[41]

Sanctuary cities do not release MS-13 or other violent predators into communities. The idea of immigrants as invaders and the implication that the caravan was about to invade the US received lots of coverage in mainstream media and was amplified across the ultra-conservative and white nationalist worlds. Conservative columnist, former Nixon speechwriter, and sometime presidential candidate Pat Buchanan amplified Trump's theme: "Yet far more critical to the future of our civilization is the ongoing invasion of the West from the Third World. . . . It also now appears that the U.S. elections, not three weeks away, may be affected by another immigration crisis on the U.S. border. As of Thursday, a caravan of 4,000 refugees without visas had crossed from Honduras into Guatemala and was heading toward Mexico. By Election Day, it will either have been stopped, or it will be here. And this caravan is a portent of things to come."[42]

Buchanan then laid out the underlying significance of the issue: "Unwanted mass migration is the issue of our time, as there is no foreseeable end to it before it alters America irremediably. As these migrants are almost all poor, not highly skilled, and do not speak English, most will join that segment of our population that pays no income taxes but qualifies for social welfare benefits like food stamps, medical care, and free education in our public schools."[43]

Buchanan closed by saying that how Trump dealt with the migrant caravan could affect the fate of the midterms and of Trump's reelection. Trump used some form of the words *invader, invasion, criminal, animal,* or *killer* with increasing frequency throughout the midterm campaign. Trump said one or more of these words between eight and ten times per rally in early October. In the three days before the election, Trump said one or more of these words more than thirty times per rally.[44] His rally speeches were further amplified by his social media posts.

As if calling the migrants invaders, criminals, animals, and infesters were not enough, Trump further stoked anti-immigrant fire by suggesting that the caravan, and therefore the invasion, was financed by Democrats. That idea led some to attribute the supposed financing of the caravan to George Soros. This is a common trope of white supremacists, and the name Soros is considered code for a globalist cabal of Jewish bankers. Soros is a Hungarian-born American investor in his late eighties. He has made billions of dollars over the years investing around the world, and is the founder of the Open Society Foundation, which promotes democracy around the world. His name has become a meme among white nationalists around the world, especially in his birth country of Hungary, for a Jewish banking conspiracy.

USA Today did an extensive analysis of how what it called "a lie about George Soros and the migrant caravan" multiplied online.[45] It noted that the president, his children, members of Congress, and conservative commentators all repeated it. For example, in mid-October, a North Carolina writer tweeted a link to a story about the caravan with a single word of commentary: *Soros.* That day, identical posts appeared on six pro-Trump Facebook pages, with 165,000 combined followers. Within four days, more than two million Twitter accounts mentioned both Soros and the caravan. On October 17, Congressman Matt Gaetz tweeted a video of people he said were in Honduras handing cash to migrants. His caption: "Soros? US-backed NGOs? Time to investigate the source!"[46] This video was retweeted by Donald Trump Jr. and by conservative commentator Ann Coulter. One conservative TV host went so far as to say that Soros was renting RVs for people in the caravan. By October 27, Twitter accounts reaching 275 million people and Facebook accounts reaching 99 million people linked Soros to the caravan.[47]

At a rally in Houston on October 22, Trump asked the fired-up crowd, "Do you know how the caravan started?"[48] He then made a gesture of handing out money. "Does everybody know what this means? I think the Democrats had something to do with it."

He then turned his attention to the midterm election and accused the Democrats of making America and Americans unsafe. "This will be the election of the caravan, Kavanaugh, law and order, tax cuts, and common sense. . . . As we speak, the Democrat party is openly encouraging millions of illegal aliens to break our laws, violate our borders, and overwhelm our nation. The Democrats have launched an assault on the sovereignty of our country, the security of our nation, and the safety of every single American."[49]

He mentioned MS-13. Members of the crowd shouted the word that they had heard Trump say many times before: "Animals!" Trump tossed that language back to them. "Yeah. Yeah, that's right. Yeah, that's right. He said it. These are—that's right—they're animals. They're animals."[50]

Adding even more potentially frightening attributes to the caravan, Trump tweeted that "criminals unknown Middle Easterners" were among the walkers.[51] A few days later, Breitbart News published a story that the caravan was bringing infectious diseases into the country.[52]

The following week, Trump tweeted that MS-13 and others had infiltrated the caravan and told them: "Please go back, you will not be admitted into the United States unless you go through the legal process. This is an invasion of our Country and our Military is waiting for you!"[53]

The next day, Trump deployed the US military to the border even though, under American law, the military is not permitted to conduct law enforcement or immigration activities. Most of the soldiers went to Texas. Most of the migrants in the "caravan" were still more than two thousand miles from the border, heading to San Diego, California. Once the military was deployed, Trump told a rally, "They're not coming in. The military is all ready. And we're going to have border protection. You watch."[54]

The *New York Times* noted the unprecedented nature of the military deployment:

> The massing of American troops comes as Mr. Trump has seized on the caravan as a closing political message in the final week before the midterms, warning darkly—and without evidence—that "Middle Eastern" people are part of a dangerous mob of migrants threatening to surge into communities here. But the caravan, which has shrunk from 7,000 people to less than 3,500, is still weeks away from reaching the United States. The rare use of the active-duty military to bolster Mr. Trump's campaign message has intensified criticism that the president is using the military for political gain.[55]

Trump justified the use of the military in several tweets. Meanwhile, Trump's dehumanization and demonization of the migrants, and the conflation of gangs with all the migrants, was being amplified by candidates for the House and Senate, and by the mainstream and conservative media. Just before the November 3 midterm election, the *New York Times* wrote that voters were energized by the talk surrounding the caravan. "For the last two weeks, Mr. Trump and his conservative allies have operated largely in tandem on social media and elsewhere to push alarmist, conspiratorial warnings about the migrant caravan more than 2,000 miles from the border. They have largely succeeded in animating Republican voters . . . around the idea of these foreign nationals posing a dire threat to the country's security, stability, and identity."[56]

The *Times* then addressed the president's language, and how it was amplified:

With the kind of dark language usually reserved for true catastrophes like the Sept. 11 attacks, conservative commentators and politicians have led a concerted push to elevate the caravan as an issue. They have called it "an invasion," "a national emergency," "an illegal alien mob," "an attack on America," and a crisis with implications that are "critical to the future of our civilization." These outcries, which have included unfounded claims about the caravan's origins and wildly fluctuating estimates of its size, are playing out in a clear pattern. They often start with right-wing commentators, conspiracy theorists, and activist groups with large followings; their talk then breaks through more broadly on Fox News, Breitbart News and other outlets that are popular with conservative voters; and ultimately Mr. Trump tweets or remarks about them, acting as an amplifier and a validator.[57]

Trump had pegged his success as president to a victory in the November midterms. He said he was the reason people would vote. And the caravan was an essential part of Trump's strategy.

But it didn't work. Trump expected Republicans to retain control of both houses of Congress. Although it took several weeks for the closest races to be certified, in the end, Democrats picked up forty seats in the House. That would fundamentally change the balance of power as of early January 2019, when the new Congress would be seated.

As soon as the election was over, so, too, was Trump's talk of the caravan, the purported existential threat to the nation on the southern border. He was silent on the topic for more than a week after the election. CNN summed up the reason for Trump's silence:

[The] discrepancy between Trump's rhetoric in the run-up
to the election and his rhetoric after it exposes, beyond a
shadow of a doubt, what most neutral observers initially sus-
pected: That Trump's decision to seize on the caravan of
migrants making their way across Mexico in hopes of entering the United States was 100% a political ploy to rev up his
base. . . . To be clear: There was *never* any evidence that what
Trump was saying about the caravan was true. . . . But now,
with the election eight days in our rear-view mirror—and
with only a handful of uncalled races remaining—the bald
cynicism of Trump's rhetoric on the migrants, and his decision to send 5,000 US troops to protect the border, is totally
revealed.[58]

October 27, 2018—
Terrorist Attack at the Tree of Life Synagogue

It was a peaceful Saturday in Squirrel Hill, an affluent neighborhood of Pittsburgh. The Tree of Life synagogue was abuzz with
the rhythms of Sabbath. Three separate congregations were at
worship in different sanctuaries of the complex. In a side room, a
family was performing a ritual circumcision and naming cere-
mony for their newborn boy. Elsewhere, children were attending
Hebrew school.

Just before 10:00 a.m. on October 27, a white supremacist
named Robert Bowers walked into the complex carrying an AR-15
assault rifle and three Glock 357 handguns. He opened fire on
the worshipers. As he fired his weapon, he shouted, "All Jews must
die!" He killed eleven worshipers and wounded two others.

The police arrived quickly. Bowers wounded four of them and
was himself wounded and taken into custody. He told one of the
SWAT officers that he wanted all Jews to die because they were
"committing genocide against my people," according to a police
complaint. At the hospital he told doctors that all Jews needed to

die. Some of the doctors were Jewish, including members of the Tree of Life congregation.

Soon after Bowers was taken into custody, the media learned of his social media posts and found that he had a long history of anti-Semitism. He was active on the social network GAB, an alternative to Twitter that arose after Twitter began enforcing its policies against racist or violent tweets. In the nineteen days before his synagogue attack, he had posted or reposted white supremacist or anti-Semitic memes sixty-eight times. An analysis by the Southern Poverty Law Center concluded that Bowers had a "conspiratorial focus on the caravan of Central Americans fleeing violence." The analysis also noted that he was particularly obsessed with Jews: "[I]t's evident he engaged with numerous anti-Semitic conspiracy theories that have long been in circulation among neo-Nazis and white nationalists."[59]

In the weeks before he attacked the synagogue, Bowers posted frequently about Jews. This included denials of the Holocaust. It also included references to Jews secretly supporting the caravan. On his social media profile, Bowers said that Jews are the children of Satan. He had recently reposted a note that said: "Open you [sic] Eyes! It's the filthy EVIL jews Bringing the Filthy EVIL Muslims into the Country!! Stop the kikes then Worry About the Muslims!"[60]

But it's a long way from anti-Semitic statements and bluster to mass murder. What made Bowers snap? He had never been physically violent before, never murdered people who were members of a group he claimed to hate. He was not on any law enforcement agency's list of possible terrorists. What would propel Bowers to move beyond the latent anti-Semitism that manifested itself mostly in hate speech and to take up arms and with a sense of urgency to slaughter innocents at worship? We can point to one change: The language he used to describe the people he hated had changed materially.

Six days before the shooting, Bowers posted on social media: "I have noticed a change in people saying 'illegals' that now say 'invaders.' I like this."[61] After that, he posted frequently about the caravan that was invading, and how it was financed by Jews. This was a direct embrace of Trump's language, which had been amplified through social and conservative media and white supremacist sites. Bowers mentioned a century-old refugee resettlement agency, the Hebrew Immigration Aid Society (HIAS), that was supported by several synagogues, including the Tree of Life. Responding to a HIAS announcement of synagogue services that would support the organization, Bowers copied the imagery and content of the announcement, and then added a threat: "Why hello there, HIAS. You like to bring in hostile invaders to dwell among us? We appreciate the list of friends you have provided."[62]

Bowers's post included a website listing synagogues where the supporting services would be held, including the Tree of Life. Two hours before the shooting, he again invoked the refugee agency in what became his final post: "HIAS likes to bring invaders that kill our people. I can't sit by and watch my people get slaughtered. Screw your optics, I'm going in."[63]

"Optics" was a reference to a debate in white supremacist circles about the best way to recruit new followers to their cause. There was no evidence that HIAS liked "to bring hostile invaders to dwell among" Americans; no evidence of any white people being "slaughtered" by refugees that HIAS or members of Jewish communities were helping to settle in the United States. No evidence that George Soros or any Jewish organization was funding the Latin American migrants walking to the US border. No evidence of any invasion.

Notice that Bowers was not a Trump supporter and had complained that Trump was not extreme enough. But he embraced the language Trump launched, that had been repeated and amplified by social media and conservative media, and that was replicated in white supremacist posts and media. The ecosystem of hate became an echo chamber that amplified, intensified, and made the president's language more relevant and more urgent— even if the end user, Bowers, was not aware that he was following the president's lead. The change in language that he used to justify his attack, and the urgency of his reaction, suggest that Bowers was triggered by the signals the president had sent.

President Trump condemned the shooting after it happened, but he also continued using the language that was implicated in triggering the violence in the first place.

We can apply to Bowers the Hamm and Spaaij radicalization model of how lone-wolf terrorists are triggered:

1. **Personal and political grievance.** Bowers was a long-time white supremacist who frequently posted about displacement levels of immigration and how immigrants were a threat to his sense that America was a white country.

2. **Affinity with an extremist group.** Bowers was active on social media and frequently reposted content generated by white supremacist groups and individuals. In particular, he quoted memes from the Christian Identity Theology movement, which interpreted the Bible as a history of the white race, that was popularized by Tom Metzger, founder of the White Aryan Resistance movement.[64]

3. **Identification with an enabler.** Trump was not directly Bowers's enabler, because Bowers believed that Trump was not extreme enough. But Bowers was inspired by the repurposing of the language Trump had put in circulation, especially the language of invasion. Bowers explicitly noted the change in language from "illegal aliens" to "invaders," and said that he liked this change.

4. **Broadcasting terrorist intent.** Bowers broadcast his intent in two ways. First, he posted on his Gab account the synagogues that were raising funds for the Hebrew Immigration Aid Society with an implied threat that those synagogues were at risk, including the Tree of Life. Then a few hours before he opened fire, he posted that he could not sit by and let his people get

slaughtered by the invaders. He closed with "I'm going in," suggesting that he would attack soon.

5. **Triggering event.** The triggering event was the intensity and frequency of the discussion of how George Soros, standing in for Jews in general, was funding and making possible the invasion by immigrants from Central America. Notice that the attack came ten days before the midterm election, at the height of Trump's intensity of language about the invasion and the sources of its funding.

October 2018—Soros, Obama, Clinton, and Others Receive Bombs in the Mail

The Monday before the synagogue shooting, George Soros received a suspicious package in the mail at his home. The police determined that it was a bomb. It did not go off.

Over the next four days, another twelve bombs were discovered, sent to former president Barack Obama; former vice president Joe Biden; former presidential candidate and secretary of state Hillary Rodham Clinton (also putting at risk former president Bill Clinton); and six other current or former officials (and two prominent people unaffiliated with government) who were all critics of the president. All of the bomb recipients had been on the receiving end of fierce criticism from President Trump. He had insulted each of them mercilessly.

On Friday, October 26, federal law enforcement agents in Florida arrested Cesar Altieri Sayoc Jr. for sending the bombs. In his home they later discovered that the names of the bomb recipients were on a list of more than a hundred targets to receive such bombs. All were people or institutions that had been similarly and persistently insulted by the president. None of the bombs had detonated. But if they had, this could have been the largest political assassination in the history of the United States.

Police confiscated the van that Sayoc owned. The van's exterior was covered with imagery, including positive portrayals of President Trump. But it also had pictures of the president's critics, including most of those who had been sent bombs. Some of their faces, including Hillary Clinton's, were covered with crosshairs resembling a rifle target. There were also slogans such as "CNN Sucks." CNN had been sent two bombs, each addressed to a different person Sayoc had thought worked at CNN. And under the heading "Drain the Swamp" were images of nineteen people who had been critical of or who had been criticized by President Trump, including five people and institutions who were sent bombs. There were also phrases such as "Benghazi Cover-Up" and "DNC/Main Stream Media Collusion."

Sayoc was not on any law enforcement watch list. As far as we know, he had never committed violence, much less mass murder. What would propel an ardent supporter of the president to move beyond adorning his van with political images and to attempt to assassinate more than a dozen of the president's critics? What could have made him snap?

A *New York Times* analysis notes that, until 2016, Sayoc's social media presence was unremarkable: food, gym, sports. But the *Times* concludes that a close study of his social media presence "reveals the evolution of a political identity built on a foundation of false news and misinformation, and steeped in the insular culture of the right-wing media. For years, these platforms captured Mr. Sayoc's attention with a steady flow of outrage and hyperpartisan clickbait and gave him a public venue to declare his allegiance to Mr. Trump and his antipathy for the president's enemies."[65]

Sayoc's posts are full of misspellings, run-on sentences, and bizarre stream-of-consciousness word salad. Below, I quote those posts verbatim. Sayoc's Facebook posts included praise for Trump, including pictures of him at Trump rallies and outside the Trump resort at Mar-a-Lago. He often tweeted directly about Trump. In March 2018, in response to the president's tax policies, he tweeted: "You don't have pay taxes on bonus yea Trump Trump Trump."[66]

In June 2018, he tweeted a happy birthday message to President Trump: "Happy Birthday to greatest gift from God President Trump Trump Trump. The greatest result President ever and economy for all American Soaring 2016–2024 Trump Trump Trump."[67]

But Sayoc didn't merely admire Trump. He adopted Trump's enemies as his own, and he sent them menacing tweets before he sent them bombs. In fact, every single person who received a bomb sent by Sayoc had been on the receiving end of the president's ire, often supercharged through the right-wing and white supremacist ecosystem.

Here is just a small sample of the president's tweets or public statements about people or institutions that were sent bombs by Sayoc.

George Soros

Trump included Soros in his frenzy of caravan-related posts and statements. Here are two from October 2018, including one made just days before Sayoc sent the bomb to Soros:

> The very rude elevator screamers are paid professionals only looking to make Senators look bad. Don't fall for it! Also, look at all of the professionally made identical signs. Paid for by Soros and others. These are not signs made in the basement from love! #Troublemakers[68]
>
> [T]he Democrat party has gone so far left that nobody knows what to do. It's become radical resistance. Have you ever seen their signs, "Resist"? They say, what will you resist? I don't know. Have you ever seen where the fake news interviews them? And they try to cut it, but they will go to a person holding a sign, who gets paid by Soros or somebody— right? That's what happens.[69]

Sayoc had a particular antipathy for Florida high school student David Hogg, a survivor of the Parkland school shooting who became a prominent gun control advocate, and for George Soros. Sayoc linked the two in a tweet: "David Hogg biggest con century fake fraud. He never attended Parkland High School. He graduated 2015 from Redondo Beach High School. He is a George Soros paid Protestor and Actor. We . . . have his real school record and real year book."[70]

An analysis of Sayoc's social media posts by online news site Talking Points Memo notes: "Sayoc appeared to harbor particular ire for Soros, who is often accused by many on the right, including Trump, of paying protesters to speak out against conservative policies. In dozens of tweets, Sayoc alleged that Soros orchestrated the February massacre at Stoneman Douglas High School in Florida and committed other 'horrors.'"[71] Sayoc was the only follower of a Facebook account named KillgeorgeSoros.[72]

On Monday, October 22, a George Soros employee found a suspicious envelope in the mailbox of Mr. Soros's Katonah, New York, home.

Barack Obama

Among the Trump statements in the months before Sayoc sent the bombs: "@foxandfriends: 'New Bombshell in the Obama Spying Scandal. Did other Agencies SPY on Trump Campaign?' Even Clapper, worlds dumbest former Intelligence Head, who has the problem of lying a lot, used the word SPY when describing the illegal activities!"[73]

Sayoc's posts include:

- A tweet saying, "People Obama Illegally Wiretapped REVEALED."[74]
- A tweet of a picture of Mar-a-Lago with the caption "Trump Mara Lago Club. Screw U Obama Terrorist."
- A link to a YouTube video, "Is Barack Obama THE ANTICHRIST—100% PROOF Is There!"

* A link to a YouTube video, "Satan Sent Obama to
  Destroy America," and a clip featuring Sean Hannity,
  the Fox News host, which was called, "MUST HEAR:
  Sean Exposes Illegal Immigrant Crime Stats."[75]

On Wednesday, October 24, the Secret Service intercepted a
mail bomb sent to President Obama by Sayoc.

Hillary Clinton

After becoming president, Trump continued to attack Hillary
Clinton, including leading people in his rallies to chant "Lock her
up!" Representative statements include: "No Collusion and No
Obstruction, except by Crooked Hillary and the Democrats. All of
the resignations and corruption, yet heavily conflicted Bob Mueller refuses to even look in that direction."[76]

Among Sayoc's posts are many Fox News clips with memes
from the 2016 campaign, and referring to Clinton as a hypocrite
and liar who would endanger the nation:

* On Facebook, Sayoc posted a photo of ISIS terrorists
  with the caption, "Wake up America FBI director warns
  an attack like never seen before here in America will
  happen. We can't afford risk American lives with Hilary
  [sic] Clinton. They will infiltrate refugees guaranteed.
  FBI clear to point."
* Sayoc posted a video of Dinesh D'Souza saying the
  Clinton Foundation was a "fake" charity and a "war chest
  for the Clintons."[77]

On Tuesday, October 23, the Secret Service intercepted a mail
bomb addressed to Clinton during a mail screening in Chap-
paqua, New York.

Robert De Niro

Actor Robert De Niro was a sharp critic of Trump, and recorded a video during the presidential campaign, calling Trump "blatantly stupid, a pig, a con, a bullshit artist, a mutt who doesn't know what he's talking about, doesn't do his homework, doesn't care, thinks he's gaming society, doesn't pay his taxes. He's an idiot."[78]

Trump did not respond directly to De Niro, who kept criticizing Trump throughout the campaign and the early part of his presidency. In June 2018, at the Tony Awards broadcast from Radio City Music Hall, the announcer introduced De Niro. The actor took the stage, stood at the microphone, looked out at the audience, and said, "I'm going to say one thing: Fuck Trump."[79] The audience broke into thunderous applause and a standing ovation. After being silent about De Niro for years, Trump respond with two tweets:

> Robert De Niro, a very Low IQ individual, has received to [sic] many shots to the head by real boxers in movies. I watched him last night and truly believe he may be "punch-drunk." I guess he doesn't . . .
> . . . realize the economy is the best it's ever been with employment being at an all time high, and many companies pouring back into our country. Wake up Punchy![80]

On Thursday, October 25, around 5:00 a.m., security personnel who worked for De Niro's film company, Tribeca Productions, discovered a bomb sent by Sayoc. It was disarmed by the New York City police.

Other Bomb Recipients

And so the pattern continued. Trump would denounce a rival or critic, Sayoc would tweet about that rival or critic, including death threats. Then he would send a bomb. These included Joe Biden, former attorney general Eric Holder, Congresswoman Maxine

Waters, Senator Cory Booker, Senator Kamala Harris, Director of National Intelligence James Clapper, former CIA Director John Brennan, and Tom Steyer, a hedge fund manager and billionaire who launched and funded a campaign to impeach Trump.

After Sayoc was arrested, a reporter asked President Trump whether he bore any blame for the attempted bombings. Trump responded, "No, not at all. There's no blame, there's no anything."[81] In late March 2019, Sayoc pleaded guilty to sixty-five felony counts, including sixteen counts of using weapons of mass destruction in an attempted terrorist attack. Although he originally said that he didn't intend to harm anyone, he acknowledged that the bombs had active explosives in them.

Earlier, I asked what could make someone like Sayoc snap, go from a social media presence that was mostly food, gym, and sports to tweeting death threats and mailing bombs filled with active explosive material. We now know the answer because he told us.

In late April 2019, Sayoc sent a handwritten thirty-one-page letter to the judge hearing his case. He described himself as a loner who found purpose and community in following Trump. In the letter he told the judge that he had attended a Trump rally and that it was fun. But it was also more. Sayoc said "it became like a new found drug."[82] He became addicted. He wrote, "Politics is a very scary dangerous ideology for a person of my nature, that never knew anything about politics before. I was not able to pull myself back from this sickness."[83]

He noted that he had not been involved in politics before. He had admired Trump from his TV show and his books on tape and his various lines of merchandise. Sayoc said, "I have never in my life ventured into politics. I did not know the difference from Democrats, Republicans, Independents, Green Party, etc. I am very neive [sic] & impressionable. I had no clue what was going to happen. All I knew was politics is very dangerous. I wish almighty God I had never ventured. I never had anything to do with again. Ever. It is a poison. It will drive you crazy like it or not. Once you get caught up you can't get out."[84]

Sayoc also noted that he had previously been inattentive to social media. He told the judge, "I did not even know about social media, TV, Facebook, or Twitter. They are weapons that twist & destroy minds. Fact. They are real weapons of mass destruction."[85]

At his first Trump rally, Sayoc found a purpose and a community. He wrote, "The first thing you here [*sic*] entering Trump rally is we are not going to take it anymore, the forgotten ones. . . . You were no longer a loner & becoming part of something, if you weren't at a rally, it was all over social media, TV, radio, Facebook, Twitter. It was political war between right & left. Facebook, Twitter, social media became like a video game. Someone would send an attack text & then you would text back. It was the most craziest political election. I was getting wrapped up in this new found fun drug."[86]

Sayoc attended his first rally in Miami. He then went to a rally in Chicago. But thousands of Trump protesters had made it into the rally venue, hoping to disrupt it. After delaying the start, the Trump campaign eventually canceled the rally outright. Four protesters were arrested for violence against police or resisting arrest. Sayoc told the judge, "I went to Chicago rally liberal left followers attacked us & shut down rally & chasing us with bats, rocks, even as far as throwing mototal [*sic*—Molotov] cocktails. We filed 6 police reports. The mayor Emmanuelle [*sic*] of Chicago had police stand down order. Violence grew on both sides. What started off as funny how people were acting on both sides right & left. I became part of a nightmare."[87]

In January 2017, Sayoc traveled to Washington to attend his hero's inauguration. As he got more and more involved, Sayoc saw himself as being "on the front lines of a war between right and left."[88] He was a foot soldier for Donald Trump. He did what he had to do to serve his leader. He also described politics as "dirty, ruthless, and deadly."[89] And if that was the nature of the fight, he was all in. Trump's targets became his targets. Having defined himself as a soldier in such a war, Sayoc also saw himself as a direct victim of political violence because his van that was covered with pro-Trump and anti-Trump-critics signage had been vandalized many times.

Sayoc described how he became increasingly agitated in the run-up to the 2018 midterm elections, attributing the calls to violence as coming from the Democrats. He wrote,

> The attacks continued day after day into midterm elections . . . the violence propaganda was so intense there was no escaping political politics. It was so bad I had friends that disassociated with myself. No matter they never before in my past ever was political. No matter where you went. You cling to it like a drug attic [*sic*]. I [*sic*] was the most scared time in my life. Weather a drug or ideology, it was same thing. . . . When you have mental problems, neive [*sic*], impressionable weakness & loner. You watch politics on both sides Right & Left. You cling to it worse than a drug. Politics you play with your life & freedoms. . . . It was at time of this nightmare happened in October 2018.[90]

Sayoc closed his letter by apologizing to the judge. Speaking of his fixation with Trump, he wrote, "Politics. It is something I wished it had never come into my life."[91]

Sayoc's attorneys submitted a pre-sentencing memorandum to the judge in late July 2019. In it they described Sayoc as having lived a difficult life on the margins of society. At the time of his arrest, said his lawyers, Sayoc had been "living alone in a decrepit and cramped van that had been his home for more than a decade."[92] The lawyers said that,

> In this darkness, Mr. Sayoc found light in Donald J. Trump. His infatuation with the President began as something personal, not political. . . . Mr. Sayoc was an ardent Trump fan and, when Trump announced he was running for President, Mr. Sayoc enthusiastically supported him. . . . He firmly believed in Donald Trump the person and wanted him to be

President. To that end, Mr. Sayoc passionately championed the President on social media and at rallies and covered his van with stickers supporting President Trump and criticizing his political opponents. Through these actions, Mr. Sayoc found the sense of community that he had been missing for so many years.[93]

Sayoc's lawyers describe him as naïve and credulous. They write:

Because of his cognitive limitations and mental illness, he believed outlandish reports in the news and on social media, which increasingly made him unhinged. He became obsessed with "attacks" from those he perceived as Trump's enemies. He believed stories shared on Facebook that Trump supporters were being beaten in the streets. He came to believe that he was being personally targeted for supporting Trump. . . . Mr. Sayoc became increasingly obsessive, paranoid, and angry. He conflated his personal situation with the perceived struggles of Trump supporters across the country, and even the President himself. . . . His paranoia bled into delusion.[94]

The lawyers explicitly pointed to Trump's congressional midterm tweets as motivation for Sayoc: "Mr. Sayoc was also an avid follower of @RealDonaldTrump, Donald Trump's Twitter page, where Trump posted prolifically about his political enemies, including all of the recipients of Mr. Sayoc's mailings. In his tweets Trump portrayed these individuals as dangerous, corrupt, and un-American. For example, he suggested that anti-Trump protestors were paid agents of billionaire George Soros and that Hillary Clinton should be prosecuted for corruption and put in jail."[95]

The lawyers said that Sayoc personalized the misinformation to which he was exposed:

He began to consider Democrats as not just dangerous in theory, but imminently and seriously dangerous to his personal safety. President Trump did nothing to dissuade this message. In the lead up to the 2018 midterm elections, President Trump warned his supporters that they were in danger from Democrats, and at times condoned violence against his critics and enemies. At a rally in October 2018, around the time Mr. Sayoc sent the packages, President Trump announced that Democrats "destroy people. They want to destroy people. These are really evil people" . . . A rational observer may have brushed off Trump's tweets as hyperbole, but Mr. Sayoc took them to heart. He was credulous, paranoid, and using large doses of steroids and supplements.[96]

They argued that Sayoc believed he was sending hoax bombs that had no detonation capability. They said that he had "no true grasp of the severity of his crimes or the potential ramifications of his actions."[97]

But recall that the FBI, Secret Service, and police departments had all characterized the devices as bombs, not as bomb lookalikes. And they were filled with an explosive powder. We can apply the Hamm and Spaaij radicalization model of how lone-wolf terrorists are formed to Sayoc:

1. **Personal and political grievance.** Sayoc was a self-described loner who lived on the fringes, suffered from mental illnesses, and thought the world had failed him. He also believed himself to have been the victim of political violence because his van, a rolling shrine to Trump and against Trump's enemies, had been vandalized many times. And he held deep animosity, evidenced in his tweets, against the president's critics.

2. **Affinity with an extremist group.** For the two-plus years before he sent the bombs, Sayoc had been active on a slew of social media sites promoting right-wing and white nationalist themes.

3. **Identification with an enabler.** Sayoc received inspiration from Trump and Trump's followers. He described himself as no longer a loner and in community with other Trump supporters. And he made Trump's enemies his own. He described himself as a soldier in a war of right against left.

4. **Broadcasting terrorist intent.** Sayoc sent death threat tweets to most of the people he later sent bombs to. He sent similar tweets to others as well.

5. **Triggering event.** The triggering event was the intensity and frequency of Trump's denunciation of his critics and rivals in the buildup to the midterm elections. The first bomb, sent to Soros, came fifteen days before the midterm, at the height of Trump's and the right-wing echo chamber's warnings about Soros funding the invasion from Central America.

Sayoc was a lone wolf who admits that he was triggered by Trump and by his rhetoric. He heard the lone-wolf whistles, and he followed them. As far back as 2011, when Trump took up the birther cause, First Lady Michelle Obama recognized the lone-wolf whistle signals. She knew that Trump's signals put her and her family in danger. She believed it was deliberately meant to stir up wingnuts and kooks. And she noted that the Secret Service knew that there are people capable of being so stirred.

Sayoc is one of those who was stirred up. He was a self-described loner, emotionally unstable, needy. His life had been a series of failures and disappointments. He lacked purpose. He found that purpose in following Trump, in working for a higher cause. He became part of something larger than himself; he was a member of a community of similarly passionate people, pulled into the Trump orbit. He was even willing to kill for Trump. And he sent a bomb intended to be received in the Obama household—just as Michelle Obama had feared.

His tweets are incoherent, as, frankly, are many of Trump's. But his intent was clear. And he followed up his tweets by sending bombs to the subjects of his tweets. Thankfully, Sayoc was an incompetent bombmaker, so no one was hurt. They could have been.

In early August 2019, Sayoc was sentenced to twenty years in federal prison.

March–July 2019—Trump Attacks Freshman Congresswoman Who Wears a Hijab

In the 2018 congressional midterm elections, the first two Muslim women ever were elected to Congress. One of them, Ilhan Omar, wears a hijab. In March 2019, the West Virginia Republican Party, in a celebration called WVGOP Day, featured a poster in the West Virginia capitol rotunda of a photograph of Congresswoman Omar, in her hijab, juxtaposed against a picture of a burning World Trade Center as the second plane exploded into it. The words "Never Forget—You Said. I Am the Proof You Have Forgotten" were written on the poster.[98]

In early April 2019, a Trump supporter was arrested for threatening to kill Congresswoman Omar. According to the US Attorney for the Western District of New York, Patrick W. Carlineo Jr. called the congresswoman's office and asked a staffer, "Do you work for the Muslim Brotherhood? Why are you working for her, she's a (expletive) terrorist. I'll put a bullet in her (expletive) skull."[99]

According to the FBI in a court filing, on being arrested suspect Patrick Carlineo justified his threat by invoking Trump: "Carlineo stated that he was a patriot, that he loves the President, and that he hates radical Muslims in our government."[100] The Council on American-Islamic Relations–New York responded to the arrest by saying in a statement: "The political environment, led by an Islamophobe in the White House, has normalized hate speech and emboldened bigots in their actions. The rising threat of Islamophobia and white supremacy must be taken seriously. We are thankful that law enforcement tracked this individual down before he could act on his hatred for Muslims."[101]

Trump did not denounce the death threat against Congress-woman Omar. Rather, three days later, Trump attacked her directly. He posted a tweet with the all-caps words "WE WILL NEVER FORGET" above a video of the congresswoman speaking at a Muslim civil rights conference, interspersed with video of the Twin Towers on 9/11 on fire and collapsing.[102] House Speaker Nancy Pelosi recognized the danger to Rep. Omar and denounced Trump: "The memory of 9/11 is sacred ground, and any discussion of it must be done with reverence. The President shouldn't use the painful images of 9/11 for a political attack. It is wrong for the President, as Commander-in-Chief, to fan the flames to make anyone less safe."[103]

Representative Omar called out the president's provocation of violence in a statement two days later, saying:

> Since the President's tweet Friday evening, I have experienced an increase in direct threats on my life—many directly referencing or replying to the President's video. I thank the Capitol Police, the FBI, the House Sergeant at Arms, and the Speaker of the House for their attention to these threats. Violent crimes and other acts of hate by right-wing extremists and white nationalists are on the rise in this country and around the world. We can no longer ignore that they are being encouraged by the occupant of the highest office in the land. . . . Violent rhetoric and all forms of hate speech have no place in our society, much less from our country's Commander in Chief. We are all Americans. This is endangering lives. It has to stop.[104]

But it did not stop. On Sunday, July 14, Trump tweeted about Congresswoman Omar and three other congresswomen of color,

each a freshman: Alexandria Ocasio-Cortez, Rashida Tlaib, and
Ayanna Pressley. Rep. Omar was born in Somalia and came to the
United States as a refugee when she was a child. She is an American citizen, which is a requirement to run for Congress. The other
three congresswomen were all born in the United States. Rep.
Ocasio-Cortez is Latina, Rep. Tlaib is a Muslim of Palestinian descent, and Rep. Pressley is African American. Trump posted three
consecutive tweets:

> So interesting to see "Progressive" Democrat Congress-
> women, who originally came from countries whose govern-
> ments are a complete and total catastrophe, the worst, most
> corrupt and inept anywhere in the world (if they even have
> a functioning government at all), now loudly......[105]
> ...and viciously telling the people of the United States, the
> greatest and most powerful Nation on earth, how our gov-
> ernment is to be run. Why don't they go back and help fix
> the totally broken and crime infested places from which they
> came. Then come back and show us how....[106]
> ....it is done. These places need your help badly, you can't
> leave fast enough. I'm sure that Nancy Pelosi would be very
> happy to quickly work out free travel arrangements![107]

Unlike most of Trump's prior tweets, this series of tweets
seemed to cross a line. Reaction was swift and fierce, with many
Trump critics labeling the tweets racist and many supporters saying that it simply proved that Trump spoke his mind. The US
Equal Opportunity Employment Commission, on its website on
Immigrants' Employment Rights, gives an explicit example of the
kind of language that may violate federal employment laws: "Examples of potentially unlawful conduct include insults, taunting,
or ethnic epithets, such as making fun of a person's foreign accent or comments like, 'Go back to where you came from,'
whether made by supervisors or by co-workers."[108]

Rep. Omar tweeted to the President: "You are stoking white nationalism bc you are angry that people like us are serving in Congress and fighting against your hate-filled agenda."[109] White supremacists cheered Trump's tweets. The neo-Nazi Daily Stormer wrote, "This is the kind of WHITE NATIONALISM we elected him for."[110]

Many other prominent white nationalists also heaped praise on Trump. The following day, with the controversy about his tweets all over the mainstream media and social media, Trump was asked whether he was concerned that white nationalists were finding common cause with him. He replied, "It doesn't concern me because many people agree with me."[111]

He also said, speaking of Rep. Omar and the other three congresswomen,

So all I'm saying is, if they want to leave, they can leave. . . . They can leave. I mean, I look at the one—I look at Omar—I don't know, I never met her. I hear the way she talks about Al-Qaeda. Al-Qaeda has killed many Americans. She said, "You can hold your chest out, you can—when I think of America . . . huh . . . when I think of Al-Qaeda, I can hold my chest out." When she talked about the World Trade Center being knocked down, "Some people." You remember the famous "some people." These are people that, in my opinion, hate our country. Now, you can say what you want, but get a list of all of the statements they've made. And all I'm saying: that if they're not happy here, they can leave. They can leave. And you know what? I'm sure that there'll be many people that won't miss them. . . . But they have to love—they have to love our country. They're Congress people. . . . These are people that if they don't like it here, they can leave.[112]

According to a fact check by the *Washington Post*, Trump falsely characterized Rep. Omar as supporting Al-Qaeda. It reports,

"Trump completely twisted and falsely characterized Omar's remarks . . . Trump appeared to be referring to an Omar comment that has circulated this year in conservative media, including Fox News. It comes from a 2013 interview on 'Bel-Ahdan,' a Twin Cities *PBS* show about Middle East issues. She did not voice approval for al-Qaeda and in fact condemned terrorist acts as 'evil' and 'heinous.' . . . Instead of proudly proclaiming support for al-Qaeda, Omar was recounting how her college professor would arch his shoulders and accentuate the name of the terrorist group for effect."[113]

The following day, the House of Representatives considered a resolution formally condemning the president's tweets. It read that the House, ". . . strongly condemns President Donald Trump's racist comments that have legitimized and increased fear and hatred of new Americans and people of color by saying that our fellow Americans who are immigrants, and those who may look to the President like immigrants, should 'go back' to other countries, by referring to immigrants and asylum seekers as 'invaders,' and by saying that Members of Congress who are immigrants (or those of our colleagues who are wrongly assumed to be immigrants) do not belong in Congress or in the United States of America."[114]

In advance of the vote, Trump issued two tweets in which he denied that the tweets were racist, but then said all four congresswomen hate the United States: "Those Tweets were NOT Racist. I don't have a Racist bone in my body! The so-called vote to be taken is a Democrat con game. Republicans should not show 'weakness' and fall into their trap. This should be a vote on the filthy language, statements and lies told by the Democrat..."[115] Further, "Congresswomen, who I truly believe, based on their actions, hate our Country."[116]

The resolution passed on a mostly party-line vote.

The next evening, President Trump hosted a rally in North Carolina. During that rally, Trump denounced Rep. Omar as the crowd chanted "Send her back!" over and over. Trump stood

upright and silent and seemed to soak in the chant for nearly fifteen seconds. The coverage of the chant was sharply critical. Many
Democratic leaders denounced the chant as dangerous and
un-American. Even some Republicans, who previously were reluctant to criticize Trump, took issue with the chant. For example,
Illinois Republican congressman Adam Kinzinger tweeted the
morning after the rally, "I deeply disagree with the extreme left
& have been disgusted by their tone. I woke up today equally
disgusted—chants like 'send her back' are ugly, wrong, & would
send chills down the spines of our Founding Fathers. This ugli-
ness must end, or we risk our great union."[117]

The Republican leader of the House of Representatives, California congressman Kevin McCarthy, told reporters, "Those
chants have no place in our party or our country." That morning,
Trump tried to distance himself from the chant. Asked by a reporter in the White House why he didn't stop the chant or ask the
audience not to do the chant, Trump suggested he had tried to
interrupt the chant by speaking over it: "Well, number one, I
think I did. I started speaking very quickly. It really was a loud—I
disagree with it, by the way. But it was quite a chant. And I felt a
little bit badly about it. But I will say this: I did, and I started speaking very quickly. But it started up rather—rather fast, as you probably noticed."[118]

The reporter then asked, "So you'll tell your supporters never
to say that again?"[119] Trump replied, "Well I would say that I was not
happy with it. I disagree with it. But again, I didn't say that, they
did."[120] But a fact check by the *Washington Post* notes that Trump
did not try to interrupt the chant or speak faster: "Video of the
rally shows Trump did not try to stop the 'Send her back!' chants
about Omar. He stood passively onstage and waited for the chants
to die down on their own before resuming his speech. Within seconds, he was back to criticizing Omar. Minutes later, he suggested
again that Omar and other critics leave the United States."[121]

But the following day, Trump changed his tune, calling those
who chanted at the rally "incredible people" and "incredible

patriots." He also escalated his incendiary rhetoric about Rep. Omar and the other three freshman congresswomen, saying that they referred to "evil Jews." CNN's fact checker noted that Rep. Omar never said that: "Trump falsely claims the congresswomen have talked about 'evil Jews,' adding, 'That's what they say, evil Jews.' None of them have said that. Omar once tweeted that Israel has committed 'evil doings.'"[122]

Omar had already received hundreds of death threats, and the Capitol Police and FBI had been investigating them. She was asked by a reporter whether she was worried for her safety. She replied, "What I am scared for is the safety [of] people who share my identity. When you have a president who clearly thinks someone like me should 'go back.' The message that he's sending is not for me, it's for every single person who shares an identity with me, and he's telling them that this is not their country. What we tell them is that this is [their country] and they are welcome here."[123]

August 3, 2019—White Nationalist Terrorist Attack Kills Twenty-Two in El Paso

El Paso is a border town in far west Texas. It is 80 percent Hispanic and has a robust relationship with its neighbor across the Mexican border, Ciudad Juarez. Thousands cross the border daily, including children who live in Ciudad Juarez but go to school in El Paso. Many Mexicans do their shopping in El Paso.

On Saturday morning, August 3, 2019, a white supremacist entered a Walmart that was part of a large shopping mall called Cielo Vista. It was a back-to-school tax-free shopping day, and the store was packed. The man was carrying an AK-47 semi-automatic assault rifle. In minutes he killed twenty people and wounded another twenty-six. The death toll eventually rose to twenty-two. The gunman was subdued by law enforcement. Police identified the shooter as Patrick Crusius, a twenty-one-year-old white man from Allen, Texas, a ten-hour drive from El Paso.

Minutes before entering the store, Crusius posted a manifesto on the extremist site 8chan. The manifesto began with a reference to the New Zealand mosque terrorist's manifesto: "In general, I support the Christchurch shooter and his manifesto."[124] But the second sentence picks up Trump's language: "This attack is a response to the Hispanic invasion of Texas. They are the instigators, not me. I am simply defending my country from cultural and ethnic replacement brought on by an invasion."[125]

The manifesto objects to both legal and illegal immigration and elaborates on a common white nationalist theme that Hispanic immigrants are replacing true Americans. Crusius warns that the continued influx of immigrants would turn Texas Democratic, which in turn would guarantee the election of Democratic presidents in the future. The manifesto also objects to marriage between Hispanics and whites and proposes separating the country into whites-only regions and minority-only regions. Crusius closed his manifesto by saying that his ideology has not changed and precedes Trump's presidency. He said, "I know the media will probably call me a white supremacist anyway and blame Trump's rhetoric. The media is infamous for fake news. Their reaction to this attack will likely just confirm that."[126]

It may be true that Crusius's white nationalism predates Trump's candidacy and election. But the language of invasion is all Trump. It's the language that the New Zealand terrorist used in his own manifesto, called "The Great Replacement," which also referred to Trump. It's the language that the Pittsburgh Tree of Life synagogue terrorist used to justify his mass murder. And the choice of location, 650 miles from where Crusius lived, was also significant. Trump had recently visited El Paso. It is one of the border towns that for weeks before the shooting had been in the news as a place where migrants were being held in crowded holding cells in squalid conditions. And Crusius's Twitter account, which was taken down hours after the shooting, included many pro-Trump posts. It also had an image he had liked of the name *Trump* spelled by arranging a number of guns to form each of the letters.

Crusius was interviewed by police detectives and, according to the arrest warrant in his case, told the police that he was specifically targeting Mexicans.[127] Within hours of the shooting, commentators were specifically connecting the shooting and the shooter's manifesto with Trump's rhetoric. Former FBI head of counterintelligence Frank Figliuzzi said that both Islamic extremist terrorism and American white nationalist terrorism have something in common: a charismatic leader who inspires followers to commit acts of violence. He said on MSNBC that day that Trump was the person inspiring violence such as the El Paso attack: "Let's understand something. This administration that we're in needs to come out and intervene. What do I mean by that? If you're on the Islamic extremism side, you've got that cleric radicalizing that young person online. He's the father figure, he's giving the license, he's facilitating and enabling. What we need is the similar figure—the President—to come out immediately . . . and say, 'I stand for something other than hate, I rebuke all the hatred going on here.' Until we see the figure do that, that's giving the license, we'll continue to have this hate problem."[128]

The Southern Poverty Law Center said,

> By describing immigrants in derogatory terms, President Trump is pushing anti-immigrant hate into the mainstream. Trump has broken the bounds of decency, and his rhetoric and tweets are normalizing anti-immigrant sentiments and fueling white supremacist conspiracy theories that engender violence. . . . We cannot ignore the role that Trump's policies, appointments, and rhetoric play in the ongoing instances of domestic terror that continue to plague our country. In referring to immigrants as "rapists" and "invaders," threatening ICE raids, separating families, and

laughing off chants of "send her back," Trump is emboldening ideologies that turn into real-life violence, making America a more dangerous place for all of us and particularly the communities Trump targets.[129]

Forty-eight hours after the El Paso shooting, President Trump stood behind a lectern in the White House and publicly denounced white supremacism. As he did after Charlottesville, his denunciation came well after the event, and after his initial statements. This time he read from a teleprompter, and in language far from his usual tone, said, "These barbaric slaughters are an assault upon our communities, an attack upon our nation, and a crime against all of humanity. We are outraged and sickened by this monstrous evil. The cruelty, the hatred, the malice, the bloodshed, and the terror. Our hearts are shattered for every family whose parents, children, husbands, and wives were ripped from their arms and their lives. America weeps for the fallen."[130]

He said, "The shooter in El Paso posted a manifesto online consumed by racist hate. In one voice this nation must condemn racism, bigotry, and white supremacy. These sinister ideologies must be defeated. Hate has no place in America. Hatred warps the mind, ravages the heart, and devours the soul."[131]

Trump then shifted the focus to the internet, gun control, and video games. He did not address his own language and its possible inspiration of the El Paso shooter and other white nationalist violence.

We can apply the Hamm and Spaaij radicalization model of how lone-wolf terrorists are formed to Crusius:

1. **Personal and political grievance.** Crusius was an active white supremacist who believed that whites were being replaced by nonwhite immigrants. He opposed even legal immigration, believing that Mexican immigration threatened to turn Texas Democratic, and advocated for separate homelands for white Americans and

Hispanic immigrants. He also objected to marriage between whites and Hispanics.

2. **Affinity with an extremist group.** Crusius was active online in white supremacist social media, including 8chan, a popular site for white supremacists to share information. He posted his manifesto to 8chan.

3. **Identification with an enabler.** Crusius was an admirer of President Trump and had a number of pro-Trump posts on his Twitter account. He also said in his own manifesto that he supported the New Zealand shooter and manifesto. And he used Trump's language of invasion in his manifesto.

4. **Broadcasting terrorist intent.** Crusius posted his manifesto on a Twitter account with no followers, to be discovered after the attack.

5. **Triggering event.** The second sentence in Crusius's manifesto was, "This attack is a response to the Hispanic invasion of Texas. They are the instigators, not me. I am simply defending my country from cultural and ethnic replacement brought on by an invasion."[132] The attack came after a year of increasingly intense and frequent language of invasion from the president. And it came after two weeks of news coverage consumed with Trump's insistence that certain people from elsewhere were going back to where they came from.

Reactions to Trump's Language

Donald Trump says his language is very nice.[133] Most Americans disagree. A Pew Research Center study published in June 2019, about two and a half years into Trump's presidency, found that, "A 55 percent majority says Trump has changed the tone and nature of political debate in this country for the worse; fewer than half as many (24 percent) say he has changed it for the better, while 20 percent say he has had little impact."[134]

More significant to the topic of this book, 78 percent of Americans say that "heated or aggressive" language directed by elected officials against certain people or groups makes violence against them more likely. This includes 61 percent of Republicans or independents who lean Republican, and 91 percent of Democrats or independents who lean Democratic.[135]

In the study, 76 percent of Americans say they are often or sometimes concerned by what President Trump says. Some 70 percent are often or sometimes confused, 69 percent are often or sometimes embarrassed, 65 percent are often or sometimes angry, and 56 percent are often or sometimes frightened by what Trump says.[136] The study further found that 69 percent of Americans said it is never or rarely appropriate for an elected official to say their opponent's position is evil; 71 percent say it is never or rarely appropriate for an elected official to say their opponent is anti-American; and 93 percent say it is never or rarely acceptable for an elected official to deliberately mislead people about their opponent's record.[137]

In late July 2019, the leaders of The National Cathedral in Washington published a response to President Trump's weeks of racially charged insults: "Make no mistake about it, words matter. And, Mr. Trump's words are dangerous. These words are more than a 'dog-whistle.' When such violent dehumanizing words come from the President of the United States, they are a clarion call, and give cover, to white supremacists who consider people of color a sub-human 'infestation' in America. They serve as a call to action from those people to keep America great by ridding it of such infestation. Violent words lead to violent actions."[138]

Figliuzzi, the former FBI counterintelligence chief, wrote in the *New York Times* in July 2019 that Trump's language creates conditions in which violence seems to be a valid solution to a problem: "The president has fallen short of calling for overt violence against minorities and immigrants, but unbalanced minds among us may fail to note the distinction. If a president paints people of color as the enemy, encourages them to be sent back to where they came from, and implies that no humans want to live in certain American cities, he gives license to those who feel compelled to eradicate what Mr. Trump calls an infestation."[139]

Soon after President Trump finally spoke, two days after the El Paso shooting, former president Barack Obama posted on his Facebook page. Without naming Trump directly, he warned about the dangers of dehumanizing language:

> We should soundly reject language coming out of the mouths of any of our leaders that feeds a climate of fear and hatred or normalizes racist sentiments; leaders who demonize those who don't look like us, or suggest that other people, including immigrants, threaten our way of life, or refer to other people as sub-human, or imply that America belongs to just one certain type of people. Such language isn't new—it's been at the root of most human tragedy throughout history, here in America and around the world. It is at the root of slavery and Jim Crow, the Holocaust, the genocide in Rwanda and ethnic cleansing in the Balkans. It has no place in our politics and our public life. And it's time for the overwhelming majority of Americans of goodwill, of every race and faith and political party, to say as much—clearly and unequivocally.[140]

6

What Is Trump Up To?

D onald Trump uses language in ways that are unprecedented among presidents of the United States. He uses a kind of language that the Holocaust Museum Simon-Skjodt Center for the Prevention of Genocide labels "dangerous speech"—speech that, under the right conditions, can influence people to accept, condone, and commit violence against members of a group.[1]

Rachel Brown, author of the Center's handbook, *Defusing Hate*, notes that speech by itself is not enough to lead people to commit violence. Four other elements are needed.

- A speaker who is influential or popular with the audience
- A medium (the means used to communicate a message) that makes the audience more likely to access, believe, or spread the speech

- A context that increases the risk that the speech will provoke violence toward a group
- An audience that is receptive to speech that promotes violence, fear, or hatred toward a group[2]

We can apply those four criteria to Trump's campaign and presidency:

- Trump certainly connects with his base and has the capacity to move them. And much of his rhetoric seems to be intended to keep his base energized and mobilized.
- Trump's tweets, rallies, and press conferences include language that is intended to generate news coverage: language of conflict, of contradiction, of controversy. And mainstream media coverage of his comments feeds into conservative media and white supremacist sites, and the language takes on a life of its own.
- Trump uses framing language that creates context: Migrants are invaders; rivals are causing American deaths.
- Both the white supremacists in his audience and those, like Sayoc, with emotional issues, respond to his language in ways that validate their own grievances, both political and personal.

But to see the real threat, we must go beyond individual words, individual incidents, or even an individual denial by the president. Civic leaders, public officials, the media, engaged citizens, and others can take steps to prevent violence provoked by language from taking place again. The first step is to recognize the patterns. And the patterns are there to see.

The Consequences of Dehumanizing Language: Activating Lone-Wolf Terrorists

I begin by reviewing key concepts on lone-wolf terrorists from Chapter 3 and applying them to the violence that has occurred in the wake of Trump's use of language.

In Chapter 3, I observed South Florida University professor Randy Borum's four-stage process of ideological development that justifies violence, including acts of terrorism. The process creates what Borum calls a "terrorist mindset." People observe some social condition and consider it both wrong and unfair. Then they identify a villain and dehumanize that villain. The process is:

1. It's not right.
2. It's not fair.
3. It's their fault.
4. They're evil/less than human.[3]

Trump doesn't wait for people to reach that conclusion. He talks his followers through all four steps. He engages in framing that creates worldviews. The final frame, "they're evil/less than human," creates social conditions in which harming or killing the person or group is seen to be an honorable thing: the remedying of an injustice by neutralizing the evil person or people who perpetuate the injustice.

Some people who committed violence against individuals or property during the 2016 presidential campaign seem to have done so impulsively, which manifested itself in an increase in hate crimes. Recall, for example, the Boston brothers who beat a sleeping man in the subway because they assumed he was a Mexican immigrant here illegally. That was a hate crime of opportunity. They hadn't gone looking for someone to harm; they just came upon him.

As Trump escalated both the intensity and frequency of his dehumanizing and demonizing language through the first two and a half years of his presidency, that violence took on a more sinister form: acts of, or attempts to commit, mass murder against symbolic targets in the service of a political purpose, what is now labeled by the FBI as domestic terrorism.

Beyond the four-stage process noted by Borum, Indiana State University criminologist Mark Hamm and Australia's Victoria University sociologist Ramon Spaaij describe how someone who has been ideologically transformed to justify acts of violence can then become activated. They observe: "An extremist must first dehumanize his victim and then raise himself to the position of moral superiority. Internalizing these psychological pre-conditions, extremists begin to think of themselves as soldiers."[4]

Notice that Bowers, the Tree of Life shooter, justified his act of terrorism by saying he was protecting his people from slaughter. Crusius, the El Paso shooter, said he was targeting Mexicans to protect Texas and the United States from invasion.

Hamm and Spaaij describe a five-stage activation model that moves people from latent haters to active terrorists. We can apply the activation model to those who were triggered by Trump's language:

1. **Blending of personal and political grievance.** Notice that Trump's language plays on grievances, both personal and group.

2. **Affinity with an extremist group.** The most prevalent extremist groups that those who engaged in the acts of terror committed in the aftermath of Trump's language had an affinity with are committed to white supremacy and white nationalism.

3. **Identification with an enabler.** One of the common elements of the acts of terror committed in the aftermath of Trump's language is that Trump was an enabler, someone the terrorists admired or who planted

language into the environment where the extremist was active.

4. **Broadcasting terrorist intent.** The US Marshals Service Lone-Wolf Terrorism Task Force concludes that manifestos and other forms of communication issued just before an act of terrorism are intended to justify not only their own attack but to shape the attitudes of others. The killings may not be the goal, but rather a catalyst to achievement of their mission or goal to force society in general to see the world from their perspective.[5]

5. **Triggering event.** In the examples of acts of terror committed in the aftermath of Trump's language, we see that a common trigger was Trump's language itself—its intensity, frequency, and escalation served as the triggering event for Bowers, Sayoc, and Crusius.

The Trump Lone-Wolf Whistle Terrorism Playbook

Donald Trump uses all twelve plays in the Lone-Wolf Whistle Terrorist Playbook. We have seen his language in the vignettes in Chapters 4 and 5. Here is a summary of the plays, with some examples for each play:

THE TRUMP PLAYBOOK
TWELVE RHETORICAL FORMS THAT MAY PROVOKE VIOLENCE

1. DEHUMANIZE: Calling groups of people animals or vermin who are infesting the nation.

- These aren't people, they're animals.
- Democrats want illegal aliens to pour into and infest our country.
- We have an infestation in certain parts of our country.
- They live in nests.
- Yes, that's right. They're animals. They're animals.

2. DEMONIZE/DELEGITIMIZE: Attributing to a rival or group a menacing or evil identity or calling into question the legitimacy or qualification of a rival or group.

- Nancy Pelosi is very bad for our country . . . She wants open borders. She doesn't mind human trafficking . . . She's costing the country hundreds of billions of dollars because what's happening is when you have a porous border, and when you have drugs pouring in, and when you have people dying all over the country because of people like Nancy Pelosi. She's doing a terrible disservice to our country.
- Democrats allow open borders, drugs, and crime!
- Beto O'Rourke even voted to shield MS-13 gang members from deportation. He doesn't want to deport them. He says they're people. They're people. They carve you up with a knife, but they're people.
- This guy [President Obama] either has a birth certificate or he doesn't. . . . If you weren't born in this country, you cannot be president.

3. SCAPEGOAT: Blaming a group for all or many of the nation's problems.

- Over the years, thousands of Americans have been brutally killed by those who illegally entered our country, and thousands more lives will be lost if we don't act right now.
- Our southern border is a pipeline for vast quantities of illegal drugs, including meth, heroin, cocaine, and fentanyl . . . 90 percent of which floods across from our southern border. More Americans will die from drugs this year than were killed in the entire Vietnam War.
- Mexicans are taking our jobs. They're taking our manufacturing jobs. They're taking our money. They're killing us.
- The federal government remains shut down for one reason and one reason only: because Democrats will not fund border security.

4. PUBLIC HEALTH THREAT: Saying people are carrying or transmitting dangerous diseases.

- Tremendous infectious diseases are coming into the country.
- People marching toward the border could bring diseases that could pose a threat to public health: exotic diseases, increasing antibiotic resistance, from the invading flood of people.

5. SAFETY THREAT: Claiming that a group or people or a political rival is a threat to public safety or civic order.

- These are evil people.
- Killers.
- They like cutting people up, slicing them, killing them like they did to two beautiful, lovely young girls going back home from school. Killing them, slicing them.
- It's like in a war, where a foreign invader, a foreign invader finally is being taken out.
- We will have many, many more World Trade Centers as sure as you're sitting there, our country will never be the same.

(continues)

TWELVE RHETORICAL FORMS
THAT MAY PROVOKE VIOLENCE (CONT.)

6. VIOLENT MOTIVE: Claiming that a group has violent or hostile intentions toward a dominant group.

- There is a great hatred toward Americans by large segments of the Muslim population.
- So as the caravan—and look, that is an assault on our country. That's an assault. And in that caravan you have some very bad people.
- The Mexican government is forcing their most unwanted people into the United States. They are, in many cases, criminals, drug dealers, rapists, etc.
- Twenty-five percent [of Muslims] agreed that violence against Americans is justified as part—think of that—as part of the global jihad. They want to change your religion.

7. SEVERELY EXAGGERATING RISK: Labeling a minor issue or routine event a major threat.

- [MS-13 has] literally taken over towns and cities of the United States.
- California's law provides safe harbor to some of the most vicious and violent offenders on Earth, like MS-13 gang members putting innocent men, women, and children at the mercy of these sadistic criminals.
- When you looked at the bridge loaded up with people. That's called an invasion of our country.

8. SINISTER IDENTITIES: Attributing vague or sinister identities to a group or its members.

- They're sending us not the right people. It's coming from more than Mexico. It's coming from all over South and Latin America, and it's coming probably from the Middle East.
- When you look at that caravan and largely, a very big percentage of young men, strong. A lot of bad people, a lot of bad people in there, people that are in gangs. We don't want them in this country.

9. CONSPIRACY: Saying that something is part of a sinister conspiracy.

- Do you know how the caravan started? [Trump then made a gesture of handing out money.] Does everybody know what this means? I think the Democrats had something to do with it.
- The Democrat party has gone so far left that it's become radical resistance. Have you ever seen their signs, "Resist"? They say, what will you resist? I don't know. Have you ever seen where the fake news will go to a person holding a sign, who gets paid by Soros or somebody.

10. DISCREDIT INFORMATION: Discrediting the source of objective information or information critical of the leader.

- Fake News.
- The Fake News Media (Mainstream).
- Disproven and paid for by Democrats Dossier used to spy on the Trump campaign.
- Has anyone looked at the mistakes that John Brennan made while serving as CIA director . . . he has become nothing less than a loudmouth, partisan, political hack who cannot be trusted with the secrets to our country!

(continues)

TWELVE RHETORICAL FORMS
THAT MAY PROVOKE VIOLENCE (CONT.)

11. CONFLATION: Conflating the leader and the state, so that any criticism of the leader is seen as an attack on the nation (i.e., negative media coverage of the leader is cast as media being an enemy of the people or unpatriotic).

- So I just heard that they broke into the office of one of my personal attorneys. . . . It's an attack on our country, in a true sense. It's an attack on what we all stand for.
- The Mainstream Media is under fire and being scorned all over the World as being corrupt and FAKE. They truly are the Enemy of the People.
- The press is doing everything within their power to fight the magnificence of the phrase MAKE AMERICA GREAT AGAIN! They are truly the ENEMY OF THE PEOPLE!
- [Investigation into Trump] is the greatest political scandal in the history of our country. Again, bigger than Watergate. Because it means so much this was a coup. This was a coup. This wasn't stealing information from an office in the Watergate apartments. This was an attempted coup.
- [Counterintelligence investigation] was a coup. This was an attempted overthrow of the United States government.
- [Investigation] was an attempted coup or an attempted takedown of the president of the United States.

12. MENACING IMAGE: Juxtaposing a menacing image (noose, crosshairs, flaming cross, swastika, etc.) with a person or person's image, a location, or a facility associated with the target.

- Online ad calls Colin Allred, a black civil rights lawyer, hostile to gun rights—accompanied by the image of a white woman with a dark-skinned hand smothering her mouth.[6]
- Trump tweet: "WE WILL NEVER FORGET" above a video of the congresswoman speaking at a Muslim civil rights conference, interspersed with video of the Twin Towers on 9/11 on fire and collapsing.[7]
- Trump tweet: Hillary Clinton's face appears with bags of cash embossed with the Star of David.[8]

Other Patterns of Trump's Language

Using the playbook is not the only pattern Trump exhibits. Other patterns of his language provide insights into him and into his possible motives for speaking the way he does.

Trump's speech—the way he uses language, the words he picks, the times he chooses to be silent—often seems improvised. And some of it may be. But we can see the patterns once we know what to look for.

The biggest pattern is that he uses all the plays in the lone-wolf-whistle terrorist playbook. But Trump also uses other patterns of speech that are not in the playbook and that seem specific to him.

One such pattern is conflation: Trump's tendency to lump to-gether genuinely dangerous people with the group from which they come and to say that the exception and the general rule are one and the same. For example, he conflates the terrorist organi-zation ISIS—whose members are Muslim—with every member of that faith. He conflates MS-13 gang members—most of whom are from Central America—with all Central Americans.

Another of Trump's patterns is the bluff: He bluffs his way through a topic by making up facts and then bluffs his way through the fallout. It could be a small matter or an important matter of state; Trump pronounces something to be true, whether it is or not, then doubles down when challenged. Yet, much of what he says is false. The *Washington Post's* Fact Checker column tracks instances of what they term Trump's lies. According to this column, the president uttered an average of seven lies per day when he took office. Two years later, the column states, the president uttered untruths an average of twenty-three times a day. Fact Checker documented more than ten thousand instances in which this sitting president made false or misleading claims during two years in office.[9] Just as the judges at the Nuremberg war crimes trials observed, even if words or beliefs are false they are still capable of moving people to commit violent acts.

In addition to conflating and bluffing, there are other patterns specific to his language that can serve as a lone-wolf whistle, and the lone wolf who answers the call can be violent.

Having It Both Ways: Building in Deniability

One frequent pattern displays Trump's tendency to contradict himself. He speaks or acts even while denying he is speaking or acting in a certain way. For example, at the same time he says something most people find racist, he says that no one is less racist than he is.

Often, the contradiction is immediate. He says one thing and in the same breath says the opposite. This is not common in his tweets, nor in his rallies in front of supporters, but he does this when speaking to reporters or to a group that may not be entirely sympathetic to his views.

This is different from political pandering, where a candidate says different things to different constituencies at different times, telling them what they want to hear so he can keep their support. When building in deniability, Trump takes a position and as soon he utters it incorporates a defense against what he has just articulated.

This tactic was evident when he made his initial 2015 announcement for the presidency. It began with an unequivocal statement: "When Mexico sends its people, they're not sending their best." He then elaborated: "They're sending people who have lots of problems, and they're bringing their problems with [them]. They're bringing crime." Trump then specified: "They're rapists." That's an unequivocal and powerful statement even if it is so general as to be inconceivable. There is a chance that a criminal might be among those coming to the US, just as there is a chance a criminal is among any group of people, but that chance is minuscule. Yet, after stating that Mexicans coming to the US are criminals and rapists, he immediately hedged: "And some, I assume, are good people."[10]

Mexico was sending its worst people, Trump affirmed a few weeks later. If that were the case, why would it also send some good people? What would be the point?

A logical conclusion is that Trump had two purposes in mentioning good and bad people in the same breath. The first was to energize his base, which was and still is inclined to be anti-immigration or anti-Muslim or anti-black or anti-LGBT. The second purpose was so that Trump could defend himself against the accusation that he is a bigot, a racist, a white nationalist, or otherwise targeting people because of their identity.

This use of contradiction is repeated over and over. Some examples:

- The same day he announced his candidacy, Trump said, "[Mexico] is sending us not the right people. It's coming from more than Mexico. It's coming from all over South and Latin America, and it's coming probably from the Middle East."

This sounds scary and sinister. The wrong people are coming to the US from an entire continent and even from the Middle East. But he instantly added this: "But we don't know. Because we have no protection and we have no competence, we don't know what's happening."[11] He was saying something provocative, that, if true, could provoke fear, while simultaneously saying it could very well be not true.

- Trump said, "I'm putting people on notice that are coming here from Syria as part of this mass migration. . . . They could be ISIS. . . . This could be one of the great tactical ploys of all time. A 200,000-man army maybe, or if you said 50,000 or 80,000 or 100,000, we got problems and it could be possible."

This is terrifying. Syrian refugees, Trump said, could be part of a huge ISIS-led army. The "maybe" seemed to express uncertainty over the number of Syrians, not over whether this is happening. But as soon as he suggested that the refugees could be terrorists, Trump added, "I don't know that it is, but it could be possible."[12] This allowed him to deny ever saying the United States was about to be invaded by an ISIS army from Syria. But a motivated follower could hear it and likely believe that an ISIS army was on its way. Or at least be scared and believe all Syrian refugees to be potential terrorists.

There are dozens of examples of Trump contradicting himself, and in most instances the media focused on the incendiary part of his utterance. Practically speaking, media and others might consider making less of a fuss about the outrageous first part of these statements or instead contrast that with the cynicism of his follow-up denial.

Dancing with White Supremacy

Looking at Trump's language from the beginning of the campaign through the first thirty months of his presidency, Trump clearly has embraced a white nationalist approach. It is evident in his patterns of speech, his choice of words, and in his behavior.

One pattern is Trump's adoption of both rhetoric and policies that have for decades been part of the white supremacy agenda, from restricting immigration to banning Muslims. Another pattern is Trump's response when asked to denounce white supremacy. J. M. Berger, a fellow at George Washington University's program on extremism, wrote an analysis for Politico just before the 2016 election in which he tracked the growth of white supremacist support for Trump.[13] He wrote, "Trump would promulgate messages with racist cues (some more subtle, some less so), then deny or disavow them, while the white nationalist community dutifully perked up and saw those messages as a call to arms."[14]

Trump follows a pattern of deflecting calls to denounce white supremacists, followed by a weak denunciation, then reverting to his prior language. When asked to denounce white supremacy, both during the campaign and during his presidency, Trump's response typically includes some or all of the four elements below.

Deflect. He does this in several ways. He ignores the call to denounce. He changes the subject. He professes ignorance about the event. He characterizes the event differently. Sometimes he expresses sympathy for victims while not addressing the event that caused them to be become victims.

Diminish. If pressed, he diminishes the significance of the event or attempts to create equivalence between the event and more benign topics.

Denounce. After an interval, sometimes of hours, but often of days, Trump issues a written denunciation or reads a statement denouncing the event or person, often in a tone of rote recitation.

Revert. Not long after the denunciation, Trump reverts to his earlier language and behavior, as if his denunciation never happened. This is a constant; it happens after every denunciation.

Not all four elements are used in every instance. Typically, if he's giving a speech and there are no reporters pressing him for clarification or challenging his explanation, he has no need to do Step 2, Diminish.

The way in which white supremacists respond to the pattern, especially the deflections, is significant. It suggests a kind of dance between Trump and the white supremacist movement. He signals to them; they signal back.

Here are some examples.

In early 2016, former Ku Klux Klan leader David Duke told his radio audience, "Voting against Donald Trump at this point is really treason to your heritage. I'm not saying I endorse everything about Trump, in fact I haven't formally endorsed him. But I do support his candidacy, and I support voting for him as a strategic action."[15] Duke directed his audience to volunteer to work on Trump's campaign. Later that day, candidate Trump was asked by a reporter how he felt about David Duke's support. Trump replied in an impatient and dismissive tone: "I didn't even know he endorsed me. David Duke endorsed me? Okay, all right. I disavow, okay?"[16]

Two days after this lukewarm disavowal, Trump interviewed with CNN's Jake Tapper and feigned ignorance of Duke. Tapper asked him, "Will you condemn David Duke and say that you do not want his vote or that of other white supremacists in this election?"[17]

Trump could very easily have said that he had already disavowed Duke, two days earlier. But he did not. Instead, he went to Step 1 of the pattern, Deflect. "Well just so you understand, I don't know anything about David Duke, okay? I don't know anything about what you're even talking about with white supremacy or white supremacists. So, I don't know. I mean, I don't know. Did he endorse me, or what's going on? Because I know nothing about David Duke. I know nothing about white supremacists. And so you're asking me a question that I'm supposed to be talking about people that I know nothing about."[18]

Tapper persevered, "Would you just say unequivocally you condemn them and that you don't want their support?"[19]

Trump continued to profess ignorance: "Well I have to look at the group. I don't know what group you're talking about. You wouldn't want me to condemn a group that I know nothing about. I'd have to look. If you would send me a list of the groups I will do research on them and certainly I would disavow if I thought there was something wrong but . . ."[20]

Tapper interrupted and said that he was speaking specifically about the Ku Klux Klan. Trump moved to Step 2, Diminish: "You may have groups in there that are totally fine, and it would be very unfair, so give me a list of the groups and I'll let you know."[21]

Tapper again clarified: "Okay, I'm now just talking about David Duke and the Ku Klux Klan here but . . ."[22] Trump replied, "I don't know anything, honestly, I don't know David Duke. I don't believe I've ever met him, I'm pretty sure I never met him, and I don't know anything about him."[23]

A few hours after the interview, Trump went to Step 3: Denounce. Trump tweeted a video clip from his press conference two days earlier, with this comment: "As I stated at the press conference on Friday regarding David Duke—I disavow."[24]

When campaigning for president in 2016, Trump clearly knew who David Duke was. In interviews years before he had called Duke a Klansman, a bigot, and a racist. In the days after his Tapper interview, Trump was confronted with the contradiction. He said that his earpiece had malfunctioned and that he hadn't heard Tapper's question.[25] But he clearly heard the name David Duke, and repeated it many times in his response.

The following Sunday, Trump appeared on CBS's *Face the Nation* and insisted that he had consistently denounced white supremacy. But he didn't make a bold new denunciation. Rather, he asserted that he had already done so. It was all in the past tense. "I have rejected, how many times do I have to reject? I have rejected David Duke. I have rejected the KKK, the Ku Klux Klan, from the time I'm five years old I have rejected that. I put it on Twitter last week."[26]

Told that Duke was advising his followers to vote for Trump, he said: "I don't want them and I don't want him to say it. I can't help if he says it . . . if he says it, he says it, okay, do I want it, no . . . I don't like any group of hate. Hate groups are not for me."[27]

We saw the same pattern again in August 2019 after a shooter killed twenty-two people in El Paso. The shooter justified his attack as a response to a "Hispanic invasion of Texas," and repeated many other themes Trump used in his campaign and during his presidency. In the aftermath of this mass murder, public officials, crime and security experts, and critics pointed to Trump's language as bearing responsibility for provoking the violence. Trump went to Step 1: Deflect. He expressed sympathy for the shooting victims. Then he went silent and ignored calls to condemn white supremacy and racially motivated violence for two days. His silence was followed by Step 3: Denounce. Standing at a lectern, he read from a teleprompter in a wooden tone: "In one voice this nation must condemn racism, bigotry, and white supremacy. These sinister ideologies must be defeated. Hate has no place in America."[28]

He read a sentence that did not remotely sound as if Trump would utter it had it not been written by a speechwriter: "Hatred warps the mind, ravages the heart, and devours the soul."[29]

After this, Trump said the internet and video games provoked individuals to violence, and then discussed gun control in general terms. Two days later, he was on Step 4: Revert. While visiting an El Paso hospital, he joked as he mischaracterized the crowd size at former El Paso congressman Beto O'Rourke's El Paso rally where O'Rourke had announced his run for president. He then spoke about the size of Trump's own crowd at an El Paso rally the same night, in which he had used the language of invasion when describing migrants.

In addition to the pattern of what Trump says and doesn't say when called on to condemn white supremacists, there's also a related pattern: how white supremacists respond to Trump. Trump appears to be in a kind of dance with the white suprema- cist movement. They respond to his patterns. He signals to them; they signal back.

In 2016, Trump told Jake Tapper he didn't know who David Duke was and later tweeted a disavowal of the former Klan leader. Duke told The Daily Beast that he wasn't troubled by Trump's need to keep a distance from him: "If he disavows me, fine. Let him do whatever he thinks he needs to do to become president of the United States. . . . It's good for him to be judicious. He can certainly disagree with David Duke."[30]

The founder of the neo-Nazi site The Daily Stormer, Andrew Anglin, has often described Trump's relationship with white su- premacists as "wink-wink-wink." It began in the first weeks of the campaign in 2015 when Trump tweeted a stock photo of Nazi SS troops. The campaign blamed an intern for posting an inappro- priate image, and the tweet was deleted. But The Daily Stormer wrote, "Obviously, most people will be like 'obvious accident, no harm done.' Meanwhile, we here at *The Daily Stormer* will be all like 'wink wink wink wink wink.'"[31]

Does this dance mean that Trump is a white nationalist? Maybe. But maybe not. It certainly empowers white nationalists. But he may be adopting their framework for his own benefit, but insincerely.

His own behavior suggests he doesn't believe some of his most powerful themes as candidate and president. He dehumanizes Mexicans and Latin Americans seeking to enter the country, and calls them criminals, an infestation, and animals. But one week after the El Paso shooting, the *Washington Post* reported that for nearly twenty years the Trump Organization, owned by Trump, has employed dozens of undocumented Latin American employees to do construction and maintenance at several Trump properties. One employee told the *Post* that he had been coached by his supervisor on how to get false immigration papers at a certain street corner in New York. Both were working for the Trump Organization at the time. Another employee was quoted in the *Post* saying, "If you're a good worker, papers don't matter."[32]

Calling Latinos rapists and criminals, saying that immigrants coming to the US are invading, is common language among white supremacists. But if Trump believed such people were dangerous, he likely would not have employed them.

In late July 2019, former FBI counterintelligence chief Frank Figliuzzi wrote in the *New York Times* about the relationship between Trump's language and violence, especially by white supremacists. He wrote: "[Trump] empowers hateful and potentially violent individuals with his divisive rhetoric and his unwillingness to unequivocally denounce white supremacy. Mr. Trump may be understandably worried about the course of congressional inquiries, but his aggressive and race-baiting responses have been beyond the pale. He has chosen a reelection strategy based on appealing to the kinds of hatred, fear, and ignorance that can lead to violence."[33]

Figliuzzi then addressed whether Trump is a racist. His conclusion: maybe. "It doesn't really matter whether Mr. Trump is truly a racist or merely playing one on television to appeal to his base. Either way, his path can lead to bloodshed. When that happens, we will hear White House officials and the Republican leadership claim their hands are clean because malicious people can't be stopped from acting out. Don't believe a word of it. Terrorists aren't born that way: They are inspired, cultivated, and directed. Our experience with online radicalization has shown there is a clear path to violence. I fear we are on it."[34]

What Is Trump's Motive?

What is Trump up to?

Without a doubt, Donald Trump's language provokes or encourages some people to commit or attempt violence against members of specific groups, as well as against Trump's critics and rivals. There are two possible explanations for Trump's incitement of violence: Either he wants the violence, or he doesn't care about the violence.

I believe that physical violence is not Trump's goal, for at least three reasons.

First, if his goal were to provoke acts of violence, he would not contradict himself. He would not simultaneously say that a group or person is an existential threat and then say that group or that person is perhaps not a threat.

Leaders in the twentieth and early twenty-first century who used dehumanizing language, who intended violence, or who ultimately planned and committed genocide used little if any contradiction. Trump's very equivocation—"And some, I assume, are good people"—suggests that he doesn't intend violence as his goal. And his persistent denial that his language is responsible for the violence suggests that he doesn't want to be directly identified with the violence.

Second, his targets continuously change. If violence were a goal, he would keep his focus on the group or rivals to whom he intends harm. But he is scattershot. Sometimes he targets Muslims, sometimes Mexicans, sometimes immigrants in general; sometimes political rivals; sometimes civic institutions such as the media or federal law enforcement.

Third, he seems unable to stick to a coherent goal-oriented strategy. Rather, he tends to adapt to the threat or opportunity day-to-day without considering long-term consequences. He acts more impulsively than strategically.

That said, even if violence is not his goal, Trump nevertheless is aware that violence is a likely consequence of his rhetoric. At virtually each instance of violence or attempted violence he has been put on notice that his words have consequences. Here are a few examples:

Coast Guard Lieutenant Christopher Hasson created a list of Trump critics to assassinate, using Trump's own language— "Pocawarren." Upon Hasson's arrest, Trump was asked whether he bore any responsibility for not moderating his language. He replied, "No, I don't. I think my language is very nice."[35]

In the aftermath of the El Paso attack there was a chorus of commentary about the link between Trump's language and violence. For forty-eight hours after the attack, he was silent on this. The president has been put on notice of the consequences of his language, and yet he persists. Trump appears to be indifferent to the harm his rhetoric causes. He doesn't specifically intend it, but he does nothing to prevent it. In fact, he acts and speaks in ways that make the violence more likely.

On a moral level this may be more frightening than if he wanted the violence to take place. It's one thing for someone affirmatively to wish harm to people, but it is much harder to make sense of why someone who doesn't intend harm would not care when his words in fact lead to violence.

On the political level, it has fundamentally changed the nature of political discourse. He is not the only leader using such language, but he is the exemplar. Although he never explicitly called for physical violence against these groups, he created conditions that made that violence likely. He could have insisted that violence stop, but he did not do so. His statements against violence often took written form and were presumably drafted by staff or read from a teleprompter or piece of paper with little vocal animation. Yet, his animated speech had the effect of encouraging such violence.

So why does he do it? On one level, it works. As a divide-and-conquer tactic, it helps him accumulate political power. Stoking fear and hatred keeps a base agitated. It keeps his base supportive.

I conclude that Trump does it because he wants to feel important, powerful. The harm his words may cause does not interest
him. He may not even believe what he says. But he does it for the
effect it causes, and he is indifferent to the negative consequences
to others. I believe that Trump is a leader who lacks humility and
is incapable of empathy. He makes choices based on what he per-
ceives will benefit him in the moment. If others are hurt in the
process, they are collateral damage.

And it seems that the route to the presidency resulted in lots of
collateral damage. Trump used dehumanizing and demonizing
language against certain groups—Mexicans, Muslims, immigrants, Democrats. And that language garnered support from
those who harbor anti-immigrant or anti-minority sentiment, including white supremacists. As Figliuzzi observed, it doesn't matter whether Trump is genuinely a white nationalist or only playing
one on TV. The consequence is the same.

The victims of the violence are not comforted by the fact that
it is unintentional. There are three categories of victim:

1. People who are treated badly because of Trump's
    language: people who are insulted or are victims of
    physical violence, and members of targeted groups,
    who live in fear that they may be physically harmed.
2. The people of the American nation, who see declines
    in civility, in civic institutions, and in social norms.
3. The lone wolves themselves who commit violent acts.
    In addition to the moral injury they suffer from
    killing or attempting to kill people, some of the lone
    wolves will end up spending much of the rest of their
    lives in prison. If they hadn't been activated in the
    first place, they would have continued in their
    ordinary lives.

One other effect of Trump's language is that acts and deeds
that seemed inconceivable until a few years ago have now come to

pass. And this, too, follows a pattern. In his book *Extremism*, J. M. Berger describes an escalation of consequences of extremist language, policies, and actions. We saw this progression in Chapter 2, in both the Nazi and Hutu examples.

Harassment: Intentionally making out-groups unwelcome in the presence of the in-group.

Discrimination: Denying out-group members benefits provided to in-group members.

Segregation: Physical separation of the in-group from out-groups.

Hate crimes: Nonsystematic violence against out-group members.

Terrorism: Public violence targeting noncombatants to advance an extremist ideology.

Oppression: Aggressive and systemic discrimination, up to and including systematic violence.

War: Open lethal fighting between an in-group and an out-group.

Genocide: Systematic slaughter of out-group members on a large scale.[36]

Even before Trump, the nation had problems with harassment, discrimination, segregation, and hate crimes, but there has been an escalation in all these since Trump began his campaign.

The nation has been subject to domestic terror for its entire history, but only during this presidency has a president's language been linked to domestic terrorism. The FBI has announced that it is treating its investigation of the El Paso shooting as an act of domestic terrorism.

Berger describes oppression as legally sanctioned curtailment of rights, discrimination, or segregation of members of a targeted group. He gives as an example the internment of Japanese Americans during World War II.[37] We have seen the beginnings of such oppression under Trump in the form of separating children from their migrant parents without any mechanism for the families to be reunited, and of holding migrants in squalid confinement.

So far we have not seen war—although since long before Trump there have been persistent calls among white supremacists for a race war. And we have not seen genocide.

But we see the pattern.

And it is terrifying.

PART III
BELIEVING
ABSURDITIES

Those who can make us believe absurdities
can make us commit atrocities.   —VOLTAIRE

The rise of Donald Trump is not a surprise. It is the predictable result of decades of degradation of political discourse,
facilitated by a media more interested in grabbing an audience's attention than in covering issues. The worst part is that we
should have seen it coming. We could have seen it coming if we
had known what to look for, and we should have known.

My purpose in this book is not to look at the Trump candidacy
and presidency in their entirety, but rather to consider certain
forms of his language and their consequences. But even in that
narrow domain, throughout the campaign and first years of

Trump's presidency, much of the media and many civic leaders and engaged citizens seemed to be grappling only with the symptoms of the problem—what Trump said in the moment, and the immediate consequences—without recognizing that there's a greater challenge that will continue regardless of how we address the immediate problem. We can solve the Trump problem but still be as vulnerable to another authoritarian figure who energizes the disenfranchised, the angry, and the scared to similar effect, and who uses the playbook to create or intensify that disenfranchisement, anger, and fear.

Much of Trump's language, both in the campaign and as president, was not about setting forth public policy but rather about creating a mindset. That mindset includes fear of a powerful Them that conflicts with Us. The conflict is so severe that if we don't do something to stop Them, They will wreak havoc on Us. Which groups were Them would change from rally to rally, from tweet to tweet, but there was always a Them.

Such a mindset, once created, allowed followers to support Trump even when he said things that were clearly not true, and even when they weren't in the followers' best interests. His support has remained steady despite Trump setbacks that are not the topic of this book. However, one of the consequences of that mindset is that it creates conditions that can lead to the acceptance of violence, against individuals and against groups. It helps to normalize what was previously unthinkable except on the fringes of society.

Believing absurdities is a precursor to committing atrocities. Part III is about the political and social conditions that made language like Trump's not only possible but predictable, and about why some people respond to the dehumanization of groups and delegitimization of critics, as well as why they believe and act on statements that are demonstrably false, or nonsensical, or contrary to evidence, or that are contrary to the followers' own interests. Why would people believe such easily refutable or nonsensical claims?

Part III is also about the media ecosystem and how it has transformed over the past twenty years in ways that can further diminish critical thinking among citizens. It is about fundamental shifts in the American political order that coincided with the shift in media. It includes a rise in incivility, a refusal to compromise, and the reflexive demonization of political opponents.

These three trends—the media ecosystem transformation, acute political polarization, and the dumbing down of the body politic—have all woven around one another, in a kind of perverse braid over time, leading to the rise of Trump and Trumpism.

We can't solve a problem or prevent its recurrence without understanding what caused it. Part III is about how we got here. Part IV is about how to prevent it from happening again.

7

Trump Not a Cause but a Consequence

Donald Trump is not the cause of the political, social, and moral divisions in the nation. Rather, he is an intensifier of them. He took a very unhealthy situation and made it worse.

Trump rose to prominence through a combination of ambition, showmanship, shamelessness, and flim-flam. But it is unlikely he would have gotten anywhere close to the White House if not for fundamental shifts in both the American news media ecosystem and political system over the past thirty years. Trump consistently toyed with the idea of seeking the highest office, and at least twice before had announced his bid, mostly to call attention to himself. Indeed, it isn't at all certain that he intended to win in 2016. Rather, he seemed to be setting himself up to launch a Trump entertainment media operation. He certainly seems to have been unprepared for the reality of office when he took over.

Rather, Trump could exploit two fundamental trends in American civic life: the transformation of the news industry and the severe polarization of politics. That, and a large portion of the citizenry that responds more to spectacle than to seriousness, made his election possible.

The Greater Content Business

Les Moonves looked out over a room full of investment analysts. It was the last day of February 2016, less than nine months before the presidential election, and more than eighteen months since the campaign had begun. Moonves was speaking at the Morgan Stanley Technology, Media, and Telecommunications Conference. His audience consisted of investors and analysts who controlled billions of dollars in investment assets, and whose job was to figure out where they could get the best return for those dollars. Moonves was one of the most powerful people in American television: Chairman and CEO of CBS Corporation.

Moonves reflected on the future fortunes of his company. He turned his attention to Donald Trump's presidential run. He referred to Trump by his first name. He called Donald's candidacy a good thing. He said, "[It] may not be good for America, but it's good for CBS."

He may as well have been speaking of much of the television news business. Moonves said the race was a "circus" full of "bomb throwing." He didn't mean that in a bad way. It would attract eyeballs, which in turn would attract advertisers. He said, "Man, who would have expected the ride we're all having right now? . . . The money's rolling in and this is fun. . . . I've never seen anything like this, and it's going to be a very good year for us. Sorry. It's a terrible thing to say. But bring it on, Donald. Keep going."[1]

The head of one of America's most respected media organizations was explicitly encouraging one of the most outrageous candidates for president to continue to be outrageous, and he fully acknowledged that doing so would probably not be good for America. Moonves had spoken a truth that had emerged only in the last twenty years: The news media, especially television news, had migrated from what had been a public service mindset to more of an entertainment mindset.

CBS had been mostly a family-owned organization until it had been sold to Westinghouse in 1995. That same year, Disney bought ABC. NBC had become part of General Electric in 1986. But CBS went through several changes of ownership. In 1990, just four years after being bought by Westinghouse, CBS was bought by Viacom. Six years later, Viacom and CBS split into two companies, although both were owned by the same parent. In 2019, Viacom and CBS Corporation merged with each other and became one entity again.[2]

As Moonves spoke in early 2016, CBS News was part of an entertainment conglomerate, and it behaved that way, as did most of the television news business at the time.

It wasn't always so.

That's the Way It Is

I grew up watching *The CBS Evening News with Walter Cronkite*, a nightly look at what was happening, intended to create an informed citizenry. Cronkite was a kind of wise uncle, filling us in on what was going on. He closed his nightly newscast with his iconic "And that's the way it is . . . " and the date.

Cronkite had reported from the battlefields of World War II as a United Press correspondent, covering the landings in North Africa and the Allied invasion of Normandy. He was also part of "The Writing Sixty-Ninth," a group of war correspondents who accompanied Allied bombers on missions over Germany. On live television in 1963, he reported the shooting of President John F. Kennedy and, holding back tears a few minutes later, announced that the president was dead. In 1968, he shared with the nation his reluctant conclusion that the Vietnam War was unwinnable, which tipped President Lyndon B. Johnson over the edge in deciding not to run for reelection. Johnson reportedly concluded, "If I've lost Cronkite, I've lost Middle America."[3]

Cronkite also narrated the US space program, from the initial Mercury and Gemini flights to the first humans to walk on the moon. During that time, he acted much like the curator of America's civic culture and the nation's collective memory. In the 1970s, he was consistently voted the most trusted person in America. Cronkite retired in 1981, some fifteen years before CBS went through a wave of mergers.

The television critic for the *New York Times*, James Poniewozik, in his book *Audience of One: Donald Trump, Television, and the Fracturing of America*, describes television at the time this way:

> For several decades in the middle of the twentieth century, first radio and then television did something that hadn't been done before or since: bring together the majority of the public to have the same cultural experiences at the same time, all the time. The mid-twentieth-century mass media took a country of regional cultures, dialects, and art forms and introduced monoculture. At the same time that the Interstate Highway System was bypassing local byways and national chains were selling the same goods and fast food coast to coast, TV gave us national news, national amusements, and national obsessions. There was even a national voice, in the mid-Atlantic neutral-speak of TV hosts and anchors.[4]

But through the 1990s with the rise of cable networks and the fragmentation of audiences, the dynamic changed dramatically. News was no longer designed to serve all of America, but just a certain, profitable few. News became fragmented, with different versions of the news being told as you switched from one channel to another.

One of Cronkite's executive producers was Don Hewitt, who later founded the CBS News magazine program *60 Minutes*. In his 2001 autobiography, *Tell Me a Story: 50 Years and 60 Minutes in Television,* Hewitt notes that the television news industry wasn't expected to make money: "The difference between then and now is that [television networks] were obliged to give something back in exchange for their public use of the airwaves. That was what the Federal Communications Commission demanded. So if news was a loss leader, that was the price of doing business."[5]

But Hewitt explained that it was possible to make a profit on the news. He tells the story about a mandate he got from the CBS News executive who green-lighted *60 Minutes*: "[O]ur marching orders in 1968: 'Make us proud.' Which may well be the last time anyone ever said 'make us proud' to anyone else in television. Because [CBS News executive Bill] Leonard said 'make us proud' and not 'make us money,' we were able to do both, which I think makes us unique in the annals of television. . . . Back then, none of us who worked in news knew anything about ratings. It was not how we or the people we worked for measured what we were worth to the company. Today, everyone's consumed with ratings."[6]

In 2004, comedian Jon Stewart of Comedy Central's *The Daily Show* confronted the co-hosts of CNN's political debate program *Crossfire.* The program, one of the most popular on the network, featured one guest each from the right and the left in a kind of debate. The co-hosts were former Clinton aide Paul Begala and conservative columnist Tucker Carlson.

The *New York Times* television critic described *Crossfire* this way: "*Crossfire* paid fealty to a particular mainstream-media idea of objectivity, that it was more important to arrive at the *center* of a controversy than at the *truth* of it. And the most entertaining way to arrive at the center was statistically—by finding two people on far opposite sides to have at it. Both sides needed to be represented, always and equally, even if both sides did not have an equal share of the evidence or of informed opinion."[7]

Stewart went on *Crossfire* ostensibly to promote a book, but he shifted instead to criticize the program itself. He asked the co-hosts to stop what they were doing on *Crossfire*, saying it was bad for the country. He called the co-hosts "partisan hacks" and asked them to "stop hurting America." He scolded them about the format, saying it was theater, more like professional wrestling than political discussion or debate. The co-hosts seemed flummoxed by the criticism. Carlson responded by criticizing Stewart about an interview he had conducted on his program. Stewart lashed back, challenging the equivalence Carlson was asserting. "You're on CNN! The show that leads into mine is puppets making crank phone calls. What's wrong with you?"[8]

It was a defining moment, for Stewart and for CNN. An editorial in The *New York Times* called the confrontation "an important milestone in the annals of popular culture" and said that Stewart was "perhaps the most influential political commentator on television."[9]

The confrontation went viral and was repeated on many other news programs. It began to be popular on the internet, even as what was later known as social media was just in its infancy. By the end of 2019, on YouTube alone, more than 12.5 million people had viewed the segment.

CNN was deeply embarrassed by the response to Stewart's critique. It fired its president and brought in a new one, Jonathan Klein, to upgrade the network's news standards. Klein canceled *Crossfire* and fired Carlson. Klein told the *New York Times*, "I agree wholeheartedly with Jon Stewart's overall premise."[10]

Tell Me a Story

Klein was profiled in the *Wall Street Journal*, in a piece about his quest to "rethink the news." It said that one of Klein's top priorities was to revamp programs so that they "focus on dramatic storytelling."[11] Six months later, *Newsweek* assessed Klein's progress, and noted that CNN's "news meetings are now singularly focused on finding characters and discussing storytelling technique."[12]

In November 2004, media critic Michael Wolff, writing in *Vanity Fair*, explained how the news business in general had become part of what he called "the greater content business," and that its primary impulse was to be interesting: "Almost everyone in the journalism and greater-content business talks about the importance and value of story (if not actually saying 'storifying'—but now they may). Not of the story, but of story. Storytelling."[13]

Wolff noted that this applies both to traditional print journalism and to twenty-four-hour cable news: "The virtues of storytelling are sung as often by Bill Keller, the executive editor of *The New York Times*, as by the Roger Ailes, the chairman of Fox News. Our business is storytelling. (At *The New York Times*, they also call it 'the narrative,' which they probably do not at Fox.)"[14]

Wolff said that the change coincided with the corporatization of the news business. He said that the impulse to be interesting requires oversimplification and appeals to emotion: "Storifying has to do with certain techniques which can make nonfiction more vivid and emotional. . . . A key part of storifying is editing out the peripheral, the random, the unresolved, the noncontributory, the complicated, the stuff that doesn't immediately move the plot forward. . . . Indeed, it is hard to go back and. . . . listen to an old Cronkite-type network news show—there's a lack of emphasis, and direction, and point of view; it seems all scattershot, unmediated."[15]

The following year, the *New York Times* television reporter Alessandra Stanley described the change in television news this way: "As television news moves further and further away from covering hard news, political issues are increasingly debated on television dramas. The finale of this season's West Wing paid more prime time attention to its fictional Democratic National Convention than the network news divisions did to the real one in the 2004 election. . . . In contrast, morning talk shows and evening newscasts race through the events of the day to dwell on the kind of personal melodramas that were once relegated to tabloids."[16]

Indeed, the ways journalists tell stories have always been predictable. For more than three decades I've prepared executives for news interviews by teaching them the five elements of storytelling that reporters put in their stories. I call them the Five Cs of News: five words that begin with the letter *C* that describe what makes a story interesting. They are:

1. **Conflict.** The most interesting element of storytelling is conflict. Throughout the history of Western civilization, conflict has been an element of the plot of every story. The *Iliad* of Homer, the oldest story from the Greek tradition, is nominally about the war between the Greeks and the Trojans. But it's really about the hatred of the two top Greek generals: commander-in-chief Agamemnon, and his field commander, Achilles.

    In 2006, the then–White House bureau chief of the *New York Times,* Elisabeth Bumiller, described the significance of conflict: "Most reporters I know are not passionately political, left or right. Our real ideology is a love of conflict, meaning that we have a bias for stories about, yes, personality feuds. But also for disputes over policy."[17]

    The "yes" in her confession is significant. It suggests a grudging acknowledgment that even at the *New York Times,* personality feuds overtake policy disputes. But it is also significant that she doesn't say that the *Times* covers policy. Rather, she emphasizes the disputes over policy.

2. **Contradiction.** Unlike conflict, which involves two parties in dispute, contradiction can be created by juxtaposing language, words, concepts, or ideas. Consider the opening to Charles Dickens's *A Tale of Two Cities:* "It was the best of times. It was the worst of times." In 1895, the *New York Sun* published a headline that is

among the most repeated headlines in English language journalism: "Man Bites Dog." This is contradiction in the form of role reversal. Other reversals that are interesting include reversals of fortune, of path, of idea, of strategy, or of approach. Other forms of contradiction include anything that is contrary to the conventional wisdom or that confounds expectations. Contradictions include negations: *no*, *not*, or words with negating prefixes, such as *unusual, insincere, atypical.* Most news stories, in print and on broadcast, begin with one or more forms of contradiction in the opening paragraphs or quotes.

3. **Controversy.** Controversy includes stories that are already in the news, and that get covered more broadly by other news organizations. By definition, they are newsworthy because they're already in the news.

4. **Colorful Language.** Colorful language begins with words that are short, lively, vivid, and pithy. It includes short sentences and simple sentence structure. It uses metaphor, simile, and other rhetorical devices to compress much meaning into few words. Technical vocabulary or complex descriptions rarely get into the news. Journalists need to simplify, and often they oversimplify.

5. **Cast of Characters.** Journalists can't write about abstractions. Rather, they write about people who embody the abstraction. The late Don Hewitt, founder of the CBS television news magazine *60 Minutes*, said in a conference I attended in the 1980s, "We don't cover issues. We cover people who are swept up by issues."[18] That's a pretty good description of news overall. Characters include the Hero, the Villain, the Victim, the Expert, the Advocate, the Scoundrel, the Everyman or Everywoman who stands in for all others in similar situations. They also include the Candidate,

the Officeholder, the Doctor, the Patient, the Movie Star, the Pop Star, the Cop, the Criminal. Journalists use characters to bring their stories to life.

Crisis Pornography

In a 2007 essay published in the book *What Orwell Didn't Know: Propaganda and the New Face of American Politics*, media professor Martin Kaplan described cable news coverage as "crisis porn." Kaplan is the Martin Lear Chair in Entertainment, Media, and Society at the University of Southern California Annenberg School. Kaplan cautioned that, "The notion that professional news judgment—a reliable journalistic rulebook—is what really drives the nature and kind of coverage is hopelessly quaint."[19]

Kaplan listed what he said cable news, especially, is good at: "[T]rapped miners, Michael Jackson, runaway brides, missing blondes, Christmas Eve murders, Princess Di, Paris Hilton, hurricanes, Tsunamis, disinformation, whiz-bang graphics, scary theme music, polls, gotcha, HeadOn ads, 'Thanks for having me,' people who begin every answer to antagonistic questions with 'look,' people who say 'I didn't interrupt you while you were talking,' and anchors who say 'We'll have to leave it there.'"[20]

Kaplan contrasted that with what he said cable news was not as good at: "[I]nsight, context, depth, reflection proportion, perspective, relevance, humility, information, proportion, perspective, relevance, humility, information, analysis, news."[21]

By 2014, this dynamic in news had escalated into severe incivility as a defining element of much television news. This phenomenon was named "the outrage industry" by two Tufts University professors. In their book, *The Outrage Industry: Political Opinion Media and the New Incivility*, Jeffrey Berry and Sarah Sobieraj argue that some form of political incivility has always existed in some parts of the media landscape. But in the past twenty-five years it has become an increasingly dominant form of coverage, characterized by "venom, vilification of opponents, and hyperbolic reinterpretations of current events."[22]

Other elements of outrage journalism include the following:

- It is personality-centered: Each show or venue is defined by "a dominant charismatic voice."[23]
- It is reactive: It rarely breaks new information. Rather, it reinterprets, reframes, and amplifies what other news organizations cover.
- It is ideologically selective: "[O]utrage commentary filters content selections through the lens of ideological coherence and superiority. The preferred focus is stories in which hosts can position themselves or their political compatriots in the role of the hero or can taint enemies, opponents, or policies they dislike as dangerous, inept, or immoral."[24]
- It is engaging: "In outrage there is performance. There are jokes. There is drama. There is conflict. There is fervor. There is even comfort, as audiences find their worldviews honored."[25]

The authors identify four distinct types of outrage language that each account for more than 10 percent of all recorded instances of outrage: mockery, misrepresentative exaggeration, insult, and name-calling. They also estimate that outrage rhetoric or behavior is used on average once during every ninety to one hundred seconds of political discussion on television, and even more frequently on radio.[26]

New York Times television critic James Poniewozik describes the state of cable television at the time that Trump began eyeing the presidency:

Cable news brought the pseudo-report: the "breaking news" that really broke hours ago, the debates that went on while we were waiting for events to happen, and the coverage of the coverage of the events and the debates. The point was to communicate constant excitement. If pseudo-events were staged by flacks to sell a product or an ideology, pseudo-reports were generated by the news outlet to sell itself. The strongest emotions to incite were fear and sadness and anger, and those could be found anywhere. Somewhere there was a war, a crime, a murdered child. . . . If you were a heavy cable news consumer—for instance, a retiree spending a lot of time at home—this was what the world became to you.[27]

It was this state of journalism that CBS CEO Les Moonves presided over when he addressed investment analysts during the 2016 presidential campaign. In this context, his encouragement of candidate Donald Trump makes sense: Trump was a perpetual outrage generator. And his persistent use of all the plays in the lone-wolf-whistle terrorist playbook was catnip to television news.

The news media couldn't resist playing into the conflict.

Consider CNN, which for years fancied itself the "Most Trusted Name in News." In the 2016 presidential debate hosted by CNN, the third debate between the candidates Trump and Clinton, CNN's advertisement for the debate was indistinguishable from an ad promoting a boxing prizefight, including the camera angles, sound effects, and juxtaposition of the contenders.

The thirty-second ad opens with a deep-voiced narrator declaring, "This. Is. It." Each word appears by itself, falling into frame and then disappearing as the narrator moves to the next word. All the while an echo sound effect amplifies the arrival and departure of each word. The narrator then declares, "Round Three!" as a bell rings. Drums play as the ad shows clips of the two candidates on the campaign trail. Clinton: "My argument is not with his supporters; it's with him." Trump: "When Bernie Sanders said she had bad judgment, she has really bad judgement." Narrator: "It all comes down to this!" Clinton: "He wants to talk about what we've been doing the last thirty years—bring it on!" Trump: "The election of Hillary Clinton would lead to the destruction of our country." The narrator then names each candidate. As he does, the candidate's face, initially in shadow, becomes bathed in light. "Clinton. Trump. The final debate. Thursday. On CNN!"[28]

Esquire noted that "CNN is pulling no promotional punches, promising what we believe will be a war of words but might apparently also explode into a devastating physical confrontation between two seemingly unstoppable warriors."[29]

It then played a mash-up of an actual prize fight promotion, featuring Floyd Mayweather and Manny Pacquaio. In tone, sound, and camera angle they were a solid match.

Keep the Camera On

Trump had toyed with presidential politics before, including in 2000 when he briefly ran for the Reform Party nomination. At the time, Reform Party head Pat Choate told the *New York Times* that he saw no evidence that Trump was a serious candidate but concluded that Trump was running for the visibility it would provide: "All this was, was a serious hustle of the media, and I think the media should send him a massive bill on it."[30]

Trump denied that he had run to promote his businesses, but said he was withdrawing because David Duke had joined the Reform party. We saw in Chapter 4 that Trump announced a run in the 2012 presidential campaign but used that visibility primarily to launch his birther initiative against President Barack Obama.

Donald Trump knew the value of being a celebrity. For much of his career, his name became his biggest asset. Poniewozik writes:

> In the 1980s, Donald Trump was a businessman who used celebrity as a helpful promotional device. By the 1990s, he was a celebrity whose calling card was the ability to play the figure of a businessman. He would leverage that performance—the self as a character, wearing the Halloween costume of a mogul—to make himself a reality-TV star in the 2000s and a

politician in the 2010s. . . . Trump had created a business whose primary product was the idea of Trump: swagger, glitter, hitting it big. . . . His job became essentially to play, on and off television, the role of Donald Trump, mascot.[31]

Trump's role as the "You're Fired" guy on *The Apprentice* solidified a perception not necessarily reflective of reality—that Donald Trump was the ideal of success, wealth, and, more generally, "winning." Poniewozik states:

> Reality TV is the art of symbol, and Trump had been amassing signifiers of wealth his entire image-obsessed career. . . . He embodied a lifestyle that was enviable yet accessible. His life looked like the last five seconds of a commercial for scratch-off lottery tickets. The author Fran Lebowitz would later say that Trump was "a poor person's idea of a rich person." But that's exactly what reality TV is about. *The Bachelor* is a lonely person's ideas of love. *Survivor* is a shut-in's idea of nature. *The Apprentice* didn't need a businessman. It needed the *idea* of a businessman. That was Donald Trump.[32]

Trump had been generally known in New York as a bit of a hustler, a con man who played the tabloid media like a musical instrument. He had transformed himself from failed casino operator to a purportedly successful billionaire and star of a wildly popular so-called "reality television" show, *The Apprentice*. That program had all the Five Cs: Conflict, Contradiction, Controversy, Colorful Language, and a Cast of Characters. Or, as the *New York Times*'s television critic James Poniewozik put it, "In actual, brick-and-mortar New York, Donald Trump was known to readers of the tabloids as a has-been. But in the virtual landscape of TV and the movies, he was New York personified."[33]

In fact, Poniewozik explains, the producers of *The Apprentice* actively worked to cultivate the perception that Donald Trump was a successful businessman: "Jonathan Braun, a supervising editor on the early seasons, described the show's mission as 'Make Trump look good, make him look wealthy, legitimate.'"[34]

Trump honed his television skills on *The Apprentice* and applied them in his 2016 campaign. Poniewozik writes:

[Trump] knew what the red light [of a television camera] wanted. . . . At his rallies, he once explained, he often didn't look at the people. The people were easy. If they got listless, you'd yell, "Build the wall!" and they'd snap back. But the red light's tastes were more exotic. It wanted something new. It wanted something dangerous. If he sensed that it might blink off—meaning that he was no longer being carried live on cable news—he told the *Washington Post*, "I would say something new to keep the red light on." If what he said got someone punched in the face—well, he didn't throw the punch, did he? If what he said was the opposite of what he said before, then that was what he believed now, until the next time. If he kept the red light sated, it would help him. The red light put you into the unreal estate of TV, the place that was everywhere, that was better than the real world.[35]

As a result, Poniewozik explained, Trump was a perfect match for the current media environment. "He and cable news were in a mind-meld. He knew what it wanted: celebrity, outrage, volatility, novelty. Give the twenty-four hour news panelists something to talk about, and the red light will stay on. He didn't even need to be on camera. A tweet would do."[36]

And the media could not (and still cannot) resist: "The idea that Trump might say something wild at any moment meant, to producers, that he was inherently newsworthy. That he might say the opposite thing tomorrow didn't matter—that just meant more material. 'Newsworthy' and 'entertaining' had long since become synonyms. Cable news carried his rallies beginning to end. Sometimes the channels would show his empty lectern, waiting for him to take the stage. The ratings went up, and Trump took his cut of the profits: $5.6 billion in free media over the election, more than every competitor, in both parties, combined."[37]

I must add that there has been some remarkable journalism during the Trump era that lives up to the definition of news as providing people with the information that they need to understand the world but doing so in a way that people are inclined to listen. This includes reporters from the *New York Times*, the *Washington Post*, *The Miami Herald* and other metropolitan newspapers, the *Wall Street Journal*, the *Atlantic*, the *New Yorker*, *Politico*, and some of the cable news programs. But the news that most Americans consume is not among that list.

The news media transformation took place as American national politics was undergoing an even more wrenching change.

Culture Wars

At the Republican National Convention in 1992, conservative pundit and former Nixon speechwriter Pat Buchanan ascended the stage:

> My friends, this election is about much more than who gets what. It is about who we are. It is about what we believe. It is about what we stand for as Americans. There is a religious war going on in our country for the soul of America. It is a cultural war, as critical to the kind of nation we will one day be as was the Cold War itself. And in that struggle for the soul of America, Clinton and Clinton are on the other side, and George Bush is on our side. And so, we have to come home, and stand beside him.[38]

CNBC political analyst Steve Kornacki, in his book, *The Red and the Blue: The 1990s and the Birth of Political Tribalism*, observed:

> The Republican Party had been aligned with religious conservatism since Reagan's ascendance, but this was something different. The Gipper had given it a soft, gentle touch, and [President George H. W.] Bush tried to do the same. Buchanan was drawing a line and telling Americans to pick a side. On CBS, Dan Rather called it a "raw meat" offering to the base. R. W. Apple in *The New York Times* wrote that Buchanan "epitomized the scowling face of conservatism." Democrats condemned him. But the discomfort included Republicans, too. "Pat's message," Senator Richard Lugar of Indiana said, "is not a very appealing one for most Americans, and it's not a winning strategy."[39]

However, today such a message from a politician would seem rather tame. A 2019 article in the *Atlantic* noted how partisan our country has become. It reads:

> [O]n both the left and the right, a visceral disdain for one's political opponents has become common, as have feelings of schadenfreude when the other side suffers a setback. In 2012, political scientists at Emory University found that fewer than half of voters said they were deeply angry at the other party's presidential nominee. In 2016, almost 70 percent of Americans were. What's worse, this partisan nastiness was also directed at fellow citizens who held opposing views. In 2016, nearly half of Republicans believed that Democrats were lazy, dishonest, and immoral, according to the Pew Research Center. Democrats returned the favor: More than 70 percent said that "Republicans are more closed-minded than other Americans," and a third said that they were unethical and unintelligent.[40]

So how did we get here?

The beginning of the political polarization we see today began with the fissures in the two political parties following the success of the Civil Rights Movement. Kornacki writes:

> Never again would either party nominate a civil rights oppo-nent for national office, but now there was an opening for Republicans to plant their flag in a place that had long been off-limits to them. It was a deal with [Strom] Thurmond that ensured the GOP nomination in 1968 for Nixon, whose "southern strategy" won over many of those aggrieved white voters. Reagan was aiming straight at them, too, when he kicked off his general election campaign in 1980 in Philadel-phia, Mississippi, the notorious scene of a triple homicide committed against civil rights activists by the local white re-sistance just sixteen years earlier.[41]

Reagan used a dog whistle at that rally. He told the crowd that he believed in states' rights. That sounds benign enough. But his-torically the phrase was a dog whistle, used as cover for states who maintained the Jim Crow segregation that relegated large swaths of their populations to second-class-citizen status. And in that Mis-sissippi town it would be recognized for what it was. Kornacki describes the reaction:

> Republicans bristled at the charge of race baiting. Civil rights, their party platform proclaimed, was a settled matter, and America was better for it. But race was so intertwined with the most contentious issues of the 1970s and '80s, from school busing and affirmative action to welfare and crime, that it was possible to stoke prejudices in ways that were po-litically advantageous. Moreover, Democrats moved in the opposite direction, embracing newly enfranchised blacks in the South and forging tighter bonds with nonwhite voters everywhere. The New Left movement of activists and

academics gained influence within the party, pushing it toward a vision of social equality and powering the nomination of George McGovern for president in 1972. Quotas to ensure diversity were imposed starting with that year's convention, and the Democratic Party became associated not just with civil rights for blacks, but with feminism, the fledgling gay rights movement, migrant rights, and a host of other cultural causes.[42]

The reorientation of the parties changed who would come to identify with each party, and who would become their most vocal supporters. Harvard professors Steven Levitsky and Daniel Ziblatt write in their book, *How Democracies Die*, that:

> For the first time in nearly a century, partisanship and ideology converged, with the GOP becoming primarily conservative and the Democrats becoming predominantly liberal. By the 2000s, the Democratic and Republican parties were no longer ideological "big tents." With the disappearance of conservative Democrats and liberal Republicans, areas of overlap between the parties gradually disappeared. Now that most senators and representatives had more in common with their partisan allies than with members of the opposing party, they cooperated less frequently and voted consistently with their own party. As both voters and their elected representatives clustered into increasingly homogenous "camps," the ideological differences between the parties grew more marked.[43]

Additionally, the authors point out, one party became more diverse, the other became more homogenous: "Realignment has gone well beyond liberal versus conservative. The social, ethnic, and cultural bases of partisanship have also changed dramatically, giving rise to parties that represent not just different policy approaches but different communities, cultures, and values. . . .

In other words, the two parties are now divided over race and religion—two deeply polarizing issues that tend to generate greater intolerance and hostility than traditional issues such as taxes and government spending."[44]

The authors argue that this polarization has weakened the guardrails of democracy, which created an environment for candidate Donald Trump to succeed:

> The erosion of our democratic norms began in the 1980s and 1990s and accelerated in the 2000s. By the time Barack Obama became the president, many Republicans, in particular, questioned the legitimacy of their Democratic rivals and had abandoned forbearance for a strategy of winning by any means necessary. Donald Trump may have accelerated this process, but he didn't cause it. The challenges facing American democracy run deeper. The weakening of our democratic norms is rooted in extreme partisan polarization—one that extends beyond policy differences into an existential conflict over race and culture. America's efforts to achieve racial equality as our society grows increasingly diverse have fueled an insidious reaction and intensifying polarization. And if one thing is clear from studying breakdowns throughout history, it's that extreme polarization can kill democracies.[45]

The extreme polarization has charged both of America's major political parties, and whole communities across the country. And with this polarization, the stage was set for democratic norms to be broken, if not outright shattered—which would make any chance of collaboration or compromise impossible.

Enter, Trump

In 1992, Pat Buchanan had posed a primary challenge against President George H. W. Bush for reelection as president. The night of the New Hampshire primary, after winning 40 percent of the Republican vote, Buchanan addressed his supporters from his New Hampshire headquarters. He said: "We are going to take our party back from those who have walked away from us and forgotten about us, and when we have taken our party back, we are going to take our country back. When we take America back, we are going to make America great again, because there is nothing wrong with putting America first."[46]

Twenty-three years later, this message became one of the key themes for candidate Donald Trump. It required both the changing culture of the media and the shift in partisanship and incivility for this message to ring true. Together, these forces created the conditions not only for Trump's victory, but also for his rhetoric to resonate with many across the country.

Trump is not a cause of these shifts; rather, he is the consequence of them. Bryan Gervais and Irwin Morris, who studied the effect of the Tea Party's actions and rhetoric on the Republican Party, warned about the way in which rhetoric could incite violence and the danger of politicians using this rhetoric for political gain:

We thus find ourselves in a time where there are bitter feelings of anger and resentment on both the left and right, as well as energized fringe groups who view violence as a legitimate tactic. It will be tempting for some political elites to try to take advantage of this energy and make subtle—and not so subtle—allusions to violence. But while this may be politically expedient, such tactics threaten to further unravel social bonds and escalate tension between the Left and Right to the point where political violence is not restricted to a few isolated events but a regular occurrence.[47]

Those same authors warned of what will happen if civic leaders do not challenge or call Trump on his rhetoric: "Unless it becomes apparent that Trump's choice of words is a liability (this is a popular talking point, but we suspect many pundits also recognize the power of Trump's incivility among a sizable segment of the electorate), then incivility among political elite is apt to increase."[48]

We did not take this warning seriously enough. And, consequently, here we are today.

Why People Believe What They Believe

AND THE DUMBING DOWN OF THE BODY POLITIC

Much of what Donald Trump says is nonsense. That is, it doesn't make sense.

Sometimes what he says is verifiably untrue: Millions of invaders are not swarming the southern border. Sanctuary cities do not release violent gangs into the community. MS-13 has not literally taken over cities in the United States. Trump did not see hundreds of Muslims in New Jersey celebrate as the Twin Towers fell.

Sometimes what he says is just illogical: Immigration is not about governments sending people to another country. Trump mobilizes the military because, he says, the "invasion" of the southern border by the "caravan" is so extreme. Yet, by law, the military is not permitted to perform immigration-related enforcement. Although the people purportedly invading are heading to

San Diego, fifteen hundred miles away, and they are still a thousand miles from the border, most of the military goes to Texas. To prevent another 9/11, Trump bans all immigrants from seven majority-Muslim countries, none of which has been implicated in terrorism against the United States, but not from any of the countries the 9/11 attackers came from.

Sometimes what he says is self-contradictory: He hasn't heard the theory that "nationalist" can mean "white nationalist," but he's heard all the theories. Mexico, to destabilize the United States, is sending rapists and drug dealers, but also some good people. Yet, the news media report that he says these things, and his followers believe what he says, even though it is nonsense. Why?

Philosophers create systems that help us understand what is true and what is not true. One such system is called the Laws of Thought. It points to three related ideas:

1. **The Law of Identity.** "Whatever is, is." Denying the existence of something does not mean it doesn't exist.
2. **The Law of Contradiction.** "Nothing can both be and not be." In practice, this means that something cannot be both true and untrue at the same time.
3. **The Law of Excluded Middle.** "Everything must either be or not be."[1] A substantive statement is either true or it is false. You can't have it both ways.

As a graduate student learning these principles in the late 1970s and early 1980s, I was astounded that such principles needed even to be stated. Of course, a statement of fact could not be both true and not true at the same time. Making a statement that is demonstrably untrue or self-contradictory, or trying to have something both ways, are examples of absurdities: of things that on their face don't make sense. And that therefore should not be relied upon.

But dangerous speech often is speech that has absurdity embedded into it. An entire group of humans cannot be somehow not-quite human. But believing that a group of people, by nature of their very identity, is somehow less than human causes some people to consider any member of that group unworthy of equal treatment, sometimes even deserving of cruelty. This isn't about how any individual may behave. It's about denying the humanity of an entire group of humans—in Trump's case, Muslims, Mexicans, sometimes all immigrants. Making a false claim that a political rival hates this country and wishes to cause it harm, when there is no evidence of such a thing, and plenty of evidence of the opposite, creates a context in which attempting or committing violence against that rival is seen as a good thing.

In the eighteenth century, the French philosopher Voltaire admonished that those who could make people believe absurdities could also make them commit atrocities. We saw in Part I that genocides typically follow the creation of false narratives about the groups that are targets of that violence: They're dangerous, they're violent, they're intent on hurting us. The emotions of anger, disgust, and fear shut down critical thinking and rally people to protect themselves and society at large. So, people miss the absurdities.

Much political discourse violates the Laws of Thought and is grounded on absurdities. So is a lot of Trump's rhetoric. The Catholic theologian and economist Michael Novak, in *The Spirit of Democratic Capitalism*, warned, "The first of all moral obligations is to think clearly."[2]

He meant this as a way of organizing society, but it applies also to engaged citizens and civic leaders. Whether in public or private life, engaged citizens and civic leaders have not only a civic duty but also a moral obligation to think clearly to get past their fear, anger, and hatred and to notice absurdities. But some politicians benefit from citizens not thinking clearly.

Donald Trump, either because he lacks the capacity to think clearly or prefers not to, speaks in ways that make little sense, but those who follow him seem not to care. They seem also unable or unwilling to think clearly. They allow falsehoods, absurdities, and outright nonsense to govern their understanding and their behavior.

Yet, it really isn't their fault. It's part of the human condition. Human beings are not as good at clear thinking as they think they are. Trump just capitalizes on this and intensifies it. Over the past several decades psychologists, neuroscientists, cognitive linguists, and other scientists have developed meaningful bodies of work that shed light into how human judgments are made.

Motivated Reasoning

In the 1950s, the Stanford University psychologist Leon Festinger famously concluded: "A man with conviction is a hard man to change. Tell him you disagree and he turns away. Show him facts and figures and he questions your sources. Appeal to logic and he fails to see your point."[3]

In 1979, psychologists Charles G. Lord, Lee Ross, and Mark R. Lepper called this phenomenon "biased assimilation." They showed that people tend to accept evidence that confirms their initial opinion and to reject evidence that fails to confirm their original opinion. They conclude: "We respond to social policies . . . in terms of the symbols or metaphors they evoke or in conformity with views expressed by opinion leaders we like or respect. When 'evidence' is brought to bear it is apt to be incomplete, biased, and of marginal probative value—typically, no more than a couple of vivid, concrete, but dubiously representative instances or cases."[4]

In 1990, social psychologist Ziva Kunda described this as "motivated reasoning." One form of motivated reasoning takes place when a person already has a strong belief, and the reasoning has the effect of justifying a preexisting conclusion or belief. Kunda says that in such goal-oriented reasoning,

People motivated to arrive at a particular conclusion attempt to be rational and to construct a justification of their
desired conclusion that would persuade a dispassionate observer . . . in other words, they maintain an "illusion of objectivity" . . . the objectivity of this justification construction
process is illusory because people do not realize that the
process is biased by their goals, that they are accessing only
a subset of their beliefs and rules in the presence of different directional goals, and that they might even be capable
of justifying opposite conclusions on different occasions. . . .
Directional goals affect reasoning by affecting which information will be considered in the reasoning process.[5]

Paradoxically, attempting to correct someone who is guided by
incorrect information may have the opposite effect, causing that
person to dig in and be even more committed to the factually
incorrect conclusion. In 2006, Professors Brendan Nyhan and Jason Reifler experimented on what happened when people, after
being given false or misleading information presented as reported
facts, were given corrections to those facts. They found that cor-
recting false information frequently failed to reduce misperceptions among the tested ideological subgroups. Additionally, they
also noticed a "backfire effect" that sometimes occurred: "The
backfire effects . . . seem to provide further support for the growing literature showing that citizens engage in 'motivated reasoning.' While our experiments focused on assessing the effectiveness
of corrections, the results show that direct factual contradictions
can actually *strengthen* ideologically grounded factual beliefs."[6]

Increasingly, neuroscientists and psychologists are noticing the
primary role emotion plays in reaching intellectual judgments,
even about deeply quantitative or empirical topics. But humans are
generally unaware that they are making such judgments emotionally and tend to rationalize their judgments by pointing to facts.

Jonathan Haidt, a psychologist of morality and my faculty colleague at the New York University Stern School of Business, notes

that social and political judgments are particularly intuitive, and that people are blind to facts and reason, especially when it comes to political issues. He writes, "Reason is merely the servant of the passions. . . . People make moral judgments quickly and emotionally and use moral reasoning to justify the judgment they've already made."[7]

Haidt observes that people believe those things even when doing so is not in their immediate self-interest, sometimes even when holding such a view harms their self-interest. He says, "[D]ecades of research on public opinion have led to the conclusion that self-interest is a weak predictor of policy preference. . . . Rather, people care about their groups, whether those be racial, regional, religious, or political. The political scientist Don Kinder summarizes the findings like this, 'In matters of public opinion, citizens seem to be asking themselves not "What's in it for me?" but rather "What's in it for my group?"'"[8]

Science confirms that evidence is less important in reaching judgments than we might otherwise want to believe. This helps to explain the phenomenon of *framing*, the creation of context that drives meaning. Frames are processed in the limbic part of the brain, the emotion-provoking part of the brain. And when the emotion-provoking part of the brain is stimulated, it tends to shut down critical thinking.[9] As cognitive linguist George Lakoff described, when facts are inconsistent with the frame, the facts bounce off and the frame remains.[10] Once people are in one frame, they cannot make sense of a contrary frame.[11] Lakoff explains that frames are giant complexes of neural circuitry we use to think, communicate, and function in everyday life. And people can understand only what fits their neural circuitry.

Even beyond the normal human condition, political language, especially when the speaker is being insincere, can intensify the effects of emotion and further reduce critical thinking.

Orwell Called It

In the years immediately following World War II, the British writer George Orwell published "Politics and the English Language." That brief essay was a warning flare, fired to call attention to a troubling trend he saw emerging in postwar Britain and around the world: the tendency of political leaders to use language that was not merely misleading, but that inhibited the capacity of citizens to think clearly.

That essay served as the nonfiction treatment for what two years later would be his novel with the same lesson: *Nineteen Eighty-Four*. That popular novel is based in a dystopian future in a continuous state of war (or the appearance of war), where an intrusive and authoritarian government keeps people uninformed, and where political language is intentionally misleading. So, the Ministry of Peace wages war. The Ministry of Truth controls all information, news, propaganda, and art. The Ministry of Plenty rations food. Our term "Orwellian" refers to the use of language to convey the opposite of reality.

But most educated Americans are not familiar with the essay that served as the novel's basis. "Politics and the English Language" helps us understand the current state of the body politic, and, sadly, it isn't pretty. Says Orwell, "In our time, political speech and writing are largely the defense of the indefensible."[12]

The problem arises when politicians use language in a disingenuous way, asserting things they don't necessarily believe and making arguments that may sound compelling but that logically don't make sense. Orwell argues that when a leader has declared aims that are inconsistent with his or her real aims, the leader turns to deception. In such circumstances, Orwell argues, "All issues are political issues, and politics itself is a mass of lies, evasions, folly, hatred, and schizophrenia. When the general atmosphere is bad, language must suffer."[13]

However damaging individual instances of political language or insincere speech or intentionally misleading statements may be, it's the effect of these that causes harm. The central ideas in "Politics and the English Language" are:

- Political speech has the effect of reducing citizens' critical thinking skills.
- This creates a self-perpetuating cycle . . .
- . . . in which as people become less discerning, they become more susceptible to political speech . . .
- . . . which further diminishes their critical thinking skills . . .
- . . . and so on . . .
- . . . and so on . . .
- . . . until a fully uninformed public creates conditions for authoritarian government to thrive.

In the essay, Orwell focuses on the relationship between cause and effect. Orwell notes that even as thought can corrupt language, language can also corrupt thought. He argues that an effect can become a cause, and a cause can become an effect. It's the cycle that matters. The result is a citizenry that remains intentionally ignorant of the issues that matter, unaware of what is happening to them, and easily manipulated by politicians.

Human beings start off being less good at critical thinking than they may believe. And the language politicians use can make it worse. But what happens when the political processes themselves are designed explicitly to reduce critical thinking?

We Don't Know That We're Misinformed

We humans aren't very good at knowing that we don't know something. In fact, we think we know more than we do. This cognitive bias is called the Dunning-Kruger effect, named after Daniel Dunning and Justin Kruger, two social psychologists who studied this phenomenon.

In May 2016, Daniel Dunning noticed how this Dunning-Kruger effect could explain the support Trump was gaining in the election. In an article in Politico, Dunning explained: "Many commentators have argued that Donald Trump's dominance in the GOP presidential race can be largely explained by ignorance; his candidacy, after all, is most popular among Republican voters without college degrees. . . . But as a psychologist who has studied human behavior—including voter behavior—for decades, I think there is something deeper going on. The problem isn't that voters are too uninformed. It is that they don't *know* just how uninformed they are."[14]

In the article, Dunning explains the Dunning-Kruger effect this way: "In studies in my research lab, people with severe gaps in knowledge and expertise typically fail to recognize how little they know and how badly they perform. To sum it up, the knowledge and intelligence that are required to be good at a task are often the same qualities needed to recognize that one is *not* good at that task—and if one lacks such knowledge and intelligence, one remains ignorant that one is not good at that task. This includes political judgment."[15]

The effect of this cognitive bias is that we become misinformed and find it easier to believe things that match our own ideologies, regardless of whether something is actually true. Dunning and his colleagues found when testing this phenomenon with people who considered themselves "well-informed" voters: "[A]ll told, it was the political lean of the fact that mattered much more than its truth-value in determining whether respondents believed it. And endorsing partisan facts both true and false led to perceptions that one was an informed citizen, and then to a greater likelihood of voting. Given all this misinformation, confidently held, it is no wonder that Trump causes no outrage or scandal among those voters who find his views congenial."[16]

The cyclical nature of the cognitive bias is that we do not have the skills necessary to correct it: "In voters, lack of expertise would be lamentable but perhaps not so worrisome if people had some sense of how imperfect their civic knowledge is. If they did, they could repair it. But the Dunning-Kruger Effect suggests something different. It suggests that some voters, especially those facing significant distress in their life, might like some of what they hear from Trump, but they do not know enough to hold him accountable for the serious gaffes he makes. They fail to recognize those gaffes as missteps."[17]

Dunning argues that this phenomenon is not unique to Trump. It does, however, clearly benefit him:

> My take is that the conditions for the Trump phenomenon have been in place for a long time. At least as long as quantitative survey data have been collected, citizens have shown themselves to be relatively ill-informed and incoherent on political and historical matters. As way back as 1943, a survey revealed that only 25 percent of college freshmen knew that Abraham Lincoln was president during the Civil War. All it took was a candidate to come along too inexperienced to avoid making policy gaffes, at least gaffes that violate received wisdom, with voters too uninformed to see the violations. Usually, those candidates make their mistakes off in some youthful election to their state legislature, or in a small-town mayoral race or contest for class president. It's not a surprise that someone trying out a brand new career at the presidential level would make gaffes that voters, in a rebellious mood, would forgive but more likely not even see.[18]

Truthiness

Early in the George W. Bush presidency, the White House chastised writer Ron Suskind about an article he had written. It was factually accurate, but the White House didn't like the story. In a 2004 *New York Times Magazine* profile of President Bush, Suskind described many serious people—from within the Bush administration's senior ranks to opposition senators to public supporters of the president—who each expressed dismay that President Bush seemed unconcerned with facts and made decisions on gut feelings. Suskind described the atmosphere six months after the inauguration: "A cluster of particularly vivid qualities was shaping George W. Bush's White House through the summer of 2001: a disdain for contemplation or deliberation, an embrace of decisiveness, a retreat from empiricism, a sometimes bullying impatience with doubters and even friendly questioners."[19]

Suskind quoted former Ronald Reagan domestic policy advisor Bruce Bartlett, who said that President Bush "dispenses with people who confront him with inconvenient facts. . . . He truly believes he's on a mission from God. Absolute faith like that overwhelms a need for analysis. The whole thing about faith is to believe things for which there is no empirical evidence.' Bartlett paused, then said, 'But you can't run the world on faith.'"[20]

A year later, the new late-night comedy host Stephen Colbert created a parody character who lampooned Fox News prime-time hosts and other conservative commentators. The role he played on *The Colbert Report* was a purportedly conservative commentator and fierce Bush supporter.

In his very first episode, Colbert coined the term "truthiness." It was a category somewhere between truth and falsity. He defined truthiness as putting forward concepts or facts one wishes to be true as if they are true, rather than concepts or facts known to be true. Colbert defined the problem this way: "[F]ace it, folks, we are a divided nation. Not between Democrats and Republicans or conservatives and liberals. . . . We are divided between those who think with their head and those who know with their heart."[21]

Colbert explained that what was true and right didn't matter; rather, what mattered was what *felt* true and *felt* right. He explained: "[T]hat's where the truth comes from, ladies and gentlemen, the gut. Do you know you have more nerve endings in your stomach than in your head? Look it up. Now, somebody is going to say I did look that up and it's wrong. Well, mister, that's because you looked it up in a book. Next time, try looking it up in your gut. I did. And my gut tells me that's how our nervous system works."[22] He then defined the purpose of his new show: "The truthiness is, anyone can read the news to you. I promise to feel the news at you."[23]

In early 2006, the American Dialectical Society named Truthiness the 2005 Word of the Year.[24] But the insidious nature of truthiness is that leaders who deploy it tend to believe those things that in fact are not true, as if they were true. So do the followers who rely on those statements. Consistent with Orwell, the result is that verifiable truth becomes suspect.

What Colbert intended as a comedic take on misdirection has proven to be a defining element of much modern political debate. Candidates argue not the truth they know but the truth they wish, and citizens don't really know the difference.

Make America Great Again

After descending the escalator in Trump Tower in 2015, Donald Trump launched a campaign slogan that resonated deeply with some people across the country: "Make America Great Again." The argument embedded within this slogan is that America is not great now. We used to be great, but we no longer are. In other words, the country has changed, and not for the better. And the United States needs a leader who will right the ship.

But what does that mean for Trump supporters? How did they define what it meant to "make America great again"?

Studies have shown that Trump's supporters are more likely to be male, older, less-educated, and to work a blue-collar job.[25] Therefore, during and shortly after the 2016 presidential election, one argument made to explain the results was that people who had been economically disenfranchised in the past several decades voted for Trump to push back against the establishment.

These people had been "left behind" as the economy favored more globalized, automated, and high-tech jobs.

Psychology professor Thomas F. Pettigrew analyzed the psychological characteristics of far-right supporters in the United States and Europe. Pettigrew found that they shared five characteristics: a tendency toward authoritarianism; an orientation toward social dominance; prejudice against out-groups; the absence of contact with other, diverse groups; and relative deprivation. He argued that these traits together explain how Trump could connect with his supporters.[26] Of note, Pettigrew found that, "Trump followers were *less* likely than others to be looking for work, unemployed, or part-time employed. And those voters living in districts with more manufacturing were actually *less* favorable to Trump. Nor were his followers largely living and working in postal areas where employment in manufacturing had declined since 1990."[27]

In fact, some studies found that Trump supporters' median annual income is between seventy and eighty thousand dollars.[28] Moreover, Pettigrew noted that: "Contrary to the popular too-simple theory . . . people who live in areas with *greater* mobility voted *more* Republican. This was even true in the crucial 'swing states,' and is a trend that can be detected in other recent elections."[29]

Pettigrew found that: "Trump adherents feel deprived relative to what they expected to possess at this point in their lives and relative to what they erroneously perceive other 'less deserving' groups have acquired. . . . Thus, Trump adherents are typically not personally economically destitute; but they are, as Thomas Edsall phrased it, 'falling behind the Joneses.' In short, they were often feeling deprived *relative* to their hopes and expectations."[30]

The combination of the five factors Pettigrew noted—authoritarianism, social dominance orientation, prejudice, lack of intergroup contact, and relative deprivation—has this effect: It makes people "vulnerable to an intense sense of threat."[31] So, what is that threat if not economic insecurity? Diana C. Mutz, a professor of political science and communication at the University of Pennsylvania, examined whether the "left behind" theory was true. Mutz found that economic hardship and financial well-being were not indicative of which candidate a voter favored. Rather, "Evidence points overwhelmingly to perceived status threat among high-status groups as the key motivation underlying Trump support. White Americans' declining numerical dominance in the United States together with the rising status of African Americans and American insecurity about whether the United States is still the dominant global economic superpower combined to prompt a classic defensive reaction among members of dominant groups."[32]

Mutz explains why members of high-status groups feel threatened today:

> For the first time since Europeans arrived in this country, white Americans are being told that they will soon be a minority race. The declining white share of the national population is unlikely to change white Americans' status as the most economically well-off racial group, but symbolically, it threatens some whites' sense of dominance over social and political priorities. Furthermore, when confronted with evidence of racial progress, whites feel threatened and experience lower levels of self-worth relative to a control group. They also perceive greater antiwhite bias as a means of regaining those lost feelings of self-worth. Second, Americans feel threatened by the increasing interdependence of the United States on other countries.[33]

Mutz found that this pattern continued into 2016. She writes that the "feeling that 'the American way of life is threatened' is a consistent predictor of Trump support."[34]

Think back to Trump's incendiary rhetoric. Much of this rhetoric plays directly into the fear that we are losing America as it was and need to win it back. In other words, the only way for our country as we know it to survive is to make America great again.

Addressing this fear is not a policy issue, it is a mindset issue. Mutz writes:

In many ways, a sense of group threat is a much tougher opponent than an economic downturn, because it is a psychological mindset rather than an actual event or misfortune. Given current demographic trends within the United States, minority influence will only increase with time, thus heightening this source of perceived status threat. Although whites will likely still be the best-educated and most well-off racial group, by 2040, they are unlikely to dominate in numbers. Likewise, despite US status as an extremely wealthy country relative to those countries perceived to threaten it economically, many Americans find that small comfort.[35]

Trump took that mindset and used it to keep his base on edge, constantly reminded that there was much to fear from people who were unlike them: Mexicans, Muslims, immigrants, and rivals who favored equal treatment of those groups.

And to keep those groups on edge, Trump spoke constantly in ways that were not reflective of objective reality, but of a dystopian present. And he counted on his base not to notice his absurdities.

PART IV

A CALL TO ACTION: PRACTICAL TOOLS FOR LEADERS AND CITIZENS

The more powerful you are, the more your actions will have an impact on people, the more responsible you are to act humbly. If you don't, your power will ruin you, and you will ruin the other.
—POPE FRANCIS, *April 2017*

E ven responsible leaders sometimes screw up.

Sometimes leaders overstep and use language in ways that provoke, or are likely to provoke, violence. They do not mean to do so, but when they realize they may have done so they become distressed at themselves and act to prevent further harm or to remedy whatever harm may have been committed.

Some leaders are not that responsible. Even though they do not intend the violence, they are unconcerned about it. The ends justify the means. Some are in denial about the harm; they just don't see it. Others see it but don't care. When pressed, they publicly deny the very possibility that their language may be responsible for violence. I believe Donald Trump is this sort of leader.

Some are outright malign and use language with the specific intent of provoking violence. I believe that the Nazis and Rwandan Hutu leaders were of this sort.

However, the forms of speech that can provoke violence are the same regardless of the leaders' motives.

In Chapter 9, I profile three leaders who stepped over the line and were called on it. All three, in their own ways and in varying time frames, stopped what they were doing.

I then describe humility as a leadership attribute that makes empathy possible. It is empathy that allows leaders to see the damage their rhetoric may cause, and humility and empathy that lead them to stop. I also observe that dehumanizing and demonizing language lessens the capacity for empathy in the first place, both in those who hear the language and those who speak it.

In Chapter 10, I provide a framework for civic leaders, engaged citizens, journalists, and public officials to recognize when a leader may have crossed the line, and a way to understand the likely consequences of dangerous speech. This includes a recap of the ways lone wolves are formed and activated, and the kinds of language that can trigger such lone wolves to commit violence. I take the lone-wolf-whistle terrorism playbook and recast it as a toolkit or checklist in the form of questions to ask that can help determine whether a leader's rhetoric is likely to inspire lone wolves to take matters into their own hands.

9

Leadership
and Accountability

Sometimes leaders overreach. They do not intend to put people or groups in danger, but their language has that effect. Trump seems not to care when this happens. But many leaders do. And all leaders should.

Often journalists, civic leaders, and commentators raise concerns when such language goes too far. Responsible leaders take those concerns seriously. Sometimes they do so right away. Sometimes they live in a state of denial, continuing to use such language, until some event forces them to snap out of denial and to take the concerns seriously.

Very often, once made aware, responsible leaders work to neutralize whatever damage they may have done, and to correct the impression their followers may have had about the leader's intention. Most important, they stop using such language.

Consider three examples.

President George W. Bush and a Crusade Against Terror

On the morning of September 11, 2001, Al-Qaeda operatives hijacked commercial airliners and flew them into the two towers of the World Trade Center and into the Pentagon. A fourth was apparently heading for the White House, but passengers prevented the flight from reaching its target. It crashed instead into a field in Pennsylvania. This was the largest assault against the United States since the Japanese attack on Pearl Harbor in 1941. And like Pearl Harbor it put the US on a war footing. But not against a nation-state. Unlike a nation, with a standing government and uniformed military, the amorphous nature of this enemy made defining the fight difficult.

As the nation's national security apparatus struggled initially to define what was happening, President George W. Bush was flown from Florida, where he was at a public event at the time of the attack, to a safe location in the middle of the country.

That night, back in the White House, he addressed the nation: "Today our nation saw evil, the very worst of human nature. And we responded with the best of America, with the daring of our rescue workers, with the caring for strangers and neighbors who came to give blood and help in any way they could."[1]

After offering comfort and contrasting the terrorists' character with those of the first responders, Bush committed to find the plotters and bring them to justice: "The search is underway for those who are behind these evil acts. I've directed the full resources of our intelligence and law enforcement communities to find those responsible and to bring them to justice. We will make no distinction between the terrorists who committed these acts and those who harbor them."[2]

The nation was scared, and the president was acting in his role both as commander-in-chief and comforter-in-chief. But in the days after the attack, some people in the United States who were perceived to be Muslim or Arab found themselves being menaced in ways that ranged from insults to death threats. Two days following the attack, President Bush tried to tamp down citizens' desire to blame all Muslims and Arabs for the attack. In an Oval Office phone call with New York State governor George Pataki and New York City mayor Rudolph Giuliani, broadcast live on TV, President Bush said,

> I know I don't need to tell you all this, but our nation must be mindful that there are thousands of Arab-Americans who live in New York City who love their flag just as much as the three of us do. And we must be mindful that as we seek to win the war that we treat Arab-Americans and Muslims with the respect they deserve. I know that is your attitudes, as well; it's certainly the attitude of this Government, that we should not hold one who is a Muslim responsible for an act of terror. We will hold those who are responsible for the terrorist acts accountable and those who harbor them.[3]

Many saw this as a positive development, including members of at-risk communities. But two days later a Sikh man, who had received several death threats since the attack, was murdered. NPR reported, "On Sept. 15, 2001, Balbir Singh Sodhi was outside of the Chevron gas station he owned in Mesa, Ariz., when he was shot and killed. Balbir was Sikh and wore a turban. In one of the first hate crime murders following the Sept. 11 terrorist attacks, a man, assuming Balbir was Muslim, shot and killed him as retaliation. Balbir and his brothers . . . emigrated from India in the 1980s, and they owned the Chevron together."[4]

The shooter was forty-eight-year-old Frank Roque, who shot Sodhi from the window of his moving pickup truck. He didn't stop, but continued driving, opening fire on a Lebanese American who was wounded but not killed. He also shot at the home of a family of Afghan descent. He then entered a local bar and said loudly, "They're investigating the murder of a turban-head down the street."[5]

The Southern Poverty Law Center reported, "Arrested later that afternoon at his home, Roque allegedly told officers he was seeking to revenge the terrorist assaults. 'I stand for America all the way,' he bellowed, complaining that he was being taken in while 'those terrorists run wild.'"[6]

Of course, Bodhi, the shooting victim, was not a terrorist. Nor was he a Muslim. But he wore a turban, as did Osama bin Laden, and some Americans could not differentiate among different religions or ethnicities.

On the day following Bodhi's shooting, CNN reported that hate crimes against Muslims and South Asians had risen exponentially in the days following the 9/11 attack. The Council on American-Islamic Relations received more than three hundred reports of harassment and abuse in the forty-eight hours after the attack, nearly half the number it received the entire year prior. It also noted that Sikhs were a particular target. A New York man was shot in the head with a BB gun as he left worship in a Sikh temple in Queens. A Virginia man was almost driven off the road by two vans while he drove to a site to give blood. The official US Sikh website reported more than three hundred incidents of hate crimes and harassment in the month following 9/11.[7]

The day after the Sikh gas station attendant was killed, President Bush did not address the growing violence against innocents. He did address the 9/11 attack. But in so doing, he made the situation less safe for those perceived to be Arab or Muslim. Speaking on the White House lawn as he was about to board Marine One, he said, "This is a new kind of—a new kind of evil. And we understand. And the American people are beginning to understand. This crusade, this war on terrorism is going to take a while, and the American people must be patient."[8]

The word "crusade" got people's attention, especially Muslims, Arabs, and those with a sense of history. The Crusades were a series of European invasions of the Holy Land over a four-hundred-year period, specifically cast as a holy war between Christians and Muslims, nominally over control of holy sites in the areas around Jerusalem.

President Bush clearly intended the word as metaphor, to describe a righteous struggle. Indeed, in 1944, General Dwight Eisenhower had used the word in his exhortation to those about to storm the beaches at Normandy. The first sentence of Eisenhower's remarks to the troops read, "You are about to embark on a great crusade, toward which we have striven these many months."[9]

But in Eisenhower's case, the metaphor was clear. The Allies consisted of nominally or majority Christian nations at war with the Axis powers, who were also nominally or majority Christian. But in President Bush's formulation, juxtaposing the word crusade with the idea of war against those who organized the 9/11 attack suggested to many that the war on terror was a war on Islam.

The *Christian Science Monitor* reported, "President Bush's reference to a 'crusade' against terrorism, which passed almost unnoticed by Americans, rang alarm bells in Europe. It raised fears that the terrorist attacks could spark a 'clash of civilizations' between Christians and Muslims, sowing fresh winds of hatred and mistrust."[10]

The newspaper quoted several prominent European leaders on the dangers of such language:

"If this 'war' takes a form that affronts moderate Arab opinion, if it has the air of a clash of civilizations, there is a strong risk that it will contribute to Osama bin Laden's goal: a conflict between the Arab-Muslim world and the West," warned the Paris daily *Le Monde* on Tuesday in an editorial. "Bush is walking a fine line," suggested Dominique Moisi, a political analyst with the French Institute for International Relations, the country's top foreign policy think tank. "The same black and white language he uses to rally Americans behind him is just the sort of language that risks splitting the international coalition he is trying to build. This confusion between politics and religion . . . risks encouraging a clash of civilizations in a religious sense, which is very dangerous," he added.[11]

The newspaper also quoted British prime minister Tony Blair, who said the war is not between Christians and Muslims but between civilized values and fanaticism. He also noted that the majority of law-abiding Muslims oppose fanaticism.[12]

President Bush heard the message and acted on it. He went out of his way to correct any misperception that the enemy was Islam. The following day, he visited Washington's Islamic Center. Flanked by Muslim leaders, he said, "Like the good folks standing with me, the American people were appalled and outraged at last Tuesday's attacks. And so were Muslims all across the world. Both Americans, our Muslim friends and citizens, taxpaying citizens, and Muslims in nations were just appalled and could not believe what we saw on our TV screens."[13]

President Bush then sought to differentiate the attackers from Islam and other Muslims:

These acts of violence against innocents violate the fundamental tenets of the Islamic faith. And it's important for my fellow Americans to understand that. The English translation is not as eloquent as the original Arabic, but let me quote from the Koran itself: "In the long run, evil in the extreme will be the end of those who do evil. For they rejected the signs of Allah and held them up to ridicule." The face of terror is not the true faith of Islam. That's not what Islam is all about. Islam is peace. These terrorists don't represent peace. They represent evil and war. When we think of Islam, we think of a faith that brings comfort to a billion people around the world. Billions of people find comfort and solace and peace. And that's made brothers and sisters out of every race—out of every race.[14]

He noted that millions of Muslims were American citizens, and valuable contributors to the success of America, and President Bush encouraged Americans to treat one another with respect:

Women who cover their heads in this country must feel comfortable going outside their homes. Moms who wear cover must not be intimidated in America. That's not the America I know. That's not the America I value. I've been told that some fear to leave; some don't want to go shopping for their families; some don't want to go about their ordinary daily routines because, by wearing cover, they're afraid they'll be intimidated. That should not and that will not stand in America. Those who feel like they can intimidate our fellow citizens to take out their anger don't represent the best of America. They represent the worst of humankind, and they should be ashamed of that kind of behavior. This is a great country. It's a great country because we share the same values of respect and dignity and human worth.[15]

He closed by showing common cause with the Islamic leaders who were hosting his visit. "And it is my honor to be meeting with leaders who feel just the same way I do. They're outraged; they're sad. They love America just as much as I do."[16]

Two days following his visit to the Washington Islamic Center, President Bush hosted the president of Indonesia in the White House. Indonesia is the largest Muslim country in the world, home to more than 12 percent of all Muslims. In public remarks President Bush said, "I've made it clear, Madam President, that the war against terrorism is not a war against Muslims, nor is it a war against Arabs. It's a war against evil people who conduct crimes against innocent people."[17]

Eight days after the 9/11 attack, President Bush addressed a joint session of Congress, televised nationally in prime time:

> We have seen the unfurling of flags, the lighting of candles, the giving of blood, the saying of prayers—in English, Hebrew, and Arabic. . . . The terrorists practice a fringe form of Islamic extremism that has been rejected by Muslim scholars and the vast majority of Muslim clerics—a fringe movement that perverts the peaceful teachings of Islam. . . .
>
> I also want to speak tonight directly to Muslims throughout the world. We respect your faith. It's practiced freely by many millions of Americans, and by millions more in countries that America counts as friends. Its teachings are good and peaceful, and those who commit evil in the name of Allah blaspheme the name of Allah. The terrorists are traitors to their own faith, trying, in effect to hijack Islam itself. The enemy of America is not our many Muslim friends; it is not our many Arab friends. Our enemy is a radical network of terrorists, and every government that supports them. . . .
>
> We are in a fight for our principles, and our first responsibility is to live by them. No one should be singled or for unfair treatment or unkind words because of their ethnic background or religious faith.[18]

On being put on notice of the unintended consequences of his language of crusade, President Bush responded responsibly. In several settings, including with religious and political leaders who were Muslim and in a joint session of Congress, he made clear to the American people that the enemy was a specific group of individuals, not an entire religion or ethnic group.

The Council on American-Islamic Relations noted that the president's comments at the Islamic Center "played a key role in defusing anti-Muslim backlash following the 9/11 terror attacks."[19] The Center for the Study of Hate & Extremism at California State University, San Bernardino, also found that hate crimes against

Muslims and those perceived to be Muslim fell dramatically following President Bush's remarks at the Islamic Center.[20]

Senator McCain Playing with Fire

By early 2008, a story began to circulate—first in American and
British press and then on conservative blogs and programs—that
Senator Barack Obama had a close personal relationship with Bill
Ayers, a University of Illinois professor who had been active in the
Weather Underground in the early 1970s. Ayers and Obama
served on a charity board together, and Ayers hosted a fundraiser
at his house in the 1990s as Obama was launching his political
career in Chicago.[21]

The question of Senator Obama's connection to Ayers reached
such intensity that Obama was asked about the connection during
a primary debate with Senator Hillary Rodham Clinton in April.
Obama's general election opponent, Senator John McCain, was
also asked about this alleged connection between Obama and
Ayers during a television interview that month.

Ultimately, as established news organizations uncovered no evidence of a deep personal connection between Ayers and Obama,
the Ayers story died down. That is, until the McCain/Palin campaign brought it back. By early October 2008, McCain was trailing
Obama in the polls. McCain had long been struggling to articu-
late his plan to address the economic crisis facing the country.
With just weeks left before the election, the McCain campaign
needed to shake things up. McCain's strategist Greg Strimple told
the Associated Press, "We are looking for a very aggressive last
thirty days. . . . We are looking forward to turning a page on this
financial crisis and getting back to discussing Mr. Obama's aggres-
sively liberal record and how he will be too risky for Americans."[22]

On October 5, the Republican vice-presidential candidate,
Alaska governor Sarah Palin, told reporters: "Our opponent . . . is
someone who sees America it seems as being so imperfect that

he's palling around with terrorists who would target their own country."[23] Further, "Turns out one of Barack's earliest supporters is a man who, according to *The New York Times*, and they are hardly ever wrong, was a domestic terrorist and part of a group that quote launched a campaign of bombings that would target the Pentagon and US Capitol. Wow."[24]

This was a marked shift from earlier campaign rhetoric. A candidate for high office was suggesting that the Democratic candidate for president was not merely unpatriotic, but also in league with a terrorist and therefore a threat to the country. She defended this rhetoric by saying, "I think it's fair to talk about where Barack Obama kicked off his political career, in the guy's living room."[25]

On October 9, the McCain/Palin campaign released a new attack ad against Senator Obama. The transcript of the ad reads:

> Barack Obama and domestic terrorist Bill Ayers. Friends. They've worked together for years. But Obama tries to hide it. Why? Obama launched his political career in Ayers' living room. We know Bill Ayers ran the violent left-wing activist group called Weather Underground. We know Ayers' wife was on the FBI's 10 Most Wanted list. We know they bombed the Capitol. The Pentagon. A judge's home. We know Ayers said, "I don't regret setting bombs. . . . I feel we didn't do enough." But Obama's friendship with terrorist Ayers isn't the issue. The issue is Barack Obama's judgment and candor. When Obama just says, "This is a guy who lives in my neighborhood," Americans say, "Where's the truth, Barack?" Barack Obama. Too risky for America.[26]

What began as a story in the conservative echo chamber now became a defining narrative of a major political campaign. Combined with rhetoric questioning Obama's citizenship, political ideology, and religion, this new rhetoric became a volatile trigger in McCain's and Palin's rallies. NBC News reported: "Shouts of 'traitor,' 'terrorist,' 'treason,' 'liar,' and even 'off with his head' have rung from the crowd at McCain and Sarah Palin rallies, and gone unchallenged by them."[27]

At one rally, someone in the crowd shouted, "Kill him," referring Senator Obama, and the Secret Service had to investigate the validity of that threat.[28] Some civic leaders recognized the danger that this shift in political rhetoric represented and called Senator McCain out for not taking that danger seriously. On October 10, *New York Times* bestselling author Frank Schaeffer recognized the lone-wolf whistle and wrote an open letter to Senator McCain. Schaeffer had campaigned for McCain, who had endorsed one of Schaeffer's books. The open letter was published in the *Baltimore Sun* and then in the *Huffington Post*. It read in part: "Senator John McCain: If your campaign does not stop equating Sen. Barack Obama with terrorism, questioning his patriotism, and portraying Mr. Obama as 'not one of us,' I accuse you of deliberately feeding the most unhinged elements of our society the red meat of hate, and therefore of potentially instigating violence."[29]

He noted that there were a lot of crazy people listening to the rhetoric of the campaign. The letter continued:

> If you do not stand up for all that is good in America and declare that Senator Obama is a patriot, fit for office, and denounce your hate-filled supporters when they scream out "Terrorist" or "Kill him," history will hold you responsible for all that follows. John McCain and Sarah Palin, you are playing with fire, and you know it. You are unleashing the monster of American hatred and prejudice, to the peril of all of us. You are doing this in wartime. You are doing this as our economy collapses. You are doing this in a country with a history of assassinations.[30]

That day, Senator McCain moved to tamp down some of the consequences of this rhetoric. During a town hall–style rally, McCain told a supporter who said he was "scared" of an Obama presidency: "I want to be president of the United States and obviously I do not want Senator Obama to be, but I have to tell you—I have to tell you—he is a decent person and a person that you do not have to be scared of."[31]

At the same rally, another woman expressed a similar, but troubling concern: "I can't trust Obama. I have read about him and he's not, he's not uh—he's an Arab. He's not—"[32]

McCain cut her off and responded: "No, ma'am. He's a decent family man [and] citizen that I just happen to have disagreements with on fundamental issues and that's what this campaign's all about. He's not [an Arab]."[33]

The next day, October 11, one of McCain's good friends rebuked the senator for his rhetoric. Esteemed civil rights leader and member of Congress John Lewis was one of McCain's heroes. In McCain's book *Why Courage Matters*, the senator had extensively praised Lewis for his role in the Civil Rights Movement, particularly the march in Selma, Alabama, at which Lewis was beaten nearly to death. McCain wrote, "I've seen courage in action on many occasions. I can't say I've seen anyone possess more of it, and use it for any better purpose and to any greater effect, than John Lewis."[34]

But Lewis was concerned about the rhetoric the campaign was using. He posted a statement on Politico titled "Rep. John Lewis On Hostility of McCain-Palin Campaign." It noted that he himself was a victim of hatred and violence. He said he was deeply disturbed by the negative tone of the campaign, and that "Sen. McCain and Gov. Palin are sowing the seeds of hatred and division, and there is no need for this hostility in our political discourse."[35]

He referred to former Alabama governor and presidential candidate George Wallace, who he said had created the climate and conditions that encouraged vicious attacks against Americans. He noted that such an atmosphere of hate had contributed to the bombing that killed four young girls at an Alabama church. He concluded: "As public figures with the power to influence and persuade, Sen. McCain and Gov. Palin are playing with fire, and if they are not careful, that fire will consume us all. They are play-ing a very dangerous game that disregards the value of the politi-cal process and cheapens our entire democracy. We can do better. The American people deserve better."[36]

McCain was stunned by the rebuke. According to the *New Yorker*, after McCain heard Lewis's remarks, "he sat in silence in-side the campaign's official bus."[37]

A CNN report also noted the seriousness of this blow: "A Mc-Cain aide described the moment that the campaign saw Lewis' comment as an emotional one and a reality check as to 'what the campaign is up against.' The aide said they all stopped, delayed McCain's flight and got on a conference call to try to figure out how to respond."[38]

Later that day, Lewis issued a clarifying statement in response to criticism that he had equated McCain with George Wallace. He denied that he had made such a comparison. But he added, "My statement was a reminder to all Americans that toxic language can lead to destructive behavior. I am glad that Sen. McCain has taken some steps to correct divisive speech at his rallies. I believe we need to return to civil discourse in this election about the pressing economic issues that are affecting our nation."[39]

The following weekend, McCain received another disappoint-ment when another friend chose to call McCain out for his rhet-oric. Former Chairman of the Joint Chiefs of Staff and Secretary of State Colin Powell had previously vowed to remain neutral in this presidential election. But he went on NBC's *Meet the Press* and endorsed Senator Obama. One of his chief reasons: his disap-pointment with the tone McCain's campaign had exhibited. He said, "This Bill Ayers situation that's been going on for weeks be-came something of a central point of the campaign. But Mr. Mc-Cain says that he's a washed-out terrorist. But then why do we keep talking about him and why do we have these robo-calls going on around the country trying to suggest that, because of this very, very limited relationship that Senator Obama has had with Mr. Ayers, somehow Mr. Obama is tainted. What they're trying to connect him to is some kind of terrorist feelings, and I think that's inappropriate."[40]

He also took issue with the demonization of Muslims, and the suggestion that Obama himself was a Muslim and therefore likely a terrorist. He said,

> I am also troubled by, not what Senator McCain says, but what members of the party say, and it is permitted to be said, such things as, "Well, you know Mr. Obama is a Muslim." Well, the correct answer is he is not a Muslim; he's a Christian, he's always been a Christian. But the really right answer is: What if he is? Is there something wrong with being a Muslim in this country? The answer is: No, that's not America. Is there something wrong with some seven-year-old Muslim American kid believing that he or she could be president? Yet I have heard senior members of my own party [make] this suggestion: "He's a Muslim and he might be associated with terrorists." This is not the way we should be doing it in America. . . . Now we have got to stop polarizing ourselves in this way.[41]

A chastened McCain scaled back his and his campaign's rhetoric and stopped talking about Senator Obama. Having been held accountable by people he admired, he saw that he and his campaign had gone too far. If he had continued to use divisive rhetoric for the days remaining in the campaign, he might have derived some incremental electoral benefit. But he chose not to do so. As a responsible leader would.

Baby Killers and Costly Grace

Reverend Robert Schenck faced a crisis of conscience and of faith. After decades on the front lines against abortion, Schenck was wondering whether he had gone too far.

Schenck and his brother had converted to Christianity as teens, and both became ministers in their twenties. Rob Schenck's early ministry in suburban Buffalo quickly expanded to helping the poor in Mexico and elsewhere. He also became involved in national movements, eventually moving to Washington, where he ministered to senior officials in all three branches of the federal government.

In his 2018 book, *Costly Grace: An Evangelical Minister's Rediscovery of Faith, Hope, and Love*, Schenck describes how he became an anti-abortion activist and leader, working with Operation Rescue founder Randall Terry and others, both in his hometown outside of Buffalo and in Wichita, Kansas. He says, "We were in a holy war, in which the forces of good would confront the forces of evil—and, perhaps, even triumph."[42]

Schenck describes how he and hundreds of others staged protests outside the Wichita clinic of Dr. George Tiller, labeled by the protesters "Tiller the Killer": "We blocked cars, chained ourselves to clinic doors, printed and distributed 'Wanted' posters of the doctors. We waved signs that read 'Babies Killed Here' and passed out countless broadsides denouncing 'baby killing' that included gruesome photos of aborted fetuses."[43]

Schenck says that he and his colleagues were confident in the rightness of their cause, but also that followers would observe boundaries: "Despite our often extreme rhetoric, we adjudged the battle was never physically violent, which would have been to stoop to the level of the abortionist."[44]

But they were mistaken, at least about the battle never being physically violent. In 1993, Dr. David Gunn, a Florida abortion provider, was murdered. Operation Rescue had published "wanted" posters with his picture, phone number, and other identifying information. But Schenck and his followers had also signed a pledge that their work would be nonviolent in both word and deed. Schenck admits to being blind to the likely consequences of their rhetoric: "I didn't appreciate, or allow myself to see, the contradiction between the pledge and our increasingly inflammatory rhetoric. We would use stark language—'baby kill-ers,' 'mass murderers,' 'pro-aborts'—and outline battle plans in which we referred to abortion providers as 'the enemy,' and as-serted that sometimes people may break lesser laws to avoid com-mitting the greater evil of murdering innocent children."[45]

Schenck says that neither he nor his colleagues considered that some people might have difficulty discriminating between literal and figurative concepts. But he acknowledges, "There were also people bent on doing harm, and all they needed was religious permission to do so."[46]

But Dr. Gunn's murder was not the turning point for Schenck. That came five years later. In 1998, an abortion provider just out-side of Buffalo, whom Schenck had protested for years, was also murdered. Dr. Barnett Slepian had just returned with his wife from Friday synagogue services. He was shot and killed by a snip-er's bullet while preparing dinner.

Schenck was shocked by the killing and flew back to Buffalo. On the way, he began to take stock: "I started asking myself the hard questions: Who in our world would ever perpetrate such a horrible act? Was it possible someone under my spiritual care was an assassin? Our people put themselves in harm's way to prevent murder; how could one of them commit one? Had I ever said or done anything that contributed to this terrible event? Could I have prevented it?"[47]

Schenck went to a makeshift memorial outside of Dr. Slepian's clinic and laid a bouquet of flowers with a note of condolences. He says that, "I would not accept any responsibility for the violent act of one madman, but I regretted, painfully at that moment, the incendiary language we used to get our point across and acknowl-edged the harm it may have caused. . . . I bowed my head, con-fused and ambivalent, praying for an end to all violence, inside and outside abortion businesses. . . . At the same time, I felt an unfamiliar but profound sense of moral culpability and grief."[48]

Dr. Slepian's widow smashed the bouquet and returned it to Schenck with a note accusing him and his colleagues of provoking her husband's murder through their incendiary rhetoric. In a 2019 interview on PBS, Schenck describes how he tried to convince himself that he wasn't responsible for Dr. Slepian's death:

> When it happened, I convinced myself that it must have been someone very far on the periphery, probably an invader, maybe even somebody who was setting us up in some way to discredit our movement. And then someone sent me a photo of the perpetrator standing in the frame of a news conference that we had held. I didn't know his name at the time, but there he was. Not on the periphery, but standing very close to the leaders of our movement. And that told me something is deeply wrong here. But it would take me years to face it and address it.[49]

In *Costly Grace*, Schenck describes his transition—he calls it a conversion—from condemning those who sought or provided abortions. He says,

> I have talked with many women who have regretted their abortions. I have comforted and counseled women who were afraid of being pregnant but then decided to go through with the pregnancy. But in none of these hundreds, maybe thousands, of conversations over the years has anyone ever asked me what I would have done as an unmarried twenty-one-year-old woman. . . . I had a shocking but authentic moment of reckoning. By characterizing women who had made this choice as a specific type of sinner—our movement labeled them "post-abortive women"—I was perpetuating exactly what I had spent much of my adult life decrying: the dehumanizing of others.[50]

And slowly he came to recognize that the very rhetoric he had used against abortion providers contributed to their deaths. In August 2019, in the aftermath of the El Paso attack on Mexicans provoked by Trump's language of invasion, Schenck wrote in *TIME* magazine: "As a national anti-abortion leader for more than thirty years, I routinely used inflammatory language from the podium. At rallies for the activist anti-abortion organization Operation Rescue, I depicted doctors who performed abortions as murderers, callous profiteers in misery, monsters and even pigs. . . . Slepian wasn't the last person to die or be gravely injured by individuals who may have taken literally what I thought of at the time as harmless rhetoric. I now live with great sorrow and regret that it took me so long to learn incendiary speechifying can too often turn deadly."[51]

It took Rev. Schenck years to come to his own reckoning with accountability. But he did so fully, redirecting his life and his ministry to stop using an Us-Them dichotomy: "As I emerged from my period of darkness, of succumbing to politics and power, I saw how expansive God's grace is and how universal his invitation is to it. I no longer believe you're excluded if . . . you've had an abortion, or if you perform them. . . . I do believe we are better off when we listen more and talk less, and that especially includes our conversations with God. And I do believe we need to seek deeply and risk greatly to act courageously in obedience to the will of God as best we can."[52]

Accountability and Humility

Responsible leaders allow themselves to be held accountable for the consequences of their actions and statements, even when there is not a direct connection between the violence or threats of violence they prompt. Yet, to be accountable requires at least a drop of humility.

Humility isn't a word we often hear in relation to leadership, whether in politics, government, or business. Humility all too often is interpreted as weakness, especially in competitive cultures like politics.

But a dollop of humility tempers other attributes and makes a leader even stronger. Humility helps a leader to recognize that maybe—just maybe—he or she might be wrong; that there may be other valid perspectives; that he or she doesn't have to be the smartest person in every room, at every meeting. Humility also allows a leader to recognize that even if his or her cause is just, there are some means that are just as inappropriate—the ends may not justify the means.

Humility also allows leaders to recognize that, whatever their intentions may have been, it is possible—even foreseeable—that their words or actions can cause unintended consequences. But just because a consequence is unintended doesn't mean it isn't foreseeable.

Emotional intelligence guru Daniel Goleman, in a *Harvard Business Review* article, "What Makes a Good Leader?" identifies self-awareness as the first leadership skill: "People with a high degree of self-awareness know their weaknesses and aren't afraid to talk about them."[53] He notes, however, that many executives mistake such candor for "wimpiness." Another key leadership discipline is self-regulation: the ability to redirect impulses and drives to a more productive place.

Jim Collins, author of *Good to Great*, says that the best leaders take responsibility in high-stakes communication through a paradoxical combination of humility and fierce resolve.[54] He also acknowledges the danger of misinterpreting humility for weakness. Collins notes that the most effective leaders are a study in duality: "[M]odest and willful, shy and fearless. To grasp this concept, consider Abraham Lincoln, who never let his ego get in the way of his ambition to create an enduring great nation. . . . Those who thought Lincoln's understated manner signaled weakness in the man found themselves terribly mistaken.[55]

Indeed, Pope Francis, in a TED Talk recorded in 2017, notes that humility is not a weakness; rather, it is a kind of fortitude. He says that with power comes responsibility. He argues that power without humility leads to ruin, of the leader and of the people and institutions the leader presides over.

The pope uses a simile to illustrate the consequences of having an imbalance of humility and resolve: "There is a saying in Argentina: 'Power is like drinking gin on an empty stomach.' You feel dizzy, you get drunk, you lose your balance, and you will end up hurting yourself and those around you, if you don't connect your power with humility. Through humility . . . power . . . becomes a service, a force for good."[56]

Humility makes empathy possible. Yale philosopher Jason Stanley observed that the dehumanization of groups lessens citizens' capacity for empathy. But the very act of dehumanizing others may also make a leader less able to empathize. Reverend Robert Schenck describes his own struggle to empathize when in the throes of his advocacy against abortion: "One of the greatest faults in the movement that I have been a part of for so long was our inability to appreciate others and empathize with them. We were sure anyone who allowed for abortion under virtually any circumstances . . . was evil, self-serving, morally bankrupt, and motivated only by financial gain. There just couldn't be—and never would be—any other rationale for such abhorrent behavior."[57]

Humility, combined with other attributes of effective leadership, allows effective leaders to become responsible and accountable. But they don't need to wait until the harm is done.

10

Be on the Lookout

WARNING SIGNS OF RHETORIC THAT MAY PROVOKE VIOLENCE

What can civic leaders, engaged citizens, journalists, and public officials do to prevent violence triggered by rhetoric?

To start, they can recognize that there is a documented phenomenon that certain kinds of speech create conditions that make violence more likely. This has been known as *stochastic terrorism*, but for many people that is an inaccessible phrase that is confusing. In addition, there is an escalating continuum of violence that may end with terrorism, but not all violence-provoking language leads to terrorism.

"Hate speech" is too broad a phrase and riddled with First Amendment concerns.

Lone-wolf-whistle violence and lone-wolf-whistle terrorism are more accessible names for these kinds of violence, pointing to who is inspired to commit such violence (lone wolves) and what the triggering event can be (the lone-wolf whistle). And it acknowledges the continuum of violence, from opportunistic hate crimes to systematic and planned terrorism.

The next step is to be able to recognize such speech when it takes place.

The signs of dangerous speech that can condition an audience to accept, condone, and commit violence are not difficult to recognize. Once recognized, it isn't difficult to call to leaders' attention the predictable consequences of their behavior.

Some examples will help make the point:

In 2011, when Donald Trump began his birther initiative, First Lady Michelle Obama recognized the lone-wolf whistle and worried that he was intentionally saying something he knew to be untrue in ways that would "stir up wingnuts and kooks" and put her family at risk. The Secret Service confirmed that there were people capable of being so stirred. She kept her concerns private until the Obamas were out of office.

In 2015, the FBI issued a public warning about lone offenders who had already vandalized or made threats against Planned Parenthood clinics. It warned that the rhetoric about Planned Parenthood's purported sale of baby parts put the lives of reproductive health workers at risk. But the rhetoric was not tamped down, and as the FBI had warned, a lone wolf acting on the lone-wolf whistles invaded a Planned Parenthood clinic and killed three people and wounded another nine.

Holding Leaders Accountable

We must have a vocabulary to be able to hold leaders who use such speech accountable. In 2017, just a week into his presidency, Trump announced a travel ban against seven majority-Muslim countries. A federal judge in Seattle suspended the ban nationwide. Trump tweeted several attacks on the judge including,

"Because the ban was lifted by a judge, many very bad and danger-ous people may be pouring into our country. A terrible decision."[1]

The government appealed. Trump tweeted, "Just cannot be-lieve a judge would put our country in such peril. If something happens blame him and court system. People pouring in. Bad!"[2] The judge received many death threats in the days immediately following this tweet. Several days later, the architect of Trump's immigration policy, White House advisor Stephen Miller, went on Fox News. Journalist Chris Wallace recognized the lone-wolf whis-tle Trump had sent about the judge and called out the president's aide to account for it: "[A]fter Judge Robart's initial order, Presi-dent Trump tweeted this, and I want to put it on the screen. 'Just cannot believe a judge would put our country in such peril. If something happens blame him and court system. People pouring in. Bad!' But now, Stephen, that judge is getting death threats. So the question is, if something happens to him, should we blame President Trump?"[3]

Miller dismissed the suggestion. He said that the media blame politicians any time a crazy person makes a death threat. Wallace pushed back: "But some people would say that personally attack-ing a judge is reckless and irresponsible. In fact, your own Su-preme Court nominee, Judge Gorsuch, called it disheartening and demoralizing."[4]

Miller responded, "Statements that you can't criticize a judge demonstrate a profound misunderstanding of what it means to have separate and equal branches. Of course one branch can crit-icize another branch of government. It is ludicrous to say that Congress can criticize the president and judges can criticize the president, but the president can't criticize judges."[5]

Miller was committing misdirection and creating a false equiv-alence. The judge hadn't criticized Trump. Rather, he had made a legal ruling in a case. Trump did not merely criticize the judge. He used incendiary language falsely accusing the judge of allow-ing terrorists into the country and claimed that it would be the judge's fault if there were to be another terror attack.

Wallace was correct in holding the administration to account for the consequences of Trump's language. But he didn't have a framework to push back further when Miller redirected the conversation to suggest that this was about a policy disagreement between the president and the judge.

Civic leaders also need a vocabulary that calls appropriate attention to the risks. A good model is the open letter that author Frank Schaeffer, a McCain supporter, wrote to Senator McCain: "If your campaign does not stop equating Sen. Barack Obama with terrorism, questioning his patriotism and portraying Mr. Obama as 'not one of us,' I accuse you of deliberately feeding the most unhinged elements of our society the red meat of hate, and therefore of potentially instigating violence."[6]

He also said: "If you do not . . . declare that Senator Obama is a patriot, fit for office, and denounce your hate-filled supporters when they scream out 'Terrorist' or 'Kill him,' history will hold you responsible for all that follows. John McCain and Sarah Palin, you are playing with fire, and you know it. You are unleashing the monster of American hatred and prejudice, to the peril of all of us. You are doing this in wartime. You are doing this as our economy collapses. You are doing this in a country with a history of assassinations."[7]

That kind of language is unambiguous and difficult for a leader to evade. But in the Trump campaign and early presidency, many civic leaders and journalists did not recognize the signals or did not act when they finally noticed the signals. One reason, perhaps, is that they were not aware of what to look for.

What to Look For

Trump's use of lone-wolf whistles is unprecedented in terms of frequency, scope, and intensity, but it is not unique. We have examples in recent years in the United States of others using language in ways that provoke, or risk provoking, violence.

Because he does it so often, and so visibly, and against so many targets, Trump provides an opportunity to understand better how lone-wolf-whistle violence works. We can study this phenomenon across a very large sample size and see the patterns emerge. Those patterns provide an opportunity for the future: to help civic leaders, engaged citizens, journalists, and public officials recognize the phenomenon and take steps to hold leaders accountable when they use such language. They can do so while Trump is still in office. We can all harvest these lessons to hold Trump accountable in ways he has not been so far.

Speech that endangers begins with leaders using language in ways that have the effect of mobilizing some people to take matters into their own hands. There is a continuum of possible actions. Some of these people may commit acts of insult or incivility against people in suspect groups. Or, they may commit hate crimes of opportunity: When they come upon someone they believe is in the group, they may assault or rob them, or deface their property, or even kill them. And some may commit or attempt acts of mass violence, usually designated as domestic terrorism. That was the case for the Tree of Life shooter and the El Paso shooter. Because the acts of violence were not directed by the speaker or any other entity, those who commit such acts are essentially lone wolves. They self-mobilize, select their targets themselves, and equip themselves without coordinating with any authority.

Not everyone who hears the language will be so provoked. Just as there are many who do not recognize dog whistle language, there are many who do not recognize lone-wolf whistles. Those who do follow predictable patterns.

Mindset

The first pattern is that those who commit violence develop a mindset where taking violent action seems like a noble thing. They see themselves as warriors in a just cause. Such people observe some social situation and conclude, in stages: It's not right; it's not fair; it's their fault; they're evil/less than human.[8]

We saw these steps take place in the labeling of Dr. George Tiller as a "baby killer." Dr. Tiller's assassin said he killed the doctor to protect babies. The Colorado Planned Parenthood shooter called himself a "warrior for babies." The Tree of Life shooter said he was protecting his people from slaughter. The El Paso shooter said he was protecting Texas, and the United States, from invasion.

And we have noted that President Trump doesn't just lead people to this mindset; he uses all four elements in his rhetoric.

Dynamic Speaker

As I observed in Chapters 2 and 6, language by itself is not enough to lead people to commit violence. As Rachel Brown, author of the US Holocaust Museum's Simon-Skjodt Center for the Prevention of Genocide's handbook, *Defusing Hate*, points out, four other elements are needed:

- The language must be used by an influential or popular speaker.
- The message must be delivered in a form or medium that makes the audience more likely to access, believe, or spread the message.
- The language must be delivered in a context that increases the risk that the message will provoke violence.
- The message must be received by an audience that is receptive to speech that promotes violence, fear, or hatred.[9]

We saw these at play when President Bush spoke about a "crusade." He was certainly influential, and immediately after 9/11 very many people listened to him. His message, delivered on the White House lawn in front of Marine One, gave it an aura of official pronouncement. There were already threats, incivility, and violence against people perceived to be Muslim or Arab, and the word seemed to validate such violence.

We also note that because the president took prompt and thorough steps to disavow the idea of a religious war and to recalibrate his rhetoric, hate crimes against Muslims, Sikhs, and others declined dramatically. His influence was such that when he told followers not to commit such acts, they followed his direction.

We saw these elements also in the Planned Parenthood shooting after the "selling baby parts" video became part of the political debate in the presidential campaign in 2015, and we saw these elements throughout the Trump campaign and presidency.

Activation

Even that is not enough. Something more is needed. Those who take the initiative to commit violence, who become lone wolves, typically are activated in ways described by Hamm and Spaaij.[10] It begins with someone with a combination of personal and political grievance. Wingnuts and kooks are not only the ones who commit such violence. People who have strong ideological commitments, whether to white nationalism or some other cause, also commit such violence. The activation includes affinity with an extremist group, being part of a cause bigger than the individual. It also includes identification with an enabler, which can be a group or an individual or event. Many lone wolves make their intent known ahead of time. For example, the Tree of Life shooter posted on social media about the Hebrew Immigrant Aid Society, and posted about synagogues that raised money for it, including the Tree of Life. And hours before he attacked the Tree of Life synagogue complex, he posted that he was "going in."

But the activation is consummated by a triggering event. The triggering event in the Planned Parenthood shooting was the persistent references in the 2015 presidential election primary campaign to Planned Parenthood allegedly selling baby parts for profit and harvesting such parts from live babies. The triggering event in the Tree of Life shooting was the persistent rhetoric suggesting that George Soros and Jews in general were sponsoring an invasion of immigrants to slaughter white Americans. The triggering event in the mail bomber was President Trump's persistent and vocal demonization of his rivals and critics. And the triggering event in the El Paso shooting was the persistent language of an invasion by Mexicans.

This escalation model applies to all lone-wolf terrorists, not just those for whom the triggering event is a lone-wolf whistle.

But in lone-wolf-whistle violence and terrorism, the triggering event is typically language spoken by a leader. And this language is public. We can recognize it when we hear it.

Lone-Wolf Whistles

The triggering event for those who commit violence in response to language is the lone-wolf whistle.

Throughout this book, I have pointed to a playbook that describes the forms of language that malign leaders use to divide, to provoke fear and anger. Sometimes they are intentionally provoking violence. That was the case with both the Nazis and the Rwandan Hutu. Sometimes they are merely seeking political advantage or social change. But violence is a foreseeable and predictable consequence of such language.

Here we use the playbook as a toolkit or checklist that civic leaders, engaged citizens, journalists, and public officials can use to determine whether any public figure's language is likely to provoke some people to commit violence. We present the playbook in the form of questions to ask. If the answer to any of the questions is *yes*, then the next step is to look for signs of whether a violent mindset is taking place, whether the reaction to the language

includes incivility, insult, or violence that may escalate i⸍
gated quickly, and whether individuals seem to be goin⸍
the activation model.

THE LONE-WOLF-WHISTLE PLAYBOOK
TWELVE WARNING SIGNS THAT
RHETORIC MAY PROVOKE VIOLENCE

1. DEHUMANIZE: Calling groups of people animals or vermin who are infesting the nation.

- Is the leader equating a group with animals, insects, or vermin?
- Is the leader using the language of infestation?

2. DEMONIZE/DELEGITIMIZE: Attributing to a rival or group a menacing or evil identity or calling into question the legitimacy or qualification of a rival.

- Is the leader attributing a menacing or evil identity to a rival or group?
- Does the leader challenge the legitimacy, patriotism, loyalty, or motive of a rival or group?

3. SCAPEGOAT: Blaming a group for all or many of the nation's problems.

- Does the leader blame the group for causing or intensifying a nation's or community's problems (crime, unemployment, civic unrest, etc.)?

(continues)

TWELVE WARNING SIGNS THAT
RHETORIC MAY PROVOKE VIOLENCE (CONT.)

4. PUBLIC HEALTH THREAT: Saying people are carrying or transmitting dangerous diseases.

- Does the leader characterize a group as diseased?
- Does the leader attribute a particular disease to members of the group (smallpox, COVID-19, HIV)?

5. SAFETY THREAT: Claiming that a group or people or a political rival is a threat to public safety or civic order.

- Does the leader claim that a group is violent, dangerous, likely to cause injury or death to society at large or to the dominant group?
- Does the leader claim that a political rival or his/her policies will lead to injury, death, or civic unrest?

6. VIOLENT MOTIVE: Claiming that a group has violent or hostile intentions toward a dominant group.

- Does the leader claim that a group intends to commit violence?
- Does the leader claim that a group or rival intends to harm the dominant group in some way?
- Does the leader claim that a group or rival is hostile toward the dominant group?
- Does the leader claim that a group or rival wants to supplant, replace, wipe out, eliminate, or kill members of the dominant group?

7. SEVERELY EXAGGERATING RISK: Labeling a minor issue or routine event a major threat.

- Does the leader characterize a minor event or issue a serious threat?
- Does the leader exaggerate a routine event as a serious threat?
- Does the leader assign a scary name to an otherwise benign event or issue?

8. SINISTER IDENTITIES: Attributing vague or sinister identities to a group or its members.

- Does the leader use vague descriptions to characterize a group or its members?
- Does the leader use a sinister name or characterization when referring to a group or its members?

9. CONSPIRACY: Saying that something is part of a sinister conspiracy.

- Does the leader claim that a sinister puppet-master is controlling the members of a group?
- Does the leader claim that an individual, representing a larger threatening group, is secretly controlling a group or its members?

10. DISCREDIT INFORMATION: Discrediting the source of objective information or information critical of the leader.

- Does the leader discredit the legitimacy of the source of information (news media, academics, scientists)?
- Does the leader refuse to accept the accuracy of information that is critical of the leader or his/her policies?
- Does the leader threaten to punish, exclude, arrest, or physically harm people who publish information or who challenge the leader's policies?

(continues)

TWELVE WARNING SIGNS THAT
RHETORIC MAY PROVOKE VIOLENCE (CONT.)

11. CONFLATION: Conflating the leader and the state, so that any criticism of the leader is seen as an attack on the nation. Negative media coverage of the leader is cast as media being an enemy of the people or unpatriotic.

- Does the leader equate criticism of him/her as criticism of or harm to the entire nation?
- Does the leader challenge the patriotism of critics or opponents?

12. MENACING IMAGE: Juxtaposing a menacing image (noose, crosshairs, flaming cross, swastika, etc.) with a person or person's image, a location, or a facility associated with the target.

- Has the leader used an image that is traditionally associated with violence?
- Has the leader juxtaposed that image with an individual's image, home, workplace, or other facility traditionally associated with the individual?
- Has the leader juxtaposed that image with representatives of an entire group?

Calling Out Leaders Who Use Such Language

When the answer to one or more of those questions is *yes*, there's a possibility that violence may follow. The next step is to monitor whether such violence happens. Is there increased incivility or insult against the target of that language? Are extremist groups picking up that language and using it to rally their followers? These are often precursors to violence. Are there death threats?

Is there a spike in hate crimes? These are evidence that violence or threats of violence are already taking place and may escalate.

When the targets are public figures, they may have the capacity to call out the speaker directly. But their voice may not be enough. Other civic leaders may also need to lend their voices. Consider, for example, Michael Cohen.

For ten years, Cohen had been Donald Trump's personal lawyer and fixer. In that role he had threatened reporters, companies, and others who were seen to be attacking Trump. He also had arranged for a secret payment to adult film actress Stephanie Clifford, who performed under the name Stormy Daniels. She and Trump had been in a sexual relationship in 2006, and the payment was to prevent public disclosure just before the election. Cohen was also involved in the *National Enquirer* buying the exclusive rights to a story by former *Playboy* model Karen McDougal and later suppressing that story.

Cohen was investigated by the US Attorney for the Southern District of New York for these two payments and for other unrelated activities. Trump defended his former lawyer until it became clear that Cohen was cooperating not only with the US Attorney but also with Special Counsel Robert Mueller.

Cohen pled guilty to eight felony counts, including campaign finance violations, tax fraud, and bank fraud. In the hearing he implicated President Trump, saying that he had made the payments in coordination with and at the direction of a candidate for federal office. He later confirmed that that candidate was Donald Trump.

As Cohen awaited sentencing in mid-December 2018, Trump began a series of tweets and public statements to discredit Cohen, including attacking his family and suggesting criminal activity by his wife and father-in-law.

On December 12, 2018, Cohen was sentenced to three years in prison and a $50,000 fine. During the sentencing hearing, Cohen told the court, "My weakness could be characterized as a blind loyalty to Donald Trump."[11]

Four days later, Donald Trump called Cohen a "Rat," which was widely reported as mob slang for "informant." Trump tweeted: "Remember, Michael Cohen only became a 'Rat' after the FBI did something which was absolutely unthinkable & unheard of until the Witch Hunt was illegally started. They BROKE INTO AN AT-TORNEY'S OFFICE! Why didn't they break into the DNC to get the Server, or Crooked's office?"[12]

The *Washington Post* told the story of mob boss Al Capone, who refused to testify against others, and asserted, "I'm no rat." The *Post* noted, "Capone's rise to power as a prohibition-era gangster roughly coincides with the use of the rodent name for someone who 'secretly aids the police to apprehend criminals,' as defined in the *Dictionary of the American Underworld Lingo.*"[13]

ABC News specifically saw the term as a lone-wolf whistle, putting Cohen's life potentially at risk when he arrived in federal prison. It reported, "A rat, commonly known as an FBI informant, often refers to someone from an organized crime family who has gotten arrested and cooperated with the federal government to provide information about a larger crime or crime family."[14]

When asked by ABC News whether Cohen being branded as a "rat" would be dangerous, Michael J. Stern, a former federal prosecutor, said that it could be: "'Trump is not disclosing anything the prison population will not already know, given Cohen's very public disclosure of his cooperation. In general, cooperators are often subject to retribution, by the people they cooperate against and by prisoners who don't like the idea of people cooperating with the government. One nuance, in this case, is that there will be prisoners who support Trump and his branding Cohen a "rat" may be perceived as a call for them to punish Cohen,' he said."[15]

On January 10, 2019, the House Oversight Committee announced that Cohen would testify on February 7. The House had recently become Democrat-controlled. Two days later, Trump appeared by telephone on Fox News and spoke with Jeanine Pirro on the *Justice with Judge Jeanine* program. Trump suggested that Cohen's father-in-law was in some way making money illegally.

This perceived threat against Cohen's father-in-law prompted concerns that Trump was trying to intimidate a witness. The three chairs of the House committees on Oversight, Intelligence, and Judiciary published a joint statement, saying, "The integrity of our process to serve as an independent check on the Executive Branch must be respected by everyone, including the President. Our nation's laws prohibit efforts to discourage, intimidate, or otherwise pressure a witness not to provide testimony to Congress. The President should make no statement or take any action to obstruct Congress' independent oversight and investigative efforts, including by seeking to discourage any witness from testifying in response to a duly authorized request from Congress."[16]

Despite that warning, Trump continued to tweet about Cohen and his family. Five days after the House committee chairs admonished Trump to stop making statements about Cohen and his family, Trump tweeted in response to a Fox News story, "Kevin Corke, @FoxNews 'Don't forget, Michael Cohen has already been convicted of perjury and fraud, and as recently as this week, the *Wall Street Journal* has suggested that he may have stolen tens of thousands of dollars. . . .' Lying to reduce his jail time! Watch father-in-law!"[17] Cohen and his family received many death threats, in writing and by phone.[18]

After much discussion with several committees of Congress, Cohen agreed to testify in front of various House and Senate committees in private, and to have a public hearing in front of the House Committee on Oversight and Reform. In the public hearing on February 27, Cohen accepted responsibility for his lying to Congress the year before, and for other acts for which he had pleaded guilty. He also addressed the threats to him and his family, and the consequences of being called a "rat" by the president:

I have asked this Committee to ensure that my family be protected from Presidential threats, and that the Committee be sensitive to the questions pertaining to ongoing investigations. Thank you for your help and for your understanding. . . .

And, by coming today, I have caused my family to be the target of personal, scurrilous attacks by the President and his lawyer—trying to intimidate me from appearing before this panel. Mr. Trump called me a "rat" for choosing to tell the truth—much like a mobster would do when one of his men decides to cooperate with the government.

Only someone burying his head in the sand would not recognize them for what they are: encouragement to someone to do harm to me and my family.[19]

As the hearing ended many hours later, committee chair Elijah Cummings (D-MD) made explicit reference to Trump's calling Cohen a rat. He closed the hearing with this admonition of the president while speaking directly to Cohen: "And when you call somebody a rat, that's one of the worst things you can call them because when they go to prison, that means a snitch. I'm just saying. And so, the president called you a rat. We're better than that! We really are."[20]

Michael Cohen began serving his prison sentence on May 6, 2019.

The Power of an Engaged Citizenry

In 2015, President Obama spoke to a room of aspiring civil society leaders from around the world. He said: "As the saying goes, the most important title is not president or prime minister; the most important title is citizen. It is citizens—ordinary men and women, determined to forge their own future—who throughout history have sparked all the great change and progress. It was citizens here in America who worked to abolish slavery, who marched for women's rights and workers' rights and civil rights. They are the reason I can stand here today as President of the United States. It's citizens who, right now, are standing up for the freedom that is their God-given right."[21]

Obama continued: "When people are free to speak their minds and hold their leaders accountable, governments are more responsive and more effective."[22]

Donald Trump is not the first leader to put people's lives and safety at risk because of the language he uses. And he won't be the last. Whether concerning Donald Trump during his tenure as president, or other leaders in government, religion, business, or other sectors, it falls to engaged citizens and civic leaders to recognize the lone-wolf whistles and their significance. And to hold both those who send the signals and the lone wolves who respond to them accountable.

This requires an active and engaged and informed citizenry.

In the United States, one of the highest duties of its citizens is to hold our leaders accountable. It is one of the reasons I am so proud to be a citizen of my adoptive country.

ACKNOWLEDGMENTS

This book was made possible by the encouragement, support, and help of a great many people.

I thank my wife and life partner, Laurel Garcia Colvin, for all of her forbearance and support during the fifteen months I worked on the book. I also thank our daughters, Katie and Juliana, for all of their encouragement and support.

I also thank my colleagues at the Logos Institute for Crisis Management and Executive Leadership: Anthony Ewing, Katie Garcia, Barbara Greene, Holly Helstrom, Raleigh Mayer, Yinnan Shen, Maida Kalic Zheng.

My book agent, Leah Nathan Spiro, had the idea for this book and was a thought partner throughout. I had great help on the proposal and early drafts from Anne Greenberg and DeeDee Slewka.

I thank the team at Radius Book Group for all of their support: Scott Waxman, Mark Fretz, and Evan Phail. Also, Henry Carrigan, who edited the manuscript, and Jeff Farr of Neuwirth Associates who worked on the book design.

I was helped mightily by a team of gifted researchers; Katie Garcia was the lead researcher, and the team included Yinnan Shen and Yifei Wu.

While writing the book, I was assisted in testing ideas in the public square by West End Strategy Team. I thank Matt Dorf, Ari Geller, Josh Glasstetter, and Alice Murawski.

I thank the leaders who have read early drafts and who have endorsed the book on the cover and in the frontmatter pages.

I thank my students, faculty colleagues, and department heads at NYU Stern School of Business, NYU School of Professional Studies, and Columbia Engineering, for all of their encouragement and support.

I applaud the civic leaders, public figures, and engaged citizens who have raised the alarm about the dangers of incendiary rhetoric, lone-wolf terrorism, and stochastic terrorism. This book builds on their work.

NOTES

PREFACE

1. Letter, page 21, *USA v. Sayoc*, No. 1:18-cr-00820-1 (S.D.N.Y. Apr. 23, 2019), at https://www.usatoday.com/documents/5975837-Letter/.

CHAPTER 1

1. Franklin Delano Roosevelt, "Inaugural Address," March 4, 1933, at https://avalon.law.yale.edu/20th_century/froos1.asp.
2. Roosevelt, "Inaugural Address."
3. Roosevelt, "Inaugural Address."
4. Roosevelt, "Inaugural Address."
5. Winston Churchill, Address to the House of Commons, May 13, 1940, at https://winstonchurchill.org/resources/speeches/1940 -the-finest-hour/blood-toil-tears-and-sweat-2/.
6. Winston Churchill, Address to the House of Commons, June 4, 1940, at https://winstonchurchill.org/resources/speeches/1940 -the-finest-hour/we-shall-fight-on-the-beaches/.
7. Josiah Wedgwood, letter of June 4, 1940, quoted in Martin Gilbert, *Finest Hour: Winston S. Churchill, 1939–1941* (London: Book Club Associates, 1983), 468.
8. Vita Sackville-West, letter of June 4, 1940, to Harold Nicolson in Nigel Nicolson (ed.), *Harold Nicolson: Diaries and Letters 1939–1945* (London: Collins, 1967), 93.
9. H. R. Knickerbocker, *Is Tomorrow Hitler's? 200 Questions on the Battle of Mankind* (Reynal & Hitchcock, 1941), 152–53.

10. John F. Kennedy, Address to a Joint Session of Congress, May 25, 1961, at https://www.space.com/11772-president-kennedy-historic -speech-moon-space.html.

11. John F. Kennedy, speech at Rice University, September 12, 1962, at https://er.jsc.nasa.gov/seh/ricetalk.htm.

12. George Lakoff, *Don't Think of an Elephant! Know Your Values and Frame the Debate—The Essential Guide for Progressives.* (White River Junction, VT: Chelsea Green Publishing Company, 2004), xv.

13. Mark Green, "7 Days in America: Lakoff on Voters' Brains and Obama's Brain, with Huffington, vanden Heuvel & Green," Huff-Post, November 26, 2008, at https://www.huffpost.com/entry /em7-days-in-americaem-lak_b_138025.

14. Lakoff, *Don't Think of an Elephant!*, xv.

15. Lakoff, *Don't Think of an Elephant!*, 17.

16. Churchill, Address to the House of Commons, May 13, 1940.

17. John F. Kennedy, Address to a Joint Session of Congress, May 25, 1961, at https://www.space.com/11772-president-kennedy-historic -speech-moon-space.html.

18. John F. Kennedy, speech at Rice University, September 12, 1962.

19. "Facing Our Fears," episode of *This Emotional Life.* PBS, January 5, 2010.

20. Lakoff, *Don't Think of an Elephant!*, 17.

21. Lakoff, *Don't Think of an Elephant!*, 17.

22. George Lakoff and Mark Johnson, *Metaphors We Live By* (Chicago: University of Chicago Press, 1980), 3–6.

23. Jason Stanley, *How Fascism Works: The Politics of US and THEM* (New York: Random House, 2018), xvi.

24. Stanley, *How Fascism Works*, xv.

25. Note: My firm published *Five Frequencies*, and I wrote the foreword to it.

26. Jeff Grimshaw, Tanya Mann, Linne Viscio, and Jennifer Landis, *Five Frequencies: Leadership Signals That Turn Culture into Competitive Advantage* (Logos Institute for Crisis Management and Executive Leadership Press, 2019), 24.

27. Jim VandeHei and Mike Allen, "Trump Creep: Bad Habits Spread Fast," Axios, February 14, 2018, at https://www.axios.com/trump -bad-habits-white-house-republicans-congress-87dc1136-b9b1-414e -a951-553bc117cd46.html.

28. Jim VandeHei and Mike Allen, "Trump Creep: Bad Habits Spread Fast."

29. Jim VandeHei and Mike Allen, "Trump Creep: Bad Habits Spread Fast."

CHAPTER 2

1. "Mein Kampf," The Holocaust Encyclopedia, United States Holocaust Memorial Museum, at https://encyclopedia.ushmm.org/content/en/article/mein-kampf.

2. "Documenting Numbers of Victims of the Holocaust and Nazi Persecution," The Holocaust Encyclopedia, United States Holocaust Memorial Museum, at https://encyclopedia.ushmm.org/content/en/article/documenting-numbers-of-victims-of-the-holocaust-and-nazi-persecution.

3. Rachel Hillary Brown, *Defusing Hate: A Strategic Communication Guide to Counteract Dangerous Speech*, 8, at https://www.ushmm.org/m/pdfs/20160229-Defusing-Hate-Guide.pdf.

4. Brown, *Defusing Hate*, 8.

5. Brown, *Defusing Hate*, 8.

6. Linda Kirschke, *Broadcasting Genocide: Censorship, Propaganda and State-Sponsored Violence in Rwanda 1990–1994* (London: ARTICLE 19: 1996), at https://www.article19.org/data/files/pdfs/publications/rwanda-broadcasting-genocide.pdf.

7. Hege Løvdal Gulseth, *The Use of Propaganda in the Rwandan Genocide: A Study of Radio-Télévision Libre des Mille Collines (RTLM)*, unpublished master's thesis, University of Oslo, 2004, at http://urn.nb.no/URN:NBN:no-9823.

8. Brown, *Defusing Hate*, 8.

9. Stanley, *How Fascism Works*, 10.

10. "Ten Commandments of the Hutu," *Rwanda Genocide blog*, October 16, 2008, at http://rwandainformation.blogspot.com/2008/10/ten-commandments-of-hutu.html.

11. Sarah Anne Fisk, *When Words Take Lives: The Role of Language in the Dehumanization and Devastation of Jews in the Holocaust*, unpublished master's thesis, University of Canterbury, 2009, at https://ir.canterbury.ac.nz/bitstream/handle/10092/2900/thesis_fulltext.pdf;sequence=1.

12. Adolf Hitler, *Mein Kampf*, trans. James Murphy (London: Hurst and Blackett, 1939, rpt. 2014), 133.

13. Hitler, *Mein Kampf*, 236.

14. Mafeza Faustin, "Preventing Genocide by Fighting Against Hate Speech," *International Journal of Advanced Research* 4(3) (2016), 117–32. doi:ISSN 2320-5407.

15. Alison Des Forges, "Call to Genocide: Radio in Rwanda, 1994," in *The Media and the Rwanda Genocide* (London: Pluto Press, 2007), 48.

16. Hitler, *Mein Kampf*, 132.

17. Hitler, *Mein Kampf*, 139.

18. Gulseth, *The Use of Propaganda in the Rwandan Genocide*, 68.

19.   "Ten Commandments of the Hutu," *Rwanda Genocide blog.*

20.   Hitler, *Mein Kampf,* 139.

21.   Hitler, *Mein Kampf,* 236.

22.   Marcel Kabana, "*Kangura:* the Triumph of Propaganda Refined," in *The Media and the Rwanda Genocide* (London: Pluto Press, 2007).

23.   Hitler, *Mein Kampf.*

24.   Hitler, *Mein Kampf,* 260.

25.   Hitler, *Mein Kampf,* 260.

26.   Des Forges, "Call to Genocide," 46.

27.   Des Forges, "Call to Genocide," 48.

28.   Hitler, *Mein Kampf,* 141.

29.   Hitler, *Mein Kampf,* 142.

30.   Charles Mironko, "The Effects of RTLM's Rhetoric of Ethnic Hatred in Rural Rwanda," in *The Media and the Rwanda Genocide* (London: Pluto Press, 2007), 123.

31.   *Kanguru* 6 (Dec. 1990): 2–19; see especially page 8. Available at http://genocidearchiverwanda.org.rw/index.php/Kangura_No_6.

32.   Hitler, *Mein Kampf,* 125.

33.   Kirschke, *Broadcasting Genocide.*

34.   Hitler, *Mein Kampf,* 133.

35.   Hitler, *Mein Kampf,* 37.

36.   Jean-Marie Vianney Higiro, "Rwandan Private Print Media on the Eve of the Genocide," in *The Media and the Rwanda Genocide* (London: Pluto Press, 2007), 74.

37.   Mary Kimani, "RTLM: the Medium that Became a Tool for Mass Murder," in *The Media and the Rwanda Genocide* (London: Pluto Press, 2007), 112.

38.   Hitler, *Mein Kampf,* 142.

39.   Hitler, *Mein Kampf,* 260.

40.   Kabana, "*Kangura:* the Triumph of Propaganda Refined," 65–66.

41.   Kimani, "RTLM: the Medium that Became a Tool for Mass Murder," 199.

42.   Hitler, *Mein Kampf,* 35.

43.   Hitler, *Mein Kampf,* 109.

44.   Kirschke, *Broadcasting Genocide.*

45.   Gulseth, *The Use of Propaganda in the Rwandan Genocide,* 88.

46.   "Origins of Neo-Nazi and White Supremacist Terms and Symbols: A Glossary," United States Holocaust Memorial Museum, at https://www.ushmm.org/confront-antisemitism/origins-of-neo-nazi-and-white-supremacist-terms-and-symbols.

47.   Richard J. Evans, "All Hailed: The Meaning of the Hitler Salute," *New York Sun,* April 16, 2008, at https://www.nysun.com/arts/all-hailed-the-meaning-of-the-hitler-salute/74744/.

48. Stephen Hicks, "A Nazi Graphic Against Capitalism, Communism, Homosexuality, and the Jews," Stephenhicks.org, March 31, 2015, at https://www.stephenhicks.org/2015/03/31/a-nazi-graphic -against-capitalism-communism-homosexuality-and-the-jews/.

49. Kabana, "*Kangura:* the Triumph of Propaganda Refined," 68.

50. Faustin, "Preventing Genocide by Fighting Against Hate Speech."

51. Brown, *Defusing Hate*, 8.

CHAPTER 3

1. Joe Stump and Monica Davey, "Abortion Doctor Shot in Kansas Church," *New York Times*, May 31, 2009, at https://www.nytimes .com/2009/06/01/us/01tiller.html.

2. Ed Pilkington, "I Shot US Abortion Doctor to Protect Children, Scott Roeder Tells Court," the *Guardian*, January 28, 2010, at https://www.theguardian.com/world/2010/jan/28/scott-roeder -abortion-doctor-killer.

3. Statement by Randall Terry, *ChristianNewsWire*, May 31, 2009, at http://www.christiannewswire.com/news/8967610531.html.

4. "Abortion Docs Decry 'Wanted' Posters as Bait," CBS News, October 26, 2010, at https://www.cbsnews.com/news/abortion-docs -decry-wanted-posters-as-bait/.

5. Bill O'Reilly, "Transcript, Countdown with Keith Olbermann," NBC News, June 1, 2009, at http://www.nbcnews.com/id/31065420 /ns/msnbc-countdown_with_keith_olbermann/t/countdown -keith-olbermann-monday-june/#.XnpHxdNKi2c; Angie Drobnic Holan, "Bill O'Reilly Called George Tiller 'A Baby Killer' Without Attribution," Politifact, June 5, 2019, at https://www.politifact .com/factchecks/2009/jun/05/bill-oreilly/bill-oreilly-called -george-tiller-baby-killer/.

6. David Daleiden, "Planned Parenthood's Top Doctor, Praised by CEO, Uses Partial-Birth Abortions to Sell Baby Parts," The Center for Medical Progress, July 14, 2015, at http://www.centerformedical progress.org/2015/07/planned-parenthoods-top-doctor-praised-by -ceo-uses-partial-birth-abortions-to-sell-baby-parts/.

7. The Center for Medical Progress, "Planned Parenthood Uses Partial-Birth Abortions to Sell Baby Parts," YouTube, July 14, 2015, at https://www.youtube.com/watch?time_continue=448&v=jjxw VuozMnU.

8. The Center for Medical Progress, "Planned Parenthood Uses Partial-Birth Abortions to Sell Baby Parts."

9. The Center for Medical Progress, "Planned Parenthood Uses Partial-Birth Abortions to Sell Baby Parts."

10. Jeb Bush, "This is a shocking and horrific reminder that we must do so much more to foster a culture of life in America: http://jeb.cm/1L7U80U," Tweet, July 14, 2015, at https://twitter.com/JebBush/status/621111166052499456.

11. Elliott Smilowitz, "Walker Calls Planned Parenthood Video 'Absolutely Horrifying,'" *The Hill*, July 15, 2015, at https://thehill.com/blogs/blog-briefing-room/news/247959-walker-calls-planned-parenthood-video-absolutely-horrifying.

12. "Sen. Cruz: Congress Should Investigate and Defund Planned Parenthood," press release, US Senator for Texas Ted Cruz, Press Office, July 14, 2015, at https://www.cruz.senate.gov/?p=press_release&id=2377.

13. Maya Rhodan, "Planned Parenthood Video: Republican Presidential Candidates Respond," *TIME*, July 15, 2015, at https://time.com/3958197/planned-parenthood-republican-video-candidates/.

14. Rhodan, "Planned Parenthood Video: Republican Presidential Candidates Respond."

15. Nina Liss-Schultz, "Attorneys: Planned Parenthood Attack Videos Could Threaten Physical Safety of Abortion Providers," Rewire. News, July 29, 2015, at https://rewire.news/article/2015/07/29/attorneys-planned-parenthood-attack-videos-threaten-physical-safety-abortion-providers/.

16. Bob Egelko, "Abortion Foes Can't Release Undercover Videos, Judge Rules," SF Gate, August 3, 2015, at https://www.sfgate.com/nation/article/Judge-extends-order-blocking-anti-abortion-group-6422800.php.

17. "Planned Parenthood's Custom Abortions for Superior Product," *Human Capital*, Episode 3. YouTube, August 19, 2015, at https://www.youtube.com/watch?time_continue=572&v=FzMAycMMXp8.

18. Alex Greig, "Mother Shares Heartbreaking Photos of Baby Son Born at Just 19 Weeks," *Daily Mail*, January 19, 2014, at https://www.dailymail.co.uk/news/article-2542212/Mother-shares-heartbreaking-photos-baby-miscarried-19-weeks.html.

19. "Wednesday's GOP Debate Transcript, Annotated," *Washington Post*, September 16, 2015, at https://www.washingtonpost.com/news/the-fix/wp/2015/09/16/annotated-transcript-september-16-gop-debate/?utm_term=.e9103d913aad#annotations:7815235.

20. "FBI Warns of Threat to Reproductive Health Care Facilities," CBS News, September 19, 2015, at https://www.cbsnews.com/news/fbi-warns-of-threat-to-reproductive-health-care-facilities/.

21. "FBI Warns of Threat to Reproductive Health Care Facilities," CBS News.

22. "FBI Warns of Threat to Reproductive Health Care Facilities," CBS News.

23. Julie Turkewitz and Jack Healy, "3 Are Dead in Colorado Springs Shootout at Planned Parenthood Center," *New York Times*, November 27, 2015, at https://www.nytimes.com/2015/11/28/us/colorado-planned-parenthood-shooting.html.

24. "Shooting Survivors Describe Tense Moments in Colorado," CBS News, November 28, 2015, at https://www.cbsnews.com/news/colorado-springs-shooting-survivors-frightening-moments-planned-parenthood/.

25. Pete Williams and Andrew Blankstein, "Planned Parenthood Shooting Suspect Made Comment About 'No More Baby Parts': Sources," NBC News, November 28, 2015, at https://www.nbcnews.com/news/us-news/planned-parenthood-shooting-suspect-made-comment-about-no-more-baby-n470706.

26. Fred Barbash and Yanan Wang, "The Twisted 'Dream' of Accused Planned Parenthood Killer Robert Dear Jr.," *Washington Post*, April 12, 2016, at https://www.washingtonpost.com/news/morning-mix/wp/2016/04/12/the-twisted-remorselessness-of-accused-planned-parenthood-killer-robert-dear-jr/.

27. Richard Fausset, "For Robert Dear, Religion and Rage Before Planned Parenthood Attack," *New York Times*, December 1, 2015, at https://www.nytimes.com/2015/12/02/us/robert-dear-planned-parenthood-shooting.html.

28. Danielle Kurtzleben, "Planned Parenthood Investigations Find No Fetal Tissue Sales," NPR, January 28, 2016, at https://www.npr.org/2016/01/28/464594826/in-wake-of-videos-planned-parenthood-investigations-find-no-fetal-tissue-sales.

29. Jennifer Ludden, "Anti-Abortion Activists Indicted on Felony Charges in Planned Parenthood Case," *All Things Considered*, NPR, January 26, 2016, transcript at https://www.npr.org/2016/01/26/464469813/anti-abortion-activists-indicted-on-felony-charges-in-planned-parenthood-case.

30. "Planned Parenthood: Fact v. Fiction," US House of Representatives, Committee on Oversight and Reform (n.d.), at https://oversight.house.gov/planned-parenthood-fact-v-fiction#_ftn1.

31. Sam Dorman, "Judge Dismisses Some Criminal Charges in Planned Parenthood Video Case," FoxNews, December 7, 2019, at https://www.foxnews.com/politics/judge-dismisses-some-criminal-charges-daleiden.

32. Bob Egelko, "Planned Parenthood Wins $2.2 Million Verdict Against Anti-abortion Activists," *San Francisco Chronicle*, November 15, 2019, at https://www.sfchronicle.com/bayarea/article/Planned-Parenthood-wins-2-2-million-verdict-14838921.php.

33. Lance Benzel, "Judge Rules Admitted Colorado Springs Planned Parenthood Shooter Still Incompetent," *Denver Post*, February 13, 2018, at https://www.denverpost.com/2018/02/13/colorado -springs-planned-parenthood-shooter-still-incompetent/.

34. Shelly Bradbury, "Admitted Planned Parenthood Killer Robert Dear Indicted by Federal Grand Jury in 2015 Rampage," *Denver Post*, December 9, 2019, at https://www.denverpost.com/2019 /12/09/robert-dear-planned-parenthood-grand-jury-indictment/.

35. Bill O'Reilly, "Transcript, Countdown with Keith Olbermann," NBC News, June 1, 2009, at http://www.nbcnews.com/id/31065420 /ns/msnbc-countdown_with_keith_olbermann/t/countdown -keith-olbermann-monday-june/#.XnpHxdNKi2c.

36. Brown, *Defusing Hate*, 2.

37. Gordon Woo, "Quantitative Terrorism Risk Assessment," *Journal of Risk Finance* 4:1 (April 1, 2002), 7–14, https://doi.org/10.1108 /eb022949.

38. Mark S. Hamm and Ramon Spaaij, *The Age of Lone Wolf Terrorism* (Columbia University Press, 2017), 84.

39. Hamm and Spaaij, *The Age of Lone Wolf Terrorism*, 84.

40. Hamm and Spaaij, *The Age of Lone Wolf Terrorism*, 84.

41. Hamm and Spaaij, *Lone Wolf Terrorism in America: Using Knowledge of Radicalization Pathways to Forge Prevention Strategies* (US Department of Justice, 2015), 3.

42. Hamm and Spaaij, *Lone Wolf Terrorism in America*.

43. Adam Levine, "Obama: Biggest Terror Fear Is the Lone Wolf," interview with Wolf Blitzer, CNN, August 16, 2011, at http://security .blogs.cnn.com/2011/08/16/obama-biggest-terror-fear-is-the -lone-wolf/.

44. Jeffrey D. Simon, *Lone Wolf Terrorism: Understanding the Growing Threat* (Amherst, NY: Prometheus Books), 23.

45. Simon, *Lone Wolf Terrorism: Understanding the Growing Threat*, 41–42.

46. Simon, *Lone Wolf Terrorism: Understanding the Growing Threat*, 201–2.

47. Simon, *Lone Wolf Terrorism: Understanding the Growing Threat*, 255.

48. Randy Borum, "Understanding the Terrorist Mind-set," *FBI Law Enforcement Bulletin* 72:7 (July 2003), 7.

49. Borum, "Understanding the Terrorist Mind-set," 7.

50. Borum, "Understanding the Terrorist Mind-set," 7.

51. Borum, "Understanding the Terrorist Mind-set," 7.

52. Borum, "Understanding the Terrorist Mind-set," 7.

53. Williams and Blankstein, "Planned Parenthood Shooting Suspect Made Comment About 'No More Baby Parts': Sources"; Barbash and Wang, "The Twisted 'Dream' of Accused Planned Parenthood Killer Robert Dear Jr."

54. Hamm and Spaaij, *Lone Wolf Terrorism in America*, 2.

55. Hamm and Spaaij, *The Age of Lone Wolf Terrorism*, 55.
56. Hamm and Spaaij, *The Age of Lone Wolf Terrorism*, 151.
57. Hamm and Spaaij, *Lone Wolf Terrorism in America*, 8.
58. Hamm and Spaaij, *The Age of Lone Wolf Terrorism*, 151.
59. Hamm and Spaaij, *Lone Wolf Terrorism in America*, 8.
60. Hamm and Spaaij, *The Age of Lone Wolf Terrorism*, 81.
61. Hamm and Spaaij, *The Age of Lone Wolf Terrorism*, 151.
62. Hamm and Spaaij, *Lone Wolf Terrorism in America*, 8.
63. Hamm and Spaaij, *The Age of Lone Wolf Terrorism*, 151.
64. Hamm and Spaaij, *Lone Wolf Terrorism in America*, 8.

PART II

1. Borum, "Understanding the Terrorist Mind-set," 7.
2. Brown, *Defusing Hate*, 2.

CHAPTER 4

1. Robert Farley, "Donald Trump Says People Who Went to School with Obama Never Saw Him," PolitiFact, February 14, 2011, at https://www.politifact.com/factchecks/2011/feb/14/donald-trump/donald-trump-says-people-who-went-school-obama-nev/.
2. Steve Nichol and Neil Santaniello, "GOP Disavows Candidate," *South Florida Sun Sentinel*, September 26, 1996, at https://www.sun-sentinel.com/news/fl-xpm-1996-09-26-9609260092-story.html.
3. Unsigned editorial, *Los Angeles Times*, December 3, 2007, at https://www.latimes.com/archives/la-xpm-2007-dec-03-ed-obama3-story.html.
4. Posted on Fight The Smears website, part of the Obama campaign, at https://web.archive.org/web/20080922222958/http://fightthesmears.com/articles/5/birthcertificate.
5. M. Johnson, "Fox Goes Birther," *Media Matters for America*, March 28, 2011. Retrieved from https://www.mediamatters.org/blog/2011/03/28/fox-goes-birther/178005.
6. Michelle Obama, *Becoming* (New York: Crown, 2018), 352–53.
7. Michelle Obama, *Becoming*, 352–53.
8. Oprah Winfrey, "Michelle Obama Gets Candid With Oprah About Her New Memoir, *Becoming*," *O, The Oprah Magazine* (November 12, 2018). Retrieved from https://www.oprahmag.com/entertainment/a24691478/oprah-michelle-obama-becoming-interview/.

9. Gallup (May 13, 2011), at https://news.gallup.com/poll/147530 /obama-birth-certificate-convinces-not-skeptics.aspx.

10. Gallup (May 13, 2011), at https://news.gallup.com/poll/147530 /obama-birth-certificate-convinces-not-skeptics.aspx.

11. Jenna Johnson, "Trump Admits Obama Was Born in U.S., but Falsely Blames Clinton for Starting Rumors," *Washington Post*, September 16, 2016, at https://www.washingtonpost.com/news/post -politics/wp/2016/09/16/trump-admits-obama-was-born-in -u-s-but-falsely-blames-clinton-for-starting-rumors/?utm_term= .bedb27923d54.

12. Laura Brady, "Remember That Time Trump Was Allegedly Cheered by Paid Actors?" *Vanity Fair,* January 20, 2017, at https:// www.vanityfair.com/hollywood/2017/01/donald-trump-campaign -announcement-actors-fec.

13. "Full Text: Donald Trump Announces a Presidential Bid," *Washington Post,* June 16, 2015, at https://www.washingtonpost.com/news /post-politics/wp/2015/06/16/full-text-donald-trump-announces -a-presidential-bid/?utm_term=.86b72196973e.

14. "Full Text: Donald Trump Announces a Presidential Bid," *Washington Post,* June 16, 2015.

15. "Full Text: Donald Trump Announces a Presidential Bid," *Washington Post,* June 16, 2015.

16. Philip Bump, "Donald Trump's Curious Defense of His Immigration Comments, Annotated," *Washington Post*, July 6, 2015, at https://www.washingtonpost.com/news/the-fix/wp/2015/07 /06/donald-trumps-lengthy-and-curious-defense-of-his-immigrant -comments-annotated/?utm_term=.89648c215737.

17. Hunter Walker, "Donald Trump Just Released an Epic Statement Raging Against Mexican Immigrants and 'Disease,'" *Business Insider,* July 6, 2015.

18. Center for Public Integrity, "Rising Hate Drives Latinos and Immigrants Into Silence," August 22, 2018, at https://publicintegrity .org/federal-politics/rising-hate-drives-latinos-and-immigrants -into-silence/.

19. "Boston Men Jailed for Trump-inspired Hate Crime Attack," Reuters, May 16, 2016.

20. Louis Jacobson, "Donald Trump Says if You're from Syria and a Christian, You Can't Come to the U.S. as a Refugee," PolitiFact, July 20, 2015, at https://www.politifact.com/truth-o-meter/statements /2015/jul/20/donald-trump/donald-trump-says-if-youre-syria -and-christianyou-/.

21. "Donald Trump Campaign Rally in Keene, New Hampshire," C-SPAN, September 30, 2015, at https://www.c-span.org/video

/?328446-1/donald-trump-campaign-rally-keene-hampshire; Ali Vitali, "Donald Trump in New Hampshire: Syrian Refugees Are 'Going Back,'" NBC News, October 1, 2015, at https://www.nbcnews .com/politics/2016-election/donald-trump-new-hampshire-syrian -refugees-are-going-back-n436616.

22. Jalelah Ahmed, "Ethnic Intimidation Charges Dismissed in Racial Attack," *Centre Daily Times*, December 9, 2015, at https://www .centredaily.com/news/local/education/penn-state/article 48797770.html.

23. Ahmed, "Ethnic Intimidation Charges Dismissed in Racial Attack."

24. Sarah Rafacz, "Man Pleads Guilty to Ethnic Intimidation," *Centre Daily Times*, October 5, 2016, at https://www.centredaily.com/news /local/crime/article106289987.html.

25. "Penn State Student Attacked Another Based on His Race. Now He's Serving Time," *Centre Daily Times*, November 18, 2016, at https:// www.centredaily.com/news/local/crime/article115708388.html.

26. Donald J. Trump, campaign rally, December 6, 2015, at https:// www.youtube.com/watch?v=mo_nYQ6ItWM.

27. "Trump Speaks Out on Plan to Ban Muslims," *Good Morning America*, ABC News, December 8, 2015, at https://abcnews.go.com/GMA /video/donald-trump-speaks-plan-ban-muslims-35640498.

28. "Trump Speaks Out on Plan to Ban Muslims," *Good Morning America*.

29. "Trump Speaks Out on Plan to Ban Muslims," *Good Morning America*.

30. "Trump Speaks Out on Plan to Ban Muslims," *Good Morning America*.

31. "Trump Speaks Out on Plan to Ban Muslims," *Good Morning America*.

32. "Trump Speaks Out on Plan to Ban Muslims," *Good Morning America*.

33. "Trump Speaks Out on Plan to Ban Muslims," *Good Morning America*.

34. "Trump Speaks Out on Plan to Ban Muslims," *Good Morning America*.

35. "Trump Speaks Out on Plan to Ban Muslims," *Good Morning America*.

36. "Trump Speaks Out on Plan to Ban Muslims," *Good Morning America*.

37. "Trump Defends Proposal to Ban Muslims Entering U.S.," interview with Jake Tapper, CNN, December 13, 2015, at https://www .youtube.com/watch?v=JKtcdn0zAqw.

38. "Trump Defends Proposal to Ban Muslims Entering U.S.," interview with Jake Tapper.

39. Council on American-Islamic Relations, *Civil Rights Report 2017: The Empowerment of Hate*, 7, at http://www.islamophobia.org/reports /188-the-empowerment-of-hate.html.

40. Aaron Williams, "Hate Crimes Rose the Day After Trump Was Elected, FBI Data Show," *Washington Post*, March 23, 2018, at https:// www.washingtonpost.com/news/post-nation/wp/2018/03/23/hate -crimes-rose-the-day-after-trump-was-elected-fbi-data-show/?utm _term=.adf72bf1287a.

41. Los Angeles County Commission on Human Relations, *2016 Hate Crimes Report*, 36, at https://www.scribd.com/document/364555731/Hate-Crime-Report-2016.

42. Ryan J. Reilly and Christopher Mathias, "Right-Wing 'Crusaders' Militia Group Plotted Terror Attack on Muslim Immigrants, FBI Charges," HuffPost, October 14, 2016, at https://www.huffpost.com/entry/militia-terror-plot-fbi-kansas_n_58014995e4b0162c043c1e90.

43. Donald Trump, rally in Costa Mesa, CA, April 28, 2016, as quoted in Theresa Berenson, "Trump Repeats False Pig's Blood Story at California Rally," *TIME*, April 29, 2016, at https://time.com/4312131/donald-trump-pigs-blood-muslim-story/.

44. Reilly and Mathias, "Right-Wing 'Crusaders' Militia Group Plotted Terror Attack on Muslim Immigrants, FBI Charges."

45. Williams, "Hate Crimes Rose the Day After Trump was Elected, FBI Data Show."

46. Ryan J. Reilly, "'Locker Room Talk': Trump Fans Charged in Anti-Muslim Plot Say It Was Just Bluster," HuffPost, March 23, 2018, at https://www.huffpost.com/entry/domestic-terrorism-kansas-militia-plot_n_5ab43c40e4b0decad04865e0.

47. Reilly, "'Locker Room Talk': Trump Fans Charged in Anti-Muslim Plot Say It Was Just Bluster."

48. Ryan J. Reilly, "Trump Fan Convicted of Anti-Muslim Terror Plot Asks Judge to Consider Trump's Rhetoric," HuffPost, October 18, 2018, at https://www.huffpost.com/entry/kansas-terror-plot-trump-anti-muslim_n_5bd742ebe4b055bc948ef751.

49. "Hate Groups Increase for Second Consecutive Year as Trump Electrifies Radical Right," Southern Poverty Law Center, February 15, 2017, at https://www.splcenter.org/news/2017/02/15/hate-groups-increase-second-consecutive-year-trump-electrifies-radical-right.

50. Richard A. Brown, District Attorney, Queens County, press release, March 16, 2017.

CHAPTER 5

1. Donald J. Trump, "Inaugural Address," January 20, 2017, at https://www.whitehouse.gov/briefings-statements/the-inaugural-address/.

2. Trump, "Inaugural Address."

3. "White Supremacists Adopt New Slogan: 'You Will Not Replace Us,'" Anti-Defamation League, June 9, 2017, at https://www.adl.org/blog/white-supremacists-adopt-new-slogan-you-will-not-replace-us.

4.   David Neiwert, "When White Nationalists Chant Their Weird Slogans, What Do They Mean?" Southern Poverty Law Center, October 10, 2017, at https://www.splcenter.org/hatewatch/2017/10/10/when-white-nationalists-chant-their-weird-slogans-what-do-they-mean.

5.   Hunton & Williams LLP, *FINAL REPORT INDEPENDENT REVIEW OF THE 2017 PROTEST EVENTS IN CHARLOTTESVILLE, VIRGINIA* (Rep.), December 1, 2017, at https://www.huntonak.com/images/content/3/4/v2/34613/final-report-ada-compliant-ready.pdf.

6.   Jason Kessler vs. City of Charlottesville and Maurice Jones, *Affidavit of City Manager Maurice Jones*, Case No: 3:17-cv-00056-GEC 2 (United States District Court for the Western District of Virginia—Charlottesville Division August 11, 2017). Retrieved from https://acluva.org/sites/default/files/field_documents/kessler_defendants briefinoppositiontopreliminaryinjunction.pdf.

7.   Jason Kessler vs. City of Charlottesville and Maurice Jones, *Brief in Opposition to Plaintiff's Motion For a Preliminary Injunction or Temporary Restraining Order.*

8.   Daily Stormer, August 8, 2017, as reprinted in Jane Coaston, "Trump's New Defense of his Charlottesville Comments Is Incredibly False," Vox, at https://www.vox.com/2019/4/26/18517980/trump-unite-the-right-racism-defense-charlottesville.

9.   Daily Stormer Facebook post, reposted by Piedmont Red Strings, Silver Valley RedneckRevolt Facebook page, at https://www.facebook.com/SilverValleyRedneckRevolt/photos/a.776473342509438/867769270046511/?type=3&theater.

10.   Elizabeth Sines et. al. v. Jason Kessler et. al., Complaint, United States District Court for the Western District of Virginia, Case 3:17-cv00072-NKM, October 12, 2017.

11.   Joe Heim, "Recounting a Day of Rage, Hate, Violence and Death," *Washington Post*, August 14, 2017, at https://www.washingtonpost.com/graphics/2017/local/charlottesville-timeline/?utm_term=.360524b418a6.

12.   Hunton & Williams LLP, *FINAL REPORT INDEPENDENT REVIEW OF THE 2017 PROTEST EVENTS IN CHARLOTTESVILLE, VIRGINIA.*

13.   "Alt-Right Charlottesville Marchers Chant 'Blood and Soil!' and 'Hail Trump!'" Hatewatch, YouTube, August 20, 2017, at https://www.youtube.com/watch?time_continue=66&v=GVDF_GkNAYA.

14.   Hunton & Williams LLP, *FINAL REPORT INDEPENDENT REVIEW OF THE 2017 PROTEST EVENTS IN CHARLOTTESVILLE, VIRGINIA.*

15.   Joe Heim, "Recounting a Day of Rage, Hate, Violence and Death."

16.   Daily Stormer, August 12, 2017, live Charlottesville blog update, 11:17 a.m., at https://dailystormer.name/unitetheright-charlottesville-live-updates/.

17. Hunton & Williams LLP, *FINAL REPORT INDEPENDENT REVIEW OF THE 2017 PROTEST EVENTS IN CHARLOTTESVILLE, VIRGINIA.*

18. Hunton & Williams LLP, *FINAL REPORT INDEPENDENT REVIEW OF THE 2017 PROTEST EVENTS IN CHARLOTTESVILLE, VIRGINIA.*

19. Hunton & Williams LLP, *FINAL REPORT INDEPENDENT REVIEW OF THE 2017 PROTEST EVENTS IN CHARLOTTESVILLE, VIRGINIA.*

20. Joe Heim, "Recounting a Day of Rage, Hate, Violence and Death."

21. "President Trump Signs Veterans Health Care Bill," C-SPAN, August 12, 2017, at https://www.c-span.org/video/?432523-1/president-trump-condemns-violence-charlottesville-va.

22. Dan Merica, "Trump Silent as Aides Look to Explain His Vague Charlottesville Statement," CNN, August 14, 2017, at https://www.cnn.com/2017/08/13/politics/trump-silent-aides-charlottesville/index.html.

23. Daily Stormer, August 12, 2017, live Charlottesville blog update, 3:46 p.m., at https://dailystormer.name/unitetheright-charlottesville-live-updates/.

24. "Statement by President Trump," The White House, August 14, 2017, at https://www.whitehouse.gov/briefings-statements/statement-president-trump/.

25. Donald Trump, "Made additional remarks on Charlottesville and realize once again that the #Fake News Media will never be satisfied . . . truly bad people!" Tweet, August 14, 2017, at https://twitter.com/realdonaldtrump/status/897223558073602049.

26. "President Trump News Conference," C-SPAN, August 15, 2017, at https://www.c-span.org/video/?432633-1/president-trump-there-blame-sides-violence-charlottesville.

27. David A. Graham, Adrienne Green, Cullen Murphy, and Parker Richards, "An Oral History of Trump's Bigotry," the *Atlantic*, June 2019, at https://www.theatlantic.com/magazine/archive/2019/06/trump-racism-comments/588067/.

28. Monika Bauerlein and Clara Jeffery, "Trump's Signals to White Supremacists Aren't Dog Whistles. They're Flares," *Mother Jones*, September 7, 2017, at https://www.motherjones.com/media/2017/09/fighting-white-supremacists/.

29. Daryl Johnson, "I Warned of Right-wing Violence in 2009. Republicans Objected. I Was Right," *Washington Post*, August 21, 2017, at https://www.washingtonpost.com/news/posteverything/wp/2017/08/21/i-warned-of-right-wing-violence-in-2009-it-caused-an-uproar-i-was-right/?utm_term=.0ac74023afc9.

30. Johnson, "I Warned of Right-wing Violence in 2009."

31. Frank Figliuzzi, "Why Does Trump Fan the Flames of Race-Based Terrorism?" *New York Times*, July 31, 2019, at https://www.nytimes.com/2019/07/31/opinion/gilroy-white-domestic-terrorism.html?smid=fb-nytopinion&smtyp=cur.

32. *Inside Edition*, August 14, 2017, at https://www.insideedition.com
/headlines/24968-charlottesville-suspect-once-called-concentration
-camp-where-the-magic-happened-classmates.

33. "Fact Sheet, Asylum in the United States," American Immigration
Council, at https://www.americanimmigrationcouncil.org/research
/asylum-united-states.

34. Donald Trump, Tweet, April 2, 2018, at https://twitter.com/real
DonaldTrump/status/980961086546632705?ref_src=twsrc
%5Etfw%7Ctwcamp%5Etweetembed%7Ctwterm%5E9809
61086546632705&ref_url=https%3A%2F%2Fwww.france24
.com%2Fen%2F20180430-mexico-usa-trump-migrant-caravan
-fits-border-wall-immigration.

35. "Immigration 101: What Is a Sanctuary City," America's Voice, April
25, 2017 (updated October 9, 2019) at https://americasvoice.org
/blog/what-is-a-sanctuary-city/.

36. "Remarks by President Trump at a California Sanctuary State
Roundtable," The White House, May 16, 2018, at https://www
.whitehouse.gov/briefings-statements/remarks-president-trump
-california-sanctuary-state-roundtable/.

37. "Remarks by President Trump at a California Sanctuary State
Roundtable," The White House, May 16, 2018.

38. "President Trump Delivers Remarks at the National Federation of
Independent Business," The White House, June 19, 2018, at
https://www.youtube.com/watch?v=jNhyPJdnXEA.

39. Tal Kopan, "Has MS-13 'literally taken over towns and cities of the
US'?" CNN, May 19, 2017, at https://www.cnn.com/2017/05/18
/politics/trump-ms-13-literally-taken-over/index.html.

40. Donald Trump, "Democrats are the problem. They don't care
about crime and want illegal immigrants, no matter how bad they
may be, to pour into and infest our Country, like MS-13. They can't
win on their terrible policies, so they view them as potential voters!" Tweet, June 19, 2018, at https://twitter.com/realdonaldtrump
/status/1009071403918864385.

41. "President Trump Rally in Topeka, Kansas," C-SPAN, October 6,
2019, at https://www.c-span.org/video/?452582-1/president-trump
-rally-topeka-kansas.

42. Patrick Buchanan, "Caravan Puts Trump Legacy on the Line," Cre-
ators, October 19, 2018, at https://www.creators.com/read/pat
-buchanan/10/18/caravan-puts-trump-legacy-on-the-line.

43. Buchanan, "Caravan Puts Trump Legacy on the Line."

44. John Fritze, "Trump Used Words Like 'Invasion' and 'Killer' to
Discuss Immigrants at Rallies 500 Times: USA TODAY Analysis,"
USA Today, August 9, 2019, at https://www.usatoday.com/story
/news/politics/elections/2019/08/08/trump-immigrants
-rhetoric-criticized-el-paso-dayton-shootings/1936742001/.

45. Brad Heath, Matt Wynn, and Jessica Guynn, "How a Lie About George Soros and the Migrant Caravan Multiplied Online," *USA Today*, October 31, 2019, at https://www.usatoday.com/in-depth /news/nation/2018/10/31/george-soros-and-migrant-caravan -how-lie-multiplied-online/1824633002/.

46. Heath, Wynn, and Guynn, "How a Lie About George Soros and the Migrant Caravan Multiplied Online."

47. Heath, Wynn, and Guynn, "How a Lie About George Soros and the Migrant Caravan Multiplied Online."

48. "President Trump Campaign Rally in Houston, Texas," C-SPAN, October 22, 2018, at https://www.c-span.org/video/?453256-1 /president-trump-campaigns-senator-ted-cruz-houston.

49. "President Trump Campaign Rally in Houston, Texas," C-SPAN, October 22, 2018.

50. "President Trump Campaign Rally in Houston, Texas," C-SPAN, October 22, 2018.

51. Donald Trump, Tweet, October 22, 2018, at https://twitter.com /realDonaldTrump/status/1054351078328885248.

52. Penny Starr, "Medical Expert: Migrant Caravan Could Pose Public Health Threat," Breitbart News, October 26, 2018, at https://www .breitbart.com/politics/2018/10/26/medical-expert-migrant -caravan-could-pose-public-health-threat/.

53. Donald Trump, "Many Gang Members and some very bad people are mixed into the Caravan heading to our Southern Border. Please go back, you will not be admitted into the United States unless you go through the legal process. This is an invasion of our Country and our Military is waiting for you!" Tweet, October 29, 2018, at https:// twitter.com/realdonaldtrump/status/1056919064906469376.

54. "President Trump Rally in Illinois," C-SPAN, October 27, 2018, at https://www.c-span.org/video/?453628-1/president-trump -campaigns-republicans-illinois.

55. Michael D. Shear and Thomas Gibbons-Neff, "Trump Sending 5,200 Troops to the Border in an Election-Season Response to Migrants," *New York Times*, October 29, 2018, at Retrieved from https://www.nytimes.com/2018/10/29/us/politics/border -security-troops-trump.html?module=inline.

56. Jeremy W. Peters, "How Trump-Fed Conspiracy Theories About Migrant Caravan Intersect with Deadly Hatred," *New York Times*, October 29, 2018, at https://www.nytimes.com/2018/10/29/us /politics/caravan-trump-shooting-elections.html.

57. Peters, "How Trump-Fed Conspiracy Theories About Migrant Caravan Intersect with Deadly Hatred."

58. Chris Cillizza, "What Trump Has Stopped Talking About Since Election Day," CNN, November 14, 2018, at https://www.cnn .com/2018/11/14/politics/donald-trump-caravan/index.html.

59. Robert Bowers, Gab post quoted in Alex Amend, "Analyzing a Ter-
     rorist's Social Media Manifesto: The Pittsburgh Synagogue Shoot-
     er's Posts on Gab," Southern Poverty Law Center, October 28, 2018,
     at https://www.splcenter.org/hatewatch/2018/10/28/analyzing
     -terrorists-social-media-manifesto-pittsburgh-synagogue-shooters
     -posts-gab.

60. Robert Bowers, Gab post at https://www.google.com/search?client
     =firefox-b-1&tbm=isch&q=Robert+Bowers+social+media+posts
     &chips=q:robert+bowers+social+media+posts,online_chips
     :gab&usg=AI4_-kTIKaS2RHw46yKUvSYheekudrlIhQ&sa=X&ved
     =0ahUKEwjb8-S-y4HfAhVp04MKHQMeCIgQ4lYIKigD&biw
     =1481&bih=858&dpr=2.22#imgrc=bJd4l4st1ahLhM:.

61. Robert Bowers, Gab post at https://www.google.com/search?client
     =firefox-b-1&tbm=isch&q=Robert+Bowers+social+media+posts
     &chips=q:robert+bowers+social+media+posts,online_chips
     :gab&usg=AI4_-kTIKaS2RHw46yKUvSYheekudrlIhQ&sa=X&ved
     =0ahUKEwjb8-S-.

62. Robert Bowers, Gab post quoted in Jason Silverstein, "Robert Bow-
     ers, Pittsburgh Shooting Suspect, Was Avid Poster of Anti-Semitic
     Content on Gab," CBS News, at https://www.cbsnews.com/news
     /robert-bowers-gab-pittsburgh-shooting-suspect-today-live
     -updates-2018-10-27/.

63. Robert Bowers, Gab post, at http://archive.li/k63LE.

64. Stuart Wexler, Guest Columnist, "The Devil Cites Scripture, as Do
     Many Who Commit Atrocities Like the Synagogue Shooting," *Clar-
     ion Ledger*, November 6, 2018, at https://www.clarionledger.com
     /story/opinion/columnists/2018/11/06/synagogue-shootings
     -devil-cites-scripture-do-many-killers/1903921002.

65. Kevin Roose, "Cesar Sayoc's Path on Social Media: From Food
     Photos to Partisan Fury," *New York Times*, October 27, 2018, at
     https://www.nytimes.com/2018/10/27/technology/cesar-sayoc
     -facebook-twitter.html.

66. Kevin Roose, "Cesar Sayoc's Path on Social Media: From Food Pho-
     tos to Partisan Fury."

67. Kevin Roose, "Cesar Sayoc's Path on Social Media: From Food Pho-
     tos to Partisan Fury."

68. Donald Trump, "The very rude elevator screamers are paid profes-
     sionals only looking to make Senators look bad. Don't fall for it!
     Also, look at all of the professionally made identical signs. Paid for
     by Soros and others. These are not signs made in the basement from
     love! #Troublemakers," Tweet, October 5, 2018, at https://twitter
     .com/realdonaldtrump/status/1048196883464818688?lang=en.

69. "President Trump Campaign Rally in Montana," C-SPAN, October
     18, 2018, at https://www.c-span.org/video/?453144-1/president
     -trump-campaigns-republicans-montana&start=3530.

70. hardrock2016, "David Hoggs biggest con century fake fraud. He never attended Parkland High School. He graduated in 2015 from Redondo Beach High School. He is a George Soros paid Protester and actor. We Unconquered Seminole Tribe have his real school record and Year Book," Tweet, July 28, 2018, at https://talking pointsmemo.com/muckraker/mail-bomb-suspect-sayoc-shared -social-media-posts-about-targets.

71. Allegra Kirkland and Josh Kovensky, "Cesar Sayoc Bombarded Social Media with Posts Disparaging Bomb Targets," Talking Points Memo, October 26, 2018, at https://talkingpointsmemo.com /muckraker/mail-bomb-suspect-sayoc-shared-social-media -posts-about-targets.

72. "Social Media Footprint Sheds New Light on Cesar Sayoc Jr.," *Velshi & Ruhle*, MSNBC, October 26, 2018, at https://www.msnbc.com /velshi-ruhle/watch/social-media-footprint-sheds-new-light-on -cesar-sayoc-jr-1354005571963?v=raila&.

73. Donald Trump, "@foxandfriends 'New Bombshell in the Obama Spying Scandal. Did other Agencies SPY on Trump Campaign?' Even Clapper, worlds dumbest former Intelligence Head, who has the problem of lying a lot, used the word SPY when describing the illegal activities!" Tweet, May 23, 2018, at https://twitter.com/real donaldtrump/status/999239924401438720.

74. Kirkland and Kovensky, "Cesar Sayoc Bombarded Social Media with Posts Disparaging Bomb Targets."

75. Roose, "Cesar Sayoc's Path on Social Media: From Food Photos to Partisan Fury."

76. Donald Trump, "No Collusion and No Obstruction, except by Crooked Hillary and the Democrats. All of the resignations and corruption, yet heavily conflicted Bob Mueller refuses to even look in that direction. What about the Brennan, Comey, McCabe, Strzok lies to Congress, or Crooked's Emails!" Tweet, August 19, 2018, at https://twitter.com/realdonaldtrump/status /1031141396776984576.

77. Kirkland and Kovensky, "Cesar Sayoc Bombarded Social Media with Posts Disparaging Bomb Targets."

78. Robert De Niro, video produced in 2016, at https://www.youtube .com/watch?v=55fJ0FgPSQk.

79. Ian Schwartz, "Robert De Niro at Tony Awards, F*** Trump," Real Clear Politics, June 11, 2018, at https://www.realclearpolitics.com /video/2018/06/11/robert_de_niro_tony_awards_f_trump.html.

80. Maria Puente, "Robert De Niro Has Dumped on Trump for Years; Why Did POTUS Wait So Long to Punch Back?" *USA Today*, June 12, 2018, at https://www.usatoday.com/story/life/2018/06/12/de-niro -dumped-trump-years-potus-waited-punch-back/696123002/.

81.   John Wagner and Anne Gearan, "Trump Says He Does Not Bear Blame for Attempted Bombings," *Washington Post*, October 26, 2018, at https://www.washingtonpost.com/politics/trump-says-media -coverage-of-explosive-devices-slowing-gop-momentum-ahead -of-elections/2018/10/26/c9e52192-d906-11e8-83a2-d1c3da 28d6b6_story.html?utm_term=.c1027ac1f2e8.

82.   Letter, 20, USA v. Sayoc.

83.   Letter, 27, USA v. Sayoc.

84.   Letter, 18 and 19, USA v. Sayoc.

85.   Letter, 19, USA v. Sayoc.

86.   Letter, 21, USA v. Sayoc.

87.   Letter, 4, USA v. Sayoc.

88.   Letter, 4, USA v. Sayoc.

89.   Letter, 23 and 24, USA v. Sayoc.

90.   Letter, 28 and 29, USA v. Sayoc.

91.   Letter, 18, USA v. Sayoc.

92.   Federal Defenders of New York, United States v. Cesar Altieri Sayoc 18 Cr. 820 (JSR), Memorandum to Judge Jed. S. Rakoff, Case 1:18-cr-00820-JSR Document 38 Filed 07/22/19, 1.

93.   Federal Defenders of New York, United States v. Cesar Altieri Sayoc, 1–2.

94.   Federal Defenders of New York, United States v. Cesar Altieri Sayoc, 2.

95.   Federal Defenders of New York, United States v. Cesar Altieri Sayoc, 1–2.

96.   Federal Defenders of New York, United States v. Cesar Altieri Sayoc, 1–2.

97.   Federal Defenders of New York, United States v. Cesar Altieri Sayoc, 1.

98.   Eli Rosenberg, "Poster Linking Rep. Ilhan Omar to 9/11 Sparks Outrage and Injury in W. Va State Capital," *Washington Post*, March 2, 2019, at https://www.washingtonpost.com/politics/2019/03/02 /poster-linking-rep-ilhan-omar-sparks-outrage-injuries-wva-state -capitol/?utm_term=.481432408c06.

99.   United States of America v. Patrick W. Carlineo, Jr., No. 19-MJ-04052 -MWP (United States District Court for the Western District of New York April 4, 2019). Retrieved from https://www.documentcloud .org/documents/5797407-12914518717.html.

100.   Scott Bixby, "Pro-Trump Man Charged with Threatening to Kill Rep. Ilhan Omar," Daily Beast, April 6, 2019, at https://www.thedailybeast .com/rep-ilhan-omar-pro-trump-man-patrick-carlineo-charged -with-threatening-to-kill-congresswoman.

101.   "CAIR-NY Welcomes Arrest of Man Threatening to Kill Rep. Ilhan Omar; Decries Increased Islamophobic Environment," press re-

lease, CAIR-NY, April 8, 2019, at https://www.cair-ny.org/news
/2019/4/8/cair-ny-welcomes-arrest-of-man-threatening-to
-kill-rep-ilhan-omar-decries-increased-islamophobic-environment.

102. Donald Trump, Tweet, April 12, 2019, at https://twitter.com/real
DonaldTrump/status/1116817144006750209.

103. Eli Rosenberg and Kayla Epstein, "President Trump Targets Rep.
Ilhan Omar with a Video of Twin Towers Burning," *Washington
Post,* at https://www.washingtonpost.com/politics/2019/04/13
/president-trump-targets-rep-ilhan-omar-with-video-twin-towers
-burning/?utm_term=.3bc980bce019.

104. Rep. Ilhan Omar, Tweet, April 14, 2019, at https://twitter.com
/Ilhan/status/1117611712679694336.

105. Donald Trump, Tweet, July 14, 2019, at https://twitter.com/real
DonaldTrump/status/1150381395078000643.

106. Donald Trump, Tweet, July 14, 2019, at https://twitter.com/real
DonaldTrump/status/1150381394234941448.

107. Donald Trump, Tweet, July 14, 2019, at https://twitter.com/real
DonaldTrump/status/1150381396994723841.

108. US Equal Opportunity Employment Commission website, at
https://www.eeoc.gov/eeoc/publications/immigrants-facts.cfm.

109. Rep. Ilhan Omar, Tweet, July 14, 2019, at https://twitter.com
/IlhanMN/status/1150456031694245888.

110. Mallory Simon and Sara Sidner, "Trump Said 'Many People' Agree
with His Racist Tweets. These White Supremacists Certainly Do,"
CNN Politics, July 16, 2019, at https://www.cnn.com/2019/07/16
/politics/white-supremacists-cheer-trump-racist-tweets-soh/index
.html.

111. "Remarks by President Trump at the 3rd Annual Made in America
Product Showcase," The White House, July 15, 2019, at https://
www.whitehouse.gov/briefings-statements/remarks-president
-trump-3rd-annual-made-america-product-showcase/.

112. "Remarks by President Trump at the 3rd Annual Made in America
Product Showcase," The White House, July 15, 2019.

113. Salvador Rizzo, "President Trump Accuses Rep. Omar of Supporting
al-Qaeda," *Washington Post,* July 17, 2019, at https://www.washington
post.com/politics/2019/07/17/president-trump-accuses-rep
-omar-supporting-al-qaeda/.

114. H.Res. 249. United States House of Representatives, passed on July
16, 2019, at https://www.congress.gov/bill/116th-congress/house
-resolution/489/text.

115. Donald Trump, Tweet, July 16, 2019, at https://twitter.com/real
donaldtrump/status/1151129281134768128.

116. Donald Trump, Tweet, July 16, 2019, at https://twitter.com/real
DonaldTrump/status/1151129281919102976.

117. Rep. Adam Kinzinger, Tweet, July 18, 2019, at https://twitter.com /RepKinzinger/status/1151843201029935105.

118. "Remarks by President Trump Welcoming Team USA for the 2019 Special Olympics World Games," The White House, July 18, 2019, at https://www.whitehouse.gov/briefings-statements/remarks -president-trump-welcoming-team-usa-201-special-olympics -world-games/.

119. "Donald J. Trump Statement from the White House," Bloomberg TV, July 18, 2019, as broadcast on at https://www.bloomberg.com /news/articles/2019-07-18/trump-says-he-s-not-happy-with-send -her-back-chanting-at-rally.

120. "Donald J. Trump Statement from the White House," Bloomberg TV, July 18, 2019.

121. Salvador Rizzo, "Fact Check Analysis: Trump Falsely Claims He Tried to Stop 'Send Her Back!' Chants About Rep. Ilhan Omar," July 18, 2019, *Washington Post*, at https://www.washingtonpost.com/politics /2019/07/18/trump-falsely-claims-he-tried-stop-send-her-back -chants-about-rep-ilhan-omar/?utm_term=.1c4e02f2a5a9.

122. Dan Dale, Tweet, July 19, 2019, at https://twitter.com/ddale8/status /1152304400439947267.

123. Julie Hirschfeld Davis, Maggie Haberman, and Michael Crowley, "Trump Disavows 'Send Her Back' Chant After Pressure from GOP," *New York Times*, July 18, 2019, at https://www.nytimes.com /2019/07/18/us/politics/ilhan-omar-donald-trump.html.

124. Patrick Crusius, "The Inconvenient Truth," unsigned manifesto, at https://egbertowillies.com/2019/08/03/patrick-crusius-manifesto/.

125. Patrick Crusius, "The Inconvenient Truth."

126. Patrick Crusius, "The Inconvenient Truth."

127. Warrant of Arrest, The State of Texas vs Crusius, Patrick Wood, Offense Report #19-215079, August 4, 2019, at https://games-cdn .washingtonpost.com/notes/prod/default/documents/48647 b82-983a-4ab4-95b7-72562d39143c/note/5db9ab18-d5b2 -4805-8d35-6e7b6a8fd1f1.pdf#page=1.

128. Frank Figliuzzi interview with Ali Velshi, MSNBC, August 3, 2019, at https://www.rawstory.com/2019/08/trump-is-radicalizing -young-people-to-commit-terrorism-like-a-radical-islamic-mullah -ex-fbi-official/#.XUbkw8_utgw.twitter.

129. "SPLC El Paso Statement: Trump's Rhetoric Continues to Fuel Hate," Southern Poverty Law Center, August 4, 2019, at https:// www.splcenter.org/presscenter/splc-el-paso-statement-trumps -rhetoric-continues-fuel-hate.

130. "Donald J. Trump, Remarks from the White House," CNN, August 5, 2019, at https://www.cnn.com/2019/08/05/politics/donald -trump-mass-shooting-response/index.html.

131. "Donald J. Trump, Remarks from the White House," CNN, August 5, 2019.

132. Patrick Crusius, "The Inconvenient Truth."

133. Peter Stubley, "Donald Trump Repeated False Claim About Voter Fraud and Border Wall, Then Said His 'Language Is Very Nice,'" the *Independent*, February 24, 2019, at https://www.businessinsider .com/donald-trump-voter-fraud-border-wall-very-nice-language -2019-2.

134. "Public Highly Critical of State of Political Discourse in the United States," Pew Research Center, June 19, 2019, at https://www .people-press.org/2019/06/19/public-highly-critical-of-state-of -political-discourse-in-the-u-s/.

135. "Public Highly Critical of State of Political Discourse in the United States," Pew Research Center.

136. "Public Highly Critical of State of Political Discourse in the United States," Pew Research Center.

137. "Public Highly Critical of State of Political Discourse in the United States," Pew Research Center.

138. "Have We No Decency? A Response to President Trump," The National Cathedral, July 31, 2019, at https://cathedral.org/have-we -no-decency-a-response-to-president-trump.html.

139. Frank Figliuzzi, "Why Does Trump Fan the Flames of Race-Based Terrorism?" *New York Times*, July 31, 2019, at https://www.nytimes .com/2019/07/31/opinion/gilroy-white-domestic-terrorism.html ?smid=fb-nytopinion&smtyp=cur.

140. Barack Obama, Facebook post, August 5, 2019, at https://www .facebook.com/barackobama/posts/10156899591071749.

CHAPTER 6

1. Brown, *Defusing Hate*, 2.

2. Brown, *Defusing Hate*, 8.

3. Borum, "Understanding the Terrorist Mind-set," 7.

4. Hamm and Spaaij, *The Age of Lone Wolf Terrorism*, 55.

5. Hamm and Spaaij, *The Age of Lone Wolf Terrorism*, 91.

6. Alexander Burns and Astead W. Herndon, "Trump and G.O.P. Candidates Escalate Race and Fear as Election Ploys," *New York Times*, October 22, 2018, at https://www.nytimes.com/2018/10/22 /us/politics/republicans-race-divisions-elections-caravan.html.

7. Donald Trump, Tweet, April 12, 2019, https://twitter.com/real DonaldTrump/status/1116817144006750209.

8. Jeremy Diamond, "Donald Trump's 'Star of David' Tweet Contro-
    versy, Explained," CNN, July 5, 2016, at https://www.cnn.com
    /2016/07/04/politics/donald-trump-star-of-david-tweet-explained
    /index.html.

9. Glenn Kessler, Salvador Rizzo, and Meg Kelly, "President Trump
    Has Made More Than 10,000 False or Misleading Claims," *Washing-
    ton Post*, April 29, 2019.

10. Brady, "Remember That Time Trump Was Allegedly Cheered by
    Paid Actors?"

11. Brady, "Remember That Time Trump Was Allegedly Cheered by
    Paid Actors?"

12. Vitali, "Donald Trump in New Hampshire: Syrian Refugees Are
    'Going Back.'"

13. J. M. Berger, "How White Nationalists Learned to Love Donald
    Trump," Politico, October 25, 2016, at https://www.politico.com
    /magazine/story/2016/10/donald-trump-2016-white-nationalists
    -alt-right-214388.

14. Berger, "How White Nationalists Learned to Love Donald Trump."

15. Andrew Kaczynski, "David Duke Urges His Supporters to Volunteer
    and Vote for Trump," Buzzfeed News, February 25, 2016, at
    https://www.buzzfeednews.com/article/andrewkaczynski
    /david-duke-urges-his-supporters-to-volunteer-and-vote-for-tr
    #.pgxVgYjy4.

16. Donald Trump, Tweet, February 28, 2016, at https://twitter.com
    /realDonaldTrump/status/703996959544250373.

17. Donald Trump interview with Jake Tapper, CNN, February 28,
    2016, at https://www.youtube.com/watch?v=e9geYl9J_Mc.

18. Donald Trump interview with Jake Tapper, February 28, 2016.

19. Donald Trump interview with Jake Tapper, February 28, 2016.

20. Donald Trump interview with Jake Tapper, February 28, 2016.

21. Donald Trump interview with Jake Tapper, February 28, 2016.

22. Donald Trump interview with Jake Tapper, February 28, 2016.

23. Donald Trump interview with Jake Tapper, February 28, 2016.

24. Donald Trump interview with Jake Tapper, February 28, 2016.

25. David Jackson, "Trump Blames Faulty Earpiece for KKK Com-
    ments," *USA Today*, February 28, 2016, at https://www.usatoday
    .com/story/news/politics/onpolitics/2016/02/28/donald-trump
    -david-duke-ku-klux-klan-cnn-state-of-the-union/81073572/.

26. Donald Trump interview with John Dickerson, *CBS Face the Nation*,
    March 6, 2016, at https://www.youtube.com/watch?v=WLukCE
    3vwwA.

27. Donald Trump interview with John Dickerson, *CBS Face the Nation*,
    March 6, 2016.

28. Donald J. Trump, remarks from the White House, August 5, 2019, at https://www.cnn.com/2019/08/05/politics/donald-trump -mass-shooting-response/index.html.

29. Donald J. Trump, remarks from the White House, August 5, 2019.

30. Gideon Resnick and Tara Wanda Merrigan, "David Duke: Trump 'Knows Who I Am,'" Daily Beast, February 28, 2016, updated April 13, 2017, at https://www.thedailybeast.com/david-duke-trump -knows-who-i-am.

31. Berger, "How White Nationalists Learned to Love Donald Trump."

32. Joshua Partlow and David A. Fahrenthold, "'If You're a Good Worker, Papers Don't Matter': How a Trump Construction Crew Has Relied on Immigrants Without Legal Status," *New York Times*, August 9, 2019, at https://www.washingtonpost.com/politics/if -youre-a-good-worker-papers-dont-matter-how-a-trump-construction -crew-has-relied-on-immigrants-without-legal-status/2019/08/09 /cf59014a-b3ab-11e9-8e94-71a35969e4d8_story.html.

33. Figliuzzi, "Why Does Trump Fan the Flames of Race-Based Terrorism?"

34. Figliuzzi, "Why Does Trump Fan the Flames of Race-Based Terrorism?"

35. Stubley, "Donald Trump Repeated False Claim About Voter Fraud and Border Wall, Then Said His 'Language Is Very Nice.'"

36. J. M. Berger, *Extremism* (MIT Press, 2018), 99–100.

37. Berger, *Extremism*, 105.

CHAPTER 7

1. Paul Bond, "Leslie Moonves on Donald Trump: 'It May Not Be Good for America, but It's Damn Good for CBS,' *Hollywood Reporter*, February 29, 2016, at https://www.hollywoodreporter .com/news/leslie-moonves-donald-trump-may-871464.

2. Edmund Lee, "CBS and Viacom to Reunite in Victory for Shari Redstone," *New York Times*, August 13, 2019, at https://www.nytimes .com/2019/08/13/business/cbs-viacom-merger.html.

3. Ken Walsh, "50 Years Ago, Walter Cronkite Changed the Nation," *USA Today*, February 28, 2018, at https://www.usnews.com/news /ken-walshs-washington/articles/2018-02-27/50-years-ago-walter -cronkite-changed-a-nation.

4. James Poniewozik, *Audience of One: Donald Trump, Television, and the Fracturing of America* (New York: Liveright Publishing, 2019), 24.

5. Don Hewitt, *Tell Me a Story: 50 Years and 60 Minutes in Television* (Public Affairs Press, 2001), 4.

6. Hewitt, *Tell Me a Story*, 3.

7. Poniewozik, *Audience of One*, 149.

8. *Crossfire*, CNN, October 14, 2004, at http://transcripts.cnn.com /TRANSCRIPTS/0410/15/cf.01.html.

9. "Exit Snarling," unsigned editorial, *New York Times*, January 5, 2005.

10. Bill Carter, "CNN Will Cancel 'Crossfire' and Cut Ties to Commentator," *New York Times*, January 6, 2005, at https://www.nytimes.com /2005/01/06/business/media/cnn-will-cancel-crossfire-and-cut -ties-to-commentator.html.

11. Joe Flint, "New CNN Head Pushes Channel to Rethink News," *Wall Street Journal*, January 13, 2005, B1.

12. Jonathan Darman, "In Jacko's Wake," *Newsweek*, June 27, 2005, 32–33.

13. Michael Wolff, "The Plot to Sell the News," *Vanity Fair*, November 2004, 186, at https://www.vanityfair.com/news/2004/11/wolff 200411.

14. Wolff, "The Plot to Sell the News," 186.

15. Wolff, "The Plot to Sell the News," 186.

16. Alessandra Stanley, "End Is Expected, but There's Still Time to Debate Morality," *New York Times*, April 13, 2005, C1, at https:// www.nytimes.com/2005/04/13/arts/television/end-is-expected -but-theres-still-time-to-debate-morality.html.

17. Elisabeth Bumiller, "White House Without a Filter," *New York Times*, June 4, 2006, WK3.

18. Personal memory of the author from a conference featuring Don Hewitt, executive producer of *60 Minutes*, and Herb Schmertz, head of public relations at Mobil, Public Relations Society of America, 1986.

19. Martin Kaplan, "Welcome to the Information Freak Show," in *What Orwell Didn't Know: Propaganda and the New Face of American Politics*, ed. András Szántó (Public Affairs Press, 2007), 143.

20. Kaplan, "Welcome to the Information Freak Show," 142.

21. Kaplan, "Welcome to the Information Freak Show," 142.

22. Jeffrey M. Berry and Sarah Sobieraj, *The Outrage Industry: Political Opinion Media and the New Incivility* (Oxford: Oxford University Press, 2014), 5.

23. Berry and Sobieraj, *The Outrage Industry*, 7.

24. Berry and Sobieraj, *The Outrage Industry*, 8.

25. Berry and Sobieraj, *The Outrage Industry*, 8.

26. Berry and Sobieraj, *The Outrage Industry*, 38 and 39.

27. Poniewozik, *Audience of One*, 148–49.

28. "3rd Presidential Debate 2016 promo," CNN, at https://www .youtube.com/watch?v=o9sDpVyZkqw.

29. "CNN's Debate Promo Feels a Lot Like an Ad for a Title Fight," *Esquire*, October 19, 2016, at https://www.esquire.com/news-politics

/news/a49777/cnns-debate-promo-feels-a-lot-like-an-ad-for-a
-title-fight/.

30. Adam Nagourny, "Reform Bid Said to Be a No-Go for Trump," *New York Times*, February 14, 2000, at https://archive.nytimes.com /www.nytimes.com/library/politics/camp/021400wh-ref-trump .html.

31. Poniewozik, *Audience of One*, 63–64.

32. Poniewozik, *Audience of One*, 118–19.

33. Poniewozik, *Audience of One*, 68.

34. Poniewozik, *Audience of One*, 127.

35. Poniewozik, *Audience of One*, 195–96.

36. Poniewozik, *Audience of One*, 205.

37. Poniewozik, *Audience of One*, 207.

38. Patrick J. Buchanan, "1992 Republican National Convention Speech," August 17, 1992, Patrick J. Buchanan—Official Website, at https://buchanan.org/blog/1992-republican-national-convention -speech-148.

39. Steve Kornacki, *The Red and the Blue: The 1990s and the Birth of Political Tribalism* (New York: HarperCollins, 2018), 195–98.

40. Charles Duhigg, "The Real Roots of American Rage," the *Atlantic*, January/February 2019, at https://www.theatlantic.com/magazine /archive/2019/01/charles-duhigg-american-anger/576424/.

41. Kornacki, *The Red and the Blue*, 24–25.

42. Kornacki, *The Red and the Blue*, 24–25.

43. Steven Levitsky and Daniel Ziblatt, *How Democracies Die* (London: Penguin Random House, 2018), 167.

44. Levitsky and Ziblatt, *How Democracies Die*, 170–72.

45. Levitsky and Ziblatt, *How Democracies Die*, 9.

46. Kornacki, *The Red and the Blue*, 157.

47. Bryan T. Gervais and Irwin L. Morris, *Reactionary Republicanism: How the Tea Party in the House Paved the Way for Trump's Victory* (New York: Oxford University Press, 2018), 251.

48. Gervais and Morris, *Reactionary Republicanism*, 252.

CHAPTER 8

1. Bertrand Russell, *The Problems of Philosophy* (Oxford University Press, 1959), 72.

2. Michael Novak, *The Spirit of Democratic Capitalism* (New York: Simon and Schuster, 1982), 20.

3. Chris Mooney, "The Science of Why We Don't Believe Science: How Our Brains Fool Us on Climate, Creationism, and the Vaccine-

Autism Link," *Mother Jones,* May/June 2011, at https://www.mother jones.com/politics/2011/04/denial-science-chris-mooney/.

4. Charles G. Lord, Lee Ross, and Mark R. Lepper, "Biased Assimilation and Attitude Polarization: The Effects of Prior Theories on Subsequently Considered Evidence," *Journal of Personality and Social Psychology* 37(11)(1979), 2098–2109. doi:10.1037/0022-3514.37.11 .2098.

5. Ziva Kunda, "The Case for Motivated Reasoning," *Psychological Bulletin* 108(3)(1990), 480–98, at http://dx.doi.org/10.1037/0033 -2909.108.3.480.

6. Brendan Nyhan and Jason Reifler, "When Corrections Fail: The Persistence of Political Misperceptions," *Political Behavior* 32(2) (2010), 303–30. doi: 10.1007/s11109-010-9112-2.

7. Jonathan Haidt, *The Righteous Mind: Why Good People Are Divided by Politics and Religion* (New York: Vintage, 2012), 37.

8. Haidt, *The Righteous Mind,* 100.

9. "Facing Our Fear," episode of *This Emotional Life,* January 5, 2010, PBS.

10. Lakoff, *Don't Think of an Elephant!,* 17.

11. Lakoff, *Don't Think of an Elephant!,* 7.

12. George Orwell, "Politics and the English Language," in *What Orwell Didn't Know: Propaganda and the New Face of American Politics,* ed. András Szántó (Public Affairs Press, 2007), 217.

13. George Orwell, "Politics and the English Language," 218.

14. David Dunning, "The Psychological Quirk That Explains Why You Love Donald Trump," Politico, May 25, 2016, at https://www. politico.com/magazine/story/2016/05/donald-trump-supporters -dunning-kruger-effect-213904.

15. Dunning, "The Psychological Quirk That Explains Why You Love Donald Trump."

16. Dunning, "The Psychological Quirk That Explains Why You Love Donald Trump."

17. Dunning, "The Psychological Quirk That Explains Why You Love Donald Trump."

18. Dunning, "The Psychological Quirk That Explains Why You Love Donald Trump."

19. Ron Suskind, "Faith, Certainty, and the Presidency of George W. Bush," *New York Times,* October 17, 2004, at https://www.nytimes .com/2004/10/17/magazine/faith-certainty-and-the-presidency -of-george-w-bush.html.

20. Suskind, "Faith, Certainty, and the Presidency of George W. Bush."

21. "The Word—Truthiness—The Colbert Report," *The Colbert Report,* Comedy Central, October 17, 2005, at http://www.cc.com/video -clips/63ite2/the-colbert-report-the-word—truthiness.

22. "The Word—Truthiness—The Colbert Report," *The Colbert Report*, Comedy Central, October 17, 2005.

23. "The Word—Truthiness—The Colbert Report," *The Colbert Report*, Comedy Central, October 17, 2005.

24. "Truthiness Voted Word of the Year," American Dialectical Society, January 6, 2008, at https://www.americandialect.org/truthiness _voted_2005_word_of_the_year.

25. Jonathan Rothwell, "Explaining Nationalist Political Views: The Case of Donald Trump," draft working paper, August 1, 2016, 7, at http://www.umass.edu/preferen/You%20Must%20Read%20 This/Rothwell-Gallup.pdf.

26. Thomas F. Pettigrew, "Social Psychological Perspectives on Trump Supporters," *Journal of Social and Political Psychology* 5(1)(2017), 108. doi:10.5964/jspp.v5i1.750.

27. Pettigrew, "Social Psychological Perspectives on Trump Supporters," 111.

28. Pettigrew, "Social Psychological Perspectives on Trump Supporters," 111.

29. Pettigrew, "Social Psychological Perspectives on Trump Supporters," 111.

30. Pettigrew, "Social Psychological Perspectives on Trump Supporters," 112.

31. Pettigrew, "Social Psychological Perspectives on Trump Supporters," 112.

32. Diana C. Mutz, "Status Threat, Not Economic Hardship, Explains the 2016 Presidential Vote," *Proceedings of the National Academy of Sciences* 115(19)(2018), E4330. doi 10.1073/pnas.1718155115.

33. Mutz, "Status Threat, Not Economic Hardship, Explains the 2016 Presidential Vote," E4331.

34. Mutz, "Status Threat, Not Economic Hardship, Explains the 2016 Presidential Vote," E4336.

35. Mutz, "Status Threat, Not Economic Hardship, Explains the 2016 Presidential Vote," E4338.

CHAPTER 9

1. George W. Bush, "Presidential Address," C-SPAN, September 11, 2001, at https://www.c-span.org/video/?165970-1/presidential -address.

2. George W. Bush, "Presidential Address," C-SPAN, September 11, 2001.

3.   Transcript, "Rhetoric of 9-11," American Rhetoric, at https://www
     .americanrhetoric.com/speeches/gwbush911calltonewyork.htm.

4.   Liyna Anwar and Cameron Jenkins, "'People Saw Only a Turban
     and a Beard': Reflecting on a Post-Sept. 11 Death," NPR, Septem-
     ber 14, 2018, at https://www.npr.org/2018/09/14/647426417
     /people-saw-only-a-turban-and-a-beard-reflecting-on-a-post-sept
     -11-death.

5.   "Remembering Victims of Hate Crimes," Southern Poverty Law
     Center, March 5, 2002, at https://www.splcenter.org/fighting-hate
     /intelligence-report/2002/remembering-victims-hate-crimes
     ?page=0,6.

6.   "Remembering Victims of Hate Crimes," Southern Poverty Law
     Center, March 5, 2002.

7.   Fact Sheet on Post-9/11 Discrimination and Violence Against Sikh
     Americans, The Sikh Coalition, at https://www.sikhcoalition.org
     /images/documents/fact%20sheet%20on%20hate%20against
     %20sikhs%20in%20america%20post%209-11%201.pdf; David
     Cole, *Enemy Aliens: Double Standards and Constitutional Freedoms in the
     War on Terrorism* (New York: The New Press, 2003), 47.

8.   Transcript, "Text of Bush's Press," *New York Times*, September 16,
     2001, at https://www.nytimes.com/2001/09/16/national/text-of
     -bushs-press-conference.html.

9.   Dwight D. Eisenhower, "Letter to the Allied Expeditionary Force,
     June 6, 1944," The National Archives, at https://www.archives.gov
     /historical-docs/todays-doc/?dod-date=606.

10. Peter Ford, "Europe Cringes at Bush 'Crusade' Against Terrorists,"
     Christian Science Monitor, September 19, 2001, at https://www
     .csmonitor.com/2001/0919/p12s2-woeu.html.

11. Ford, "Europe Cringes at Bush 'Crusade' Against Terrorists."

12. Ford, "Europe Cringes at Bush 'Crusade' Against Terrorists."

13. George W. Bush, "Presidential Visit to Islamic Center," C-SPAN,
     September 17, 2001, at https://www.c-span.org/video/?166111-1
     /presidential-visit-islamic-center.

14. George W. Bush, "Presidential Visit to Islamic Center," C-SPAN,
     September 17, 2001.

15. George W. Bush, "Presidential Visit to Islamic Center," C-SPAN,
     September 17, 2001.

16. George W. Bush, "Presidential Visit to Islamic Center," C-SPAN,
     September 17, 2001.

17. George W. Bush, "Terrorist Attacks in U.S.," C-SPAN, September
     19, 2001, at https://www.c-span.org/video/?166175-1/terrorist
     -attacks-us.

18. George W. Bush, "Address to the Joint Session of the 107th Con-
     gress," Washington, DC, September 2001, 71. Retrieved from

https://georgewbush-whitehouse.archives.gov/infocus/bush
record/documents/Selected_Speeches_George_W_Bush.pdf.

19. Council on American-Islamic Relations, *Civil Rights Report 2017:
     The Empowerment of Hate*, 14, at http://www.islamophobia.org
     /reports/188-the-empowerment-of-hate.html.

20. Brian H. Levin, "Statement of Professor Brian H. Levin—
     'Responses to the Increase in Religious Hate Crimes' (Rep.)," May
     2, 2017, at https://csbs.csusb.edu/sites/csusb_csbs/files/Statement,
     by Prof. Brian Levin Responses to the Increase in Religious Hate
     Crime for the US Senate—Committee on the Judiciary—May 2,
     2017.pdf.

21. Julie Bosman, "Palin Plays to Conservative Base in Florida Rallies,"
     New York Times, October 8, 2008, at https://www.nytimes.com
     /2008/10/08/us/politics/08palin.html.

22. Jimmy Orr, "Palin: Obama 'Palling Around with Terrorists,'" *Chris-
     tian Science Monitor*, October 5, 2008, at https://www.csmonitor
     .com/USA/Politics/The-Vote/2008/1005/palin-obama-palling
     -around-with-terrorists.

23. Orr, "Palin: Obama 'Palling Around with Terrorists.'"

24. Orr, "Palin: Obama 'Palling Around with Terrorists.'"

25. "Obama Accuses McCain of Smear Tactics," NBC News, October 5,
     2008, at http://www.nbcnews.com/id/27034817/ns/politics
     -decision_08/t/obama-accuses-mccain-smear-tactics/#.Xan5
     -iV7lR0.

26. Andy Barr, "McCain Launches Ayers Ad," Politico, October 9, 2008,
     at https://www.politico.com/story/2008/10/mccain-launches
     -ayers-ad-014419.

27. "Anti-Obama Anger Erupts at McCain Events," NBC News, October
     10, 2008, at http://www.nbcnews.com/id/27123224/ns/politics
     -decision_08/t/anti-obama-anger-erupts-mccain-events/#.XaSjn
     SV7lR0.

28. "Anti-Obama Anger Erupts at McCain Events," NBC News, October
     10, 2008.

29. Frank Schaeffer, "An Open Letter to John McCain," HuffPost, No-
     vember 10, 2008, at https://www.huffpost.com/entry/an-open
     -letter-to-john-mc_b_133489.

30. Schaeffer, "An Open Letter to John McCain."

31. Elisabeth Bumiller, "McCain Draws Line on Attacks as Crowds Cry
     'Fight Back,'" *New York Times*, October 10, 2008, at https://www
     .nytimes.com/2008/10/11/us/politics/11campaign.html.

32. Jonathan Martin and Amie Parnes, "McCain: Obama Not an Arab,
     Crowd Boos," Politico, October 11, 2008, at https://www.politico
     .com/story/2008/10/mccain-obama-not-an-arab-crowd-boos
     -014479.

33. Martin and Parnes, "McCain: Obama Not an Arab, Crowd Boos."

34. John McCain with Mark Salter, *Why Courage Matters: The Way to a Braver Life* (Random House, 2004), 104.

35. Jonathan Martin and Mike Allen, "Civil Rights Icon Says McCain Stirs Hate," Politico, October 11, 2008, at https://www.politico .com/story/2008/10/civil-rights-icon-says-mccain-stirs-hate -014488.

36. Martin and Allen, "Civil Rights Icon Says McCain Stirs Hate."

37. David Grann, "The Fall," *New Yorker*, November 8, 2008, at https://www.newyorker.com/magazine/2008/11/17/the-fall -david-grann.

38. "McCain Calls Lewis Remarks 'Outrageous,'" CNN, October 13, 2008, at https://www.cnn.com/2008/POLITICS/10/13/mccain .interview/.

39. Martin and Allen, "Civil Rights Icon Says McCain Stirs Hate."

40. "Colin Powell Endorses Barack Obama for President," YouTube, October 19, 2008, at https://www.youtube.com/watch?v=b2U63f XBlFo.

41. "Colin Powell Endorses Barack Obama for President," YouTube, October 19, 2008.

42. Rob Schenck, *Costly Grace: An Evangelical Minister's Rediscovery of Faith, Hope, and Love* (Harper, 2018), 106.

43. Schenck, *Costly Grace*, 106.

44. Schenck, *Costly Grace*, 108.

45. Schenck, *Costly Grace*, 132–33.

46. Schenck, *Costly Grace*, 132–33.

47. Schenck, *Costly Grace*, 189–90.

48. Schenck, *Costly Grace*, 189–90.

49. "Rob Schenck on the Consequences of Inflammatory Rhetoric," *Amanpour & Co.*, PBS, August 16, 2019, at http://www.pbs.org /wnet/amanpour-and-company/video/rob-schenck-on-the -consequences-of-inflammatory-rhetoric/.

50. Schenck, *Costly Grace*, 290–91.

51. Rob Schenck, "My Words Led to Violence. Now Trump's Are Too," *TIME*, August 6, 2019, at https://time.com/5645371/trump -rhetoric-violence/.

52. Schenck, *Costly Grace*, 324.

53. Daniel Goleman, "What Makes a Good Leader?" *Harvard Business Review*, January 2004, at https://hbr.org/2004/01/what-makes -a-leader.

54. Jim Collins, "Level 5 Leadership: The Triumph of Humility and Fierce Resolve, *Harvard Business Review*, July–August 2005, at https://hbr.org/2005/07/level-5-leadership-the-triumph-of -humility-and-fierce-resolve.

55.   Jim Collins, "Level 5 Leadership."

56.   His Holiness Pope Francis, TED Talk, transcript translated by Elena Montrasio, at https://www.ted.com/talks/pope_francis_why_ the_only_future_worth_building_includes_everyone/transcript ?language=en.

57.   Schenck, *Costly Grace*, 297.

CHAPTER 10

1.   Donald Trump, "Because the ban was lifted by a judge, many very bad and dangerous people may be pouring into our country. A terrible decision," Tweet, February 4, 2017, at https://twitter.com /realdonaldtrump/status/827996357252243456.

2.   Donald Trump, "Just cannot believe a judge would put our country in such peril. If something happens blame him and court system. People pouring in. Bad!" Tweet, February 5, 2017, at https://twitter .com/realdonaldtrump/status/828342202174668800.

3.   "Stephen Miller on Trump's Efforts to Secure the Homeland," FoxNews, February 12, 2017, at https://video.foxnews.com/v /5320735275001/#sp=show-clips.

4.   "Stephen Miller on Trump's Efforts to Secure the Homeland," Fox-News, February 12, 2017.

5.   "Stephen Miller on Trump's Efforts to Secure the Homeland," Fox-News, February 12, 2017.

6.   Schaeffer, "An Open Letter to John McCain."

7.   Schaeffer, "An Open Letter to John McCain."

8.   Borum, "Understanding the Terrorist Mind-set," 7.

9.   Brown, *Defusing Hate*, 8.

10.   Hamm and Spaaij, *Lone Wolf Terrorism in America*, 8.

11.   Matt Zapatosky and Devlin Barrett, "Michael Cohen Sentence to Three Years in Prison for Crimes He Committed While Working for Trump," *Washington Post*, December 12, 2018, at https://www .washingtonpost.com/world/national-security/michael-cohen -scheduled-to-be-sentenced-for-crimes-committed-while-working -for-trump/2018/12/11/57226ff2-fcbf-11e8-83c0-b06139e540e5 _story.html.

12.   Donald Trump, Tweet, December 16, 2018, at https://twitter.com /realDonaldTrump/status/1074313153679450113.

13.   Isaac Stanley-Becker, "Calling Michael Cohen a 'Rat,' Trump Brings 'American Underworld' Lingo to the White House," *Washington Post*, December 17, 2018, at https://www.washingtonpost.com

/nation/2018/12/17/calling-michael-cohen-rat-trump-brings
-american-underworld-lingo-white-house/.

14. Luke Barr, "What Does Trump Mean When He Calls Cohen a 'Rat'?" ABC News, December 17, 2018, at https://abcnews.go .com/Politics/trump-calls-cohen-rat/story?id=59862349.

15. Barr, "What Does Trump Mean When He Calls Cohen a 'Rat'?"

16. Committee on Oversight and Reform, US House of Representatives, press release, January 13, 2019, at https://oversight.house .gov/news/press-releases/house-chairmen-issue-warning-after -president-s-statements-on-cohen-testimony.

17. Donald Trump, Tweet, January 18, 2019, at https://twitter.com /realDonaldTrump/status/1086277705916502017.

18. Personal discussion with the author, January 27, 2018.

19. "Full Transcript of Michael Cohen's Opening Statement to Congress," *New York Times*, February 27, 2019, at https://www.nytimes .com/2019/02/27/us/politics/cohen-documents-testimony.html.

20. "Full Transcript: Rep. Elijah Cummings' Closing Statements at Michael Cohen Hearing," *Baltimore Sun*, February 27, 2019, at https:// www.baltimoresun.com/news/maryland/politics/bs-md-cummings -transcript-20190228-story.html.

21. "Remarks by the President at Clinton Global Initiative," Office of the Press Secretary. The Obama White House, September 23, 2014, at https://obamawhitehouse.archives.gov/the-press-office/2014 /09/23/remarks-president-clinton-global-initiative.

22. "Remarks by the President at Clinton Global Initiative," Office of the Press Secretary. The Obama White House, September 23, 2014.